# Learning to Dance

'A landmark in the exploration of contemporary spirituality . . . This is the kind of book – a rare event – that one would happily take away to the mythical desert island.'
Margaret Silf, *The Tablet*

'It is Mayne at his best. A real contribution to our understanding of the complexities and tensions of the faith.'
Nick Mercer, *Church Times*

'A much-needed book . . . Have your spirit emboldened by a great teacher.'
John Austin Baker, *Salisbury Cathedral News*

'It deserves to be a kind of spiritual classic.'
Hugh Montefiore

'This is a book which heightens awareness, which in the very best way comforts the soul.'
Ronald Blythe

'A rich gift to us all, a wise, kind, artful book.'
Frederick Buechner

# Learning to Dance

MICHAEL MAYNE

*Foreword by*
DAME CICELY SAUNDERS

DARTON · LONGMAN + TODD

First published in 2001 by
Darton, Longman and Todd Ltd
1 Spencer Court
140–142 Wandsworth High Street
London SW18 4JJ

Reprinted 2002 (twice)

ISBN 0–232–52434–3

A catalogue record for this book is available from the British
Library.

Designed by Sandie Boccacci
Set in 9/12.25pt Stone Serif by Intype London Ltd
Printed and bound in Great Britain by
The Bath Press, Bath

In memory of my parents
and for Alison, who
in the 'daunsing, signifying matrimonie'
has taught me most about the dance

One never knows, do one?

*Fats Waller*

# CONTENTS

# FOREWORD

Over many years of working alongside mortally ill people, like countless other hospice workers around the world, I have witnessed the importance of delight. 'I just want to see the trees come out,' said a patient in St Christopher's Hospice, moving with open eyes to the end of her life. I took a photograph of another of my patients in St Joseph's Hospice in 1963, just a few days before he became one of the first to know that I had received a grant for the land on which to build St Christopher's. In the photograph, he is looking with total concentration and an entranced smile at a white hyacinth on his bed table. He had watched it coming into bloom and it had just reached its peak of loveliness. I have often used this as a slide in lectures to emphasise the importance of beauty as we make our farewell to earth. Somehow, that flower seems to me to be giving a strong and comforting message: the universe, to which you also belong, is good and to be trusted.

This seems to me to be the overall message of this enchanted and enchanting book. Michael Mayne has brought us through a dance of the treasures of nature and a fascinating store of literature, from the mystery of the galaxies to the intricacies of the snowflake. Like Julian of Norwich, the fourteenth-century mystic whom he quotes several times, he has seen God in a point, the still point at the centre. As she writes,

> All this he showed me with great joy. See, I am God. See, I am in all things. See, I do all things. See, I never take my hands off my work, nor ever shall through all eternity. See, I lead all things to the end I have prepared for them.[1]

But, like her, he has also met the challenge of 'whatever brute or blackguard made the world'[2] with its injustice, cruelty and suffering.

'Dancing in the dark' is for me the centre of this searching book – as was Julian's anguished question of how all can be well when such pain, trouble and distress come to God's loved creatures. Both hold the paradox in the context of the creative suffering of an almighty God who chooses to be vulnerable love. Julian looks to the Great Deed unknown till the end of all things for an answer and, like Michael Mayne, is content to live with the questions.

The overall theme is of an immense yet personally concerned universe in which we can wait for answers. The beauty of nature, to which we are returned at the beginning of each chapter, reminds me of the story of the Victorian man who, gathering his household for prayers every morning, would say each time the day was especially lovely, 'This is a Psalm 103 day.' He would then proceed to read that paean of praise to the end, when the Psalmist says,

> O speak good of the Lord,
> all ye works of his,
> in all places of his dominion:
> praise thou the Lord, O my soul.

One imagines hearing that one voice in the midst of an echoing universe, with its unique part to play in that symphony. Here, with this book, we have a rare voice to bring such a message to a world of longing today. Above all, it is full of thanksgiving. Once again, I turn to Julian.

> Thanksgiving is the deep inward certainty which moves us with reverent and loving fear to turn with all our strength to the work to which God stirs us, giving thanks and praise from the depths of our hearts.

This is a book to hearten and to stir us to gratitude for all the experience (not all easy) that lies behind it, and to a renewed sense of wonder and encouragement in our own stories.

Dame Cicely Saunders, OM, DBE, FRCP

# The Dance of the Bees

True ease in writing comes from art, not chance,
As those move easiest who have learned to dance.

*Alexander Pope*[1]

Mind you, Hugh Gaitskell was a very good dancer.
And to me, that is more important than politics in
a man.

*Barbara Castle*[2]

The year has turned. In Salisbury, the Avon has burst its
banks. On the water meadows, where the Avon meets the
Nadder, there is a lake half-a-mile wide on which confused
swans congregate; from the footpath on a still evening, lit
by a low sun, the cathedral spire is perfectly mirrored. Most
mornings bring a hard frost. Crows court in the high
branches; at dusk last year's rooks' nests are silhouetted in
the treetops, and great shoals of starlings, moving as one
in tightly controlled formation, whirr and chatter as they
dive and soar and move away. Bunches of mistletoe hang
high in the bare lime trees, like unravelling balls of wool
caught in a net of branches. Beside the river a solitary robin
perches on a bent reed, its scarlet somewhat shop-worn; a
wren calls from a tangle of old man's beard. At Welney in

the Cambridgeshire Fens hundreds of wild whooper and Bewick's swans will have flown from Arctic Russia to winter, gliding in daily to land as the light fades with their unforgettable honking cry and booming wing-beats. On the bitter salt marshes of the Norfolk coast, the huge skies will be threaded by the needles of the flights of wildfowl and waders. Redwing are feeding on the unflooded patches of grass beside the Test at Stockbridge. On most days long-tailed tits make brief raids on the bugs in our solitary apple tree. Grovely woods are silent, the moss and lichen on certain tree trunks a startling green when lit by the pale winter sun, and on the horse chestnut trees the sticky buds are beginning to grow fat.

Nothing so marks the difference in my life in the move away from the heart of London than observing and revelling in the changing seasons. There the concrete office blocks hide the sky; here, from my high study window, I watch the clouds and the light altering daily, sometimes hourly. Cities mask the dance of nature and the rhythms of the changing year. In the Middle Ages the prayers, hymns and texts sung in countless religious houses were closely tied to the natural cycle of day and night, the Canonical Hours indicating the time of day. With their changing festivals, each season's passing, and indeed each day's passing, were small images of the great annual swing of stellar and solar time. You lived close to the earth, looked on nature as basically hostile, its forests dangerous, its beauty only visible when safely contained in walled gardens. The medieval Books of Hours, those richly decorated volumes which contain both Missal and Breviary, begin with a Calendar which displays the labours or occupations of each month taken from the seasonal labours of the peasants and the pastimes of their feudal lords. The occupation for a freezing January was **feasting**, a time to stay indoors, take stock, tell stories and feed on memories.

So now, starting at this dead time of the year, with many

more comforts than the medieval peasant and a much wiser diet that their feudal lords, I want to feast a little: to look at my life, my beliefs, my faith, and feed on my memories, in as honest and personal a way as I can. Most of our lives are about doing: they should also be about being and becoming, and now in retirement they can be. While my words will come from my centre, this is not an autobiography in the sense of being the story of me, the roles I've played, the jobs I've done: rather, it is a story about what the dance of life looks like from where I sit, and therefore (in all essential details) it is doubtless also a story about you. As Henry Thoreau said: 'I should not talk so much about myself if there were anybody else whom I knew so well.' Writers have been likened to those who put messages into bottles, seal them up and cast them into the sea; and are sometimes rewarded when others find the bottles and with a frisson of delight discover that the words speak to them. Messages which don't simply say: 'I was here', but rather: 'This is how it was for me: was it also like this for you?'

Among the monks in the Middle Ages were some who might spend their whole lives painting and repainting the face of Christ. It was always the same face, yet always subtly different. So with us: each life, if it is imaginatively and truthfully explored, reveals much more than itself, for the general is found in the particular. We all exist poised between those two unimaginable darknesses, birth and death, and, notes E. M. Forster, 'the two entities who might enlighten us, the baby and the corpse, cannot do so'. In between, and over all too brief a time, we take and fashion what we are given. We explore, we respond to beauty, we learn the meaning of love and trust and hope, and (often in direct, desolating proportion to the joy and tenderness of a shared love) we endure grief and suffering; and we make of all this what we can. Ultimately, of course, each of us is alone, for that is the flip side of our uniqueness, our wonderfully distinctive selves: what I experience is *my* birth, *my* feelings, *my* sickness, *my* solitude and suffering and dying. Yet because, in Wordsworth's words, 'we all share one human heart', while my memories and experiences are unique to me, they have so much in common with yours, and I can enter imaginatively into your world and your vulnerability as you can enter into mine. We use language to tell the truth in the best way we know, and where my experience fails to resonate with yours, then language fails its most challenging test. That now-forgotten minor poet, Paul Potts, wrote in his autobiography:

> It is only those parts of one's life, whose roots go deep enough into the ground of human experience to cause language to flower when it is used to describe them, that are worthy of being written about . . . [My] book is concerned with . . . what I have thought and felt, more than with what I have done.[3]

So is this one. The sort of hybrid, hard to categorise, which infuriates neat-minded librarians.

In Anthony Powell's great sequence of novels, *A Dance to the Music of Time*, the central character Nicholas Jenkins sees in the Wallace Collection a painting by Poussin with that title, a scene of dancers treading a stately measure to Time's tune. Later that day he sees a group of workmen warming themselves at a coke-fire in falling snow.

> Something in the physical attitudes of the men as they turned from the fire suddenly suggested Poussin's scene in which the Seasons . . . tread in rhythm to the notes of the lyre . . . The image of Time brought thoughts of . . . [human beings] . . . moving hand in hand in intricate measure: stepping slowly, methodically, sometimes a trifle awkwardly, in evolutions that take recognisable shape: or breaking into seemingly meaningless gyrations, while partners disappear only to reappear again, once more giving pattern to the spectacle: unable to control the melody, unable, perhaps, to control the steps of the dance.[4]

The twelve novels, full of the world's tragi-comic absurdities, see life as a sort of formalised dance and are a rich portrait of the generation that grew up in the shadow of the First

World War only to find their lives dislocated by the Second. When Powell died in 2000, Hilary Spurling ended her obituary of him:

> He took the generous, capacious, humanistic view shared down the ages by unprejudiced observers from Lucretius to Shakespeare and Montaigne, and he gave it characteristically lapidary expression in the *Dance*: 'All human beings, driven as they are at different speeds by the same Furies, are at close range equally extraordinary.'[5]

In many ways I am an unlikely dancer, having only fully mastered the waltz and the Dashing White Sergeant and, at the age of ten, a passable Sailors' Hornpipe; yet the ideas of the invitation to the cosmic dance and of dance as a metaphor for our assorted lives in this mysterious, dancing universe have gone on expanding in my mind during the broody months in which this book has been generating. But what sort of a book? 'I am myself' wrote Montaigne at the start of his Essays, 'the substance of my book,' (though he had the modesty to add) 'and there is no reason why you should waste your leisure on so frivolous and unrewarding a subject'.[6] If what is personal is also most universal, then it needs to be about what it feels like to be human. Other people do not often get close enough to know us as we truly are, and perhaps perceptions of the roles we play must always differ from how we see ourselves. In 1555 the first European missionaries hit Japan, and an observer wrote:

> there came one who appeared to have human form at first glance but might as well be a long-nosed goblin, or a long-necked demon . . . Careful enquiry revealed that the creature was called a 'Padre'.

In an interview Seamus Heaney put it like this: 'Imagine you were an oyster. The public would see you as an infrangible nut, a kind of sea-raid shelter, but you would see yourself as all mother-of-pearly inwardness and vulnerability.' In three previous books I have sought to speak a little of that vulnerability. As a result, a large number of people wrote or came to see me because two matters seemed to touch a deep nerve: the accounts of a long illness in the first, and of my father's suicide in the third. This taught me that a common public sharing of personal wounds, done with care and with proper reticence and restraint, can help authenticate what others experience. There will be something of that sharing in the pages that follow.

But there will be something else: a deliberate absence in much of this book of explicitly 'religious' language and that gentle (often not-so-gentle) scattering of biblical references on page after page, as if that *in itself* guaranteed that the words were true. The God in whose presence I knelt to be confirmed in a wartime chapel (what had been the garage of a swish Cornish hotel in a previous incarnation), and the God I worshipped this morning in a medieval chapel in Salisbury cathedral, has not changed, but my perception of him has changed profoundly. In a richly varied life and ministry my understanding of what human beings are (and what they can be) has also shifted. Trained to anticipate the worst in human nature, I have so often found the best: generosity, compassion and a natural goodness, and great courage in the face of unlooked-for suffering. Churches always tend to exclusivity, with their own special language and liturgies, often failing to connect to where most people are. Some reject on intellectual grounds the concept of God; others are rejecting images of God, gathered at random, which are a million miles from the truth. But there are many who are what have been called 'wistful agnostics', those who are aware of the mystery that faces us at every turn of the stair, and the sense of a 'beyondness' at the heart of things, but who cannot put their names to credal statements which list so confidently what God is like and what he has done, especially as scientists from Darwin to Dawkins appear to have demolished the whole antiquated structure. Which is why, with that mixture of arrogance and trepidation of someone who specialised in the arts from the age of fifteen,

I want to bring together these two worlds: that of evolution, relativity and quantum physics and that of faith, and suggest that those of us who affirm both in a single integrity are not the clowns we are sometimes taken for.

If I have the sense of writing with one hand tied behind my back it is because my three books are still in print. And as you get older the familiar themes, those few truths that have grown more central to your life, are played again and again. While, in Eliot's words in *East Coker*,

> Old men ought to be explorers
> Here or there does not matter,

they can also be repetitive. I'll try, at least, to put new words to the old tunes. As for exploring, I guess that what most of us are looking for is the place called home. 'Home is where one starts from', wrote Eliot a few lines earlier, but my father committed suicide when I was three, and I have no memory of that sleepy Northamptonshire village of which he was the parish priest and seem to have been moving around ever since. The poet Elizabeth Bishop asks,

> Should we have stayed at home,
> Wherever that may be?[7]

while the novelist Kurt Vonnegut writes somewhere that 'unanticipated invitations to travel are dancing lessons from God'. Edwin Muir, a fine poet undeservedly out of fashion, declares his need to

> Seek the beginnings, learn from whence you came,
> And know the various earth of which you are made;

and in his imagination goes 'from place to place' seeking

> To find the secret place
> Where is my home.[8]

Leonard Woolf believed that 'what cuts the deepest channels in our lives are the different houses in which we live – deeper even than marriage and death and division'.[9] I would opt instead for *places*, perhaps because of a pretty rootless child-hood in a succession of houses that were not homes. I have often envied those embedded in a particular locality, those whose sense of 'home' is deeply rooted in feelings about the place in which they first felt secure and learned to move easily in a familiar and ordered world: the young Laurie Lee in the seventeenth-century cottage in Slad that 'smelled of pepper and mushrooms'; Edwin Muir, whose idyllic child-hood on a remote island in Orkney haunted him all his life, and became his universal landscape, a vision of a longed-for Eden; John Clare, intimate with the paths, hedgerows and woods around his native Helpston, the inner map by which his world was measured; John Bunyan, who danced and played on the green at Elstow, and walked by the Ouse among the flat fields of Bedfordshire, those endless acres of Brussels sprouts; William Blake, observing the familiar streets of London with a mystic's eye and finding 'the infinite in everything'; William Langland, dressed like a shepherd, roaming the Malvern hills in May; Constable, only happy to paint 'when he had truly made a place his own'; Thomas Traherne and Henry Vaughan, natives of the rolling country of the Welsh borders, who saw God in every hill and valley; and Francis Kilvert, also in that lovely borderland where England tips over into Wales, poorly paid but enriched by the familiar round of baptising babies, chasing birds out of the church, planting lettuces and visiting the sick. The characters in Hardy's Wessex are never lonely because they

> know all about those invisible ones of the days gone by, whose feet have traversed the fields which look so grey from his windows; recall whose creaking plough has turned those sods from time to time; whose hands planted the trees that form a crest to the opposite hill; whose horses and hounds have torn through that underwood; what birds affect that particular brake; what bygone domestic dramas of love, jealousy, revenge, or disappointment have been enacted in the cottages, the mansion, the street or on the green. The spot may have beauty,

grandeur, salubrity, convenience; but if it lacks memories it will ultimately pall upon him who settles there without opportunity of intercourse with his kind.[10]

To a great extent these are lost worlds. Yet our need to find a place where we belong and which we can call home runs deep. Many never know such a sense of intimate belonging in town or country. After that first parting, that necessary claiming of independence, when

selfhood begins with a walking away,
And love is proved in the letting go,[11]

we spend our lives coming and going, carrying snail-like our home on our back, settling for a time and then moving on. Yet as we grow old we need to find a place that is our own, a place we have chosen in which to root ourselves and feed on our memories. Stored in my memory, instantaneously available, are those places where I have been happy and fulfilled, the houses in which my children grew up, where meals were shared with friends and visitors entertained, and dogs lived and died; and there are places where certain landscapes, certain patterns and contours of field and wood, the spaces in familiar buildings, still come to mind; and other places – Iona in every kind of weather, the bird-filled Norfolk coast at Cley, a beach in Devon, a small mountain village in the high meadows of the Dolomites – visited again and again because there is a different depth to the silence, a difference in the very quality of light. These are the yardsticks against which we measure what we mean by 'home'. They have been claimed by us and now have a claim on us. We get homesick for their sights and sounds and smells. They may come to haunt us. And often it is through the healing power of memory, a reliving of the past in the present, that our fragmented selves find a unity. In recollection, one of the great gifts of old age, by combining memory and imagination, we are able to recreate our lives. Barry Lopez writes:

The power of observation, the gifts of eye and ear, of tongue and nose and finger, allows a landscape to rise up in the mind; it is memory that carries the place, that allows it to grow in depth and complexity. For as long as records go back, we hold these two things dear: landscape and memory.[12]

For all of us, such places become storied spaces, some of them even sacred spaces, spaces which help us tell ourselves something deep and important about ourselves, our inner story. The Bible has a sacramental view of such spaces: God is identified with a range of particular places, from Mount Sinai to Bethlehem, and he is encountered in this or that specific place in order that he may then be found everywhere.

And now, for me, the place that feels more and more like home is Wiltshire, whose gently rolling landscape was likened by Virginia Woolf to the long curved waves of the sea. 'It is as though the land here, all molten once, & rolling in vast billows had solidified while the rocks were still swollen & on the point of breaking.'[13] She was less kind about the 'small red houses that have marched out in the van & rear of Salisbury', in one of which I now live. E. M. Forster's *The Longest Journey* reflects Forster's great love of the English landscape. (I can see him in my mind's eye standing on the backs at Trinity College, Cambridge, in 1953, with cap and stick, gazing rapt at the blossoming cherry trees.) In the novel, Rickie sits on a hill in Wiltshire and reflects that

> this is the heart of our island: the Chilterns, the North Downs, the South Downs, radiate here. The fibres of England unite in Wiltshire, and did we condescend to worship her, here we should erect our national shrine.[14]

When the novelist William Golding, whose home was in Bowerchalke, wrote of Wiltshire, he spoke of its uniqueness in 'having a particularly ancient and mysterious history that has left its mark in every corner'.[15] There are Stonehenge,

Avebury, Silbury Hill and the remains of the castle at Old Sarum where I now walk so often, a castle built by William the Conqueror inside an Iron Age fort that is inside a Bronze Age one. When Golding drove home across the downs from Winchester to Salisbury he would experience a moment when he crossed some invisible barrier, the point at which the two cities with their two cathedrals were balanced, and heard a distinct 'Ping!' as he passed through it, and knew that he was coming home.

It is good, too, to have known and loved those places so central in the life of the poet who more than any other reveals that understanding of the Christlike God that shapes my life: George Herbert. Herbert served as Public Orator in Cambridge and often worshipped in my old church of Great St Mary's. He had been a pupil at Westminster School and would sometimes worship in Dean Lancelot Andrewes' private chapel in the Deanery that for ten years was our home. A window in the Abbey's nave shows him, dressed in his cassock, standing in the church porch of Bemerton, his tiny parish on the outskirts of Salisbury where he spent the three years of his priesthood in what John Aubrey called 'a pitifull little chapell', and from where twice a week he walked beside the Nadder to evensong in Salisbury Cathedral. And in these astonishing three years, in which he produced a definitive work on the role of a parish priest and wrote his incomparable poetry, he knew he had finally, and in every sense, come home. Ronald Blythe, one of the best living authorities on the significance of landscape in our lives, writes:

> Herbert celebrates an England which he believed God had made 'a land of Light, a storehouse of treasures and mercies', and his work ceaselessly tracks down every link it can between earthly experience and paradise. It is the poetry of a blessed continuum, with Wiltshire sprawling, quite naturally, across the frontiers of heaven.[16]

A few miles from here, in the lovely Ebble valley, a friend keeps bees. In this bleak January the hive is silent, the bees packed together in a furry mass where the temperature is that of mid-summer. If dance is a metaphor for the human journey, the beehive is a metaphor for human society. At the start of Shakespeare's *Henry V*, after a tedious speech from the Archbishop of Canterbury explaining the ancient Salic Law and urging his king to assert his right to invade France, the Archbishop's words take wing as he tells the story of the honey bees:

> Creatures that by a rule in nature teach
> The act of order to a peopled kingdom.
> They have a king and officers of sorts;
> Where some, like magistrates, correct at home,
> Others, like merchants, venture trade abroad,
> Others, like soldiers, armed in their stings,
> Make boot upon the summer's velvet buds;
> Which pillage they with merry march bring home
> To the tent-royal of their emperor:
> Who, busied in his majesty, surveys
> The singing masons building roofs of gold,
> The civil citizens kneading up the honey;
> The poor mechanic porters crowding in
> Their heavy burdens at his narrow gate;
> The sad-eyed justice with his surly hum,
> Delivering o'er to executors pale
> The lazy yawning drone.[17]

Shakespeare got the sex wrong, but then it was not known that the 'king' was a queen until just before his death, an offensive thought to King Charles II's bee master who believed it denied the divine right of kings.

With the coming of spring the bees begin their work. The queen, who has been fed with royal jelly, lays up to 2000 eggs a day, and is helped by up to 80,000 female workers, who are also responsible for gathering and storing pollen and honey with which to feed the young; and a few hundred male drones. The workers also build in the dark the 100,000 wax cells that form the heart of the hive with an instinctive knowledge of angles and planes to create a structure that is both efficient and exquisite. 'Insects' eyes' writes the geneticist Steve Jones, 'are built with not one but hundreds of (six-sided) lenses, each of which concentrates light upon a sensor . . . Bees' eyes have an upright strip of sensors adapted to the vertical world of trees and branches.'[18] When the foraging scouts buzz around alone, they use their multi-lensed eyes to navigate by the sun, using one eye for the outgoing, the other for the return, journey. They also have good colour vision and sense of smell which enables them to locate flowers, and while the search for food can cover 40 square miles from the hive, it is mostly within a four-mile radius. Each bee's hind leg bears a basket-like structure for storing large amounts of pollen, and much nectar can be packed in its honey stomach and regurgitated. But it is what the scout does on returning to the hive after finding a large enough meal that astonishes: it executes the dance of the bees.

There are two kinds of dance: the round dance and the waggle dance, performed either on the landing-board outside the hive or inside, against the face of the comb. While the nature of the flowers is conveyed by the scent permeating the pollen and nectar the scout brings back, the worker bees need to know the exact location of the patch of blossom that yields the food. Where the food is close, the round dance – quick, circular movements flown first in one direction and then in the other – is performed; where the food source is further away, it is a more sedate waggle dance, a figure-of-eight with the loops separated by a straight run. At a distance of 100 metres this is performed some 40 times a minute, at 500 metres 6 times a minute, at 1000 metres 4 times, and at 5000 metres just twice. In this dance, the bee waggles her abdomen from side to side, emitting a high-pitched buzz, the others following her as she dances; if the dance is in the comb, those closest to her touch her abdomen with their outstretched antennae. The duration of the dance and the length of the abdominal flicks show the distance: its speed reveals the amount of nectar and pollen. If she dances upwards on the comb the food is in the direction of the sun; if the upward wagging is at 60 degrees to the comb's vertical axis, the flower source will be 60 degrees to the right of the sun. Other workers take off in their turn, only collecting nectar from flowers that have the same scent as that on the returned scout, and they too dance on their return, until the food supply is gone and the dance stops.

This extraordinary dance was first discovered and decoded by Karl von Frisch in 1923 and it brought him a Nobel prize. It was in that year that the poet Rainer Maria Rilke was first struck down by the illness that was to be diagnosed as leukaemia. He may not have known of the dance of the bees, but when he wanted a metaphor for the role of the poet he wrote (and he italicised the phrase): '*We are the bees of the Invisible.*' In his poetry he sets about transforming the given world into something fruitful, and he does so by praising it. He imagines the artist as a polished surface like a mirror who, by not demanding anything of the world and learning to see it with a disinterested intensity, makes it real. Things are not simply objects, but objects seen and wondered at and loved by human beings and so capable of being transformed:

> one earthly thing
> truly experienced, even once, is enough for a lifetime . . .
> *Truly* being here is glorious.[19]

So, in a letter written to his Polish translator, Witold Hulewitz, a year before he died, he writes:

> It is our task to imprint this temporary, perishable earth into ourselves so deeply, so painfully and passionately, that its essence can rise again, invisibly, inside us. *We are the bees of the Invisible.* We wildly collect the honey of the visible, to store it in the great golden hive of the invisible.[20]

My theme is the dance: the dance of life; the dance of the cosmos, of the natural world and of the tiniest particle of matter; the dance of music and paint and words, whereby artists may make journeys into the unknown in order to recapture lost parts of themselves for our mutual healing; of those cruel times which feel like dancing in the dark; the dance of relationships, of forgiveness, friendship and love; the dance of faith; and finally, that hidden dance that some call heaven; all interwoven with how I have sought to learn to dance. I can think of no better metaphor to convey my desire in sharing what I have come to value than this dance of the bees, each with its distinctive, individual scent, carrying home the valued nectar and pollen and showing the others where such treasure may be found.

# *Learning to Dance I*

---

Why should not chickens be born and clergymen be laid and hatched? Or why, at any rate, should not the clergyman be born full grown into Holy Orders, not to say already beneficed? The present arrangement is not convenient.

*Samuel Butler*[1]

Not to go back is somewhat to advance,
And men must walk at least before they dance.

*Alexander Pope*[2]

Can't act, can't sing, slightly bald. Can dance a little.

*Hollywood executive*
*after Fred Astaire's first screen test*

I thought life was going to be like Brahms ... Instead it's, well, it's been Eric Coates.

*Enid in Alan Bennett's* Getting On

---

In certain old proverbs February is known as fill-dyke, when the rain and melted snow filled the ditches to overflowing, and it was said that if the weather is fine and frosty at the

16

close of January, as it is this year, there is more winter ahead than behind. On clear nights Venus is at her most brilliant in the south-western sky, and in the early morning, as I make my way down to the cathedral, blackbirds are starting to sing in the Close. There are few signs of life in fields and gardens, though willows are changing colour and glow in the muted landscape, in some lights a rich orange, in others a deep gold. Snowdrops cut a broad swathe through the wood at Heale House, among them patches of bright yellow aconites, known in Suffolk as 'choirboys' on account of their ruffs. In the milder days at the month's end, six fieldfare are grubbing and rootling in the puddles of mud on Martin Down, and larks are singing. As we walk on the Plain, surrounded by the ancient burial mounds and with Stonehenge in the distance, three ragged flocks of lapwing take to the air, over a hundred birds in each, and in the unexpected warmth of the sun half-a-dozen hares, golden brown, lie in the flint-strewn fields.

In the Books of Hours the unlaborious seasonal labour for bitter Februaries was **sitting by the fire**. In the French Hours of 1423, known as the Bedford Hours, a man of about my age, wrapped in a scarlet tunic and blue cloak and wearing a hat, has removed one boot and is toasting his foot before a blazing fire, over which a hanging pot of water is boiling. The fireside is a reflective space, where to the crackling of logs stories might be told to ease the long, dark evenings.

Sharing and coming to understand our own and each other's story may be a valued part of the process of learning to dance. For what is it to learn to dance but to spend a lifetime learning to love, slowly (and often painfully) coming to understand the nature of that giving, offering and sharing of yourself which is how the image of God within us is most commonly glimpsed. Learning to love starts (or falters) at our mother's knee, ideally within the safe confines of a two-parent family, but often now in a single-parent setting, which in turn may call upon all the motherly qualities latent in good fathers. Freud said that a person thrives throughout life if he or she has received as a child 'his mother's entire devotion'. Too often children are starved of love and consequently emotionally crippled. The poet Mary Oliver writes: 'After a cruel childhood, one must reinvent oneself. Then reimagine the world.' During over forty years as a priest, like every pastor or counsellor, I have sought to help people in that painful process. I have listened for countless hours to those many individuals whose sense of worth, of being loved unconditionally, has withered on the branch because one or both parents have failed in that most demanding of tasks – usually because they in their turn missed out on the enviable confidence of those who walk through the world knowing what it means to be loved.

I cannot remember my father, though he seems to have left a good taste in the memories of those few people who have spoken to me about him; in my own life he simply left an immense emptiness. So if I am to speak honestly of my own hesitant growth in the dance of life, then I must begin with that 30-year-old woman who came home from shopping in Northampton on an afternoon in May 1932 to find her deeply private husband dead, having left her a brief note before jumping from the tower of the church of which he was the parish priest. Overnight, she found herself homeless, with a 3-year-old son and £40 in the world. She took me to London. My one surviving grandparent was a grandmother, herself widowed at 37, a tiny, nervous sparrow of a woman whose passion was playing bridge and snooker. (She was to do so daily to the age of 98, and died after a fall aged 101.) She lived in London, in a small hotel beside St Marylebone station. For a year we joined her there, sharing her room; and one of my earliest memories is lying in bed and watching her hook herself, inch by inch, into a pink corset which seemed to stretch from neck to knee. In a while I went to nursery school (Miss Betty's in Regent's Park): the blond child and his beautiful mother turned out to be John Julius Norwich

18

and Lady Diana Cooper. Eventually my godfather rented a house for us in St John's Wood and for five years my undomesticated mother ran it as a boarding house, though looking back I cannot imagine a less likely combination. It was my first home, the memories still vivid after over sixty years. On the top floor, across the landing from our bedroom, lodged Elizabeth French, blonde and glamorous, an actress who, each Christmas, played the principal boy in a London pantomime. I adored her, and a lifelong passion for the theatre began in 1936 in her dressing room at the King's Theatre, Hammersmith, as I strapped on the sword with which, as Jack, she had just climbed the beanstalk and despatched the Giant. Each summer we spent two weeks on the Isle of Wight, the first at Seaview, from where I watched the pre-War liners sailing into Southampton; the next at Shanklin (Arthur Askey on the sea front, Tommy Trinder on the Pier); and a final week with my grandmother and her bridge cronies in Bexhill, from where in 1939 we listened in a hotel bedroom to Chamberlain's fateful announcement.

The five good years ended overnight, and the three of us, plus a greatly loved bull terrier (recipient over the years of many of my childhood's lonely secrets) took the long train journey to south Devon, where for the next ten years my home was a succession of meagre boarding houses and dingy small hotels: Anstey's Cove at Babbacombe, the Belvedere (with a fruit machine to which my grandmother became addicted), Aros Cove, where steam trains passed within a few yards of the bedroom, and Redlands, all in that bit of coast which is a kind of buffer state, no longer Torquay but not quite Paignton, where we survived on dried egg, spam, Woolton pie, one egg and two pints of milk a week, six ounces of butter, two ounces of cooking fat, and (from 1942) two ounces of sweets; fatless pastry, eggless cakes, sugarless puddings and meatless soup; sticky tape criss-crossed on the windows as protection against infrequent tip-and-run raids, and the nightly hum of German bombers on their way to devastate Plymouth. I remember the troops weary from Dunkirk, many bandaged, gathered for tea and buns in the front garden of the Belvedere; watching Paignton pier cut in two to deter an invasion force; climbing on the slowly rusting scaffolding frames set up as anti-tank devices on all the beaches, and seeing a German plane shot down on Torquay sands. I remember the jagged gaps in nearby roads after the occasional stray bomb, and my mixture of pride and embarrassment at being publicly commended for vigilance at a school assembly for reporting a very small bomb in the gutter which had turned out to be a bicycle horn; and listening endlessly to the wireless.

Those years are a rich bran-tub of radio memories: listening as I lay behind the sofa to *Garrison Theatre* with Jack Warner and his sisters Elsie and Doris Waters; to *ITMA*, with Mrs Mopp the office cleaner, Claude and Cecil the brokers' men, Ali Oop the persistent pedlar, Signor So-So the hopeless Italian spy, the alcoholic Colonel Chinstrap, the ominous Funf and the gloomy Diver ('Every penny makes the water warmer'). There was *Hi Gang!* with Ben Lyon, Bebe Daniels and Churchill's unlikely son-in-law, Vic Oliver; Askey and Richard Murdoch in *Bandwagon*; and, on the twice-weekly *Workers' Playtime* from a factory canteen, Flanagan and Allan or the incomparable Robb Wilton, with his impeccable timing and, it was said, the sort of ruminative style which Shakespeare might have given to one of the yokels in Dogberry's Watch; all interspersed with the sometimes-devastating news bulletins introduced by Bruce Belfrage, John Snagge or Alvar Liddell; and the speeches of Churchill. Even to an 11-year-old the powerful oratory of Churchill's wartime broadcasts was arresting, and the exploits of the RAF's Rockfist Rogan in my weekly *Hotspur* were forgotten while we gathered to listen in the cramped kitchen.

The delights of radio and weekly comics compensated for the misery of school. For one horrendous term in 1939 the only space was in a girls' school, where my final humiliation was to be sat on by several girls during break and forced to eat acorns; but the real anguish was to come. I was the classic case study in the bullying syndrome: an only child, living with a mother and grandmother, timid, useless at games, and happy with my own company. The headmaster of my private school ruled his small kingdom with an unforgivably sadistic regime of threats and beatings. Never have I been so frightened as I was of him, and I carried the scars of his impact for far too long. Many times I feigned illness; twice I played truant. An ancient member of staff, employed in wartime far beyond retirement age, sometimes met me in the town and slipped me a comforting sixpence; I was forced to box, and when battered into the floor by a much larger boy was (to my indignation) commended for 'courage'; only one member of staff, an elderly English teacher with hair coiled like great earphones on each side of her head, read us Browning and Shakespeare and lit a fuse which went on burning. In the absence of wood for carpentry we were encouraged to knit very long scarves for sailors.

Meanwhile my mother had become, with huge enjoyment and enthusiasm, a baker's roundsman, and in the holidays I would ride with her in the van, delivering the wartime luxury of currant buns, some filled with synthetic cream; while my grandmother spent afternoons at her bridge club, returning home with tales of foolish partners and failed grand slams, and in the evening knitted unforgettable peach or baby-blue bedjackets (ten rows on needles the size of chopsticks alternating with ten on needles the size of mature asparagus, which made them kind of baggy). She sold them throughout the war for 30 shillings each, topping her century just before VE Day. And then, as Italy surrendered and the Russians were finally beating back the Germans, came the time for me to move school.

Nicky de Bobrov, a 12-year old Muscovite, spoke recently of acting in a school performance of *Hamlet*: 'Hamlet has got a lot of problems very similar to mine. There is the problem with his mother, and his father is dead.' (An echo there of the woman who was heard saying to her friend as they emerged from a performance of *Anthony and Cleopatra* at Stratford: 'You know, dear, the very same thing happened to Maureen.' But then, Shakespeare is nothing if not contemporary.) I, too, had a dead father and a problem with my mother. Overprotective, realising the need for me to go away to school, yet with little in the bank, she settled for the only option: she came too. She had been an outstanding tennis player, playing at Wimbledon for 12 years and once being trounced on the Centre Court by the legendary Suzanne Lenglen. Now she did a deal with the headmaster: she would come as tennis coach (where she would be a huge success) and assistant matron (another story), and in return I would receive free education. It was not a good plan. Bullied and unhappy, I would run to her at every opportunity. I could not escape her and she could not let me go. Salvation finally came 18 months later when she fell in love, remarried, and (to my initial consternation) went to live for the next 12 years in Africa. That began to solve the problem at school: it did not restore the holidays to anything resembling normality for a bookish teenager.

For the next four years I spent practically all of them at my grandmother's small hotel. Although I loved her, it was not the best setting in which to learn the dance. Each Sunday I reluctantly accompanied her to a church which was so unbelievably boring that it nearly put paid to my faith. Each weekday morning there was distress if I did not go with her to have coffee with one of her friends at the Gay Heart (not a likely name for a genteel teashop today). And five times a week I would go alone to one of Torquay or Paignton's seven cinemas. In those days of non-stop, double feature performances, sometimes with a singalong organ interlude where the coloured lights on the organ matched the mood, one would often arrive in the middle of the plot and have to stay to see it round to the point where you came in. I would return to write a short private review, before spending the evening in the lounge at Redlands, reading James Agate's diaries or C. A. Lejeune's film reviews to the sound of clicking knitting needles or Captain Ward (who had a wooden leg) rumbling on about life at sea. A craving for the radio had given way to a passion for Hollywood.

In *A Cinemagoer's Autobiography*, the Italian novelist Italo Calvino writes of the years of his adolescence when he too went to the cinema once or even twice a day, and when

> the cinema became the world for me ... There was a hero available for every temperament: for those who aimed to tackle life through action, Clark Gable represented a sort of brutality leavened with boastful swagger; Gary Cooper was cold blood filtered through irony; for those who counted on overcoming obstacles with a mixture of humour and savoir faire, there was the aplomb of William Powell and the discretion of Franchot Tone; for the introvert who masters his shyness there was James Stewart ... and we were even given a rare example of the intellectual hero in Leslie Howard.

Startled as I am now to recall such a massive amount of cinema-going, there is comfort in Calvino's words:

> [It was] a different world from the one around me, but my feeling was that only what I saw on the screen possessed the qualities required of a world, the fullness, the necessity, the coherence, while away from the screen were only heterogenous elements lumped together at random, the materials of a life, mine, which seemed to be utterly formless. The cinema ... satisfied a need for disorientation, for the projection of my attention into a different space, a need which I believe corresponds to a primary function of our assuming our place in the world, an indispensable stage in any character formation.[3]

I guess what was important was not so much the gathering of factual knowledge, for the world of American films was a world unto itself and had little connection with the real world of school and Redlands, food rationing and drinking coffee at the Gay Heart, but it helped provide at that uniquely impressionable age what Calvino calls 'the storehouse of images, private sensations'. Christmas was always the worst time: dressing-up and word games for a dozen residents united by nothing but the same small hotel, and music hall songs led by Bertie, the landlady's elderly beau.

And then there was my mother, departing from my side after a mutually dependent relationship to an unimaginable life at the far side of the world. Three times married, three times widowed, she was a remarkable woman of boundless energy. One of her very few friends in her final years – she lived to 96 – wrote to me after she died: 'I have lit a candle for dear Bay. So lovable! So impossible! So unforgettable!' She was all those things: lovable, for she had an extraordinary enthusiam for life and a fine sense of humour; she loved people and was naturally kind, full of fun and laughter. But sometimes she was indeed impossible, and those who crossed her path did not quickly forget her. Her Wimbledon years had made her fiercely competitive, which could be exhausting, for everything was a challenge. Enormously interested in her health, and unable to understand the failure of doctors to make home-visits several times a week, she moved from practice to practice but found no satisfaction. She believed that laws were there to be challenged: if caught for speeding or parking, a frequent offence, she would go straight to the top and invariably (infuriatingly) get away with it. It was this fierce energy that kept her young. Aged nearly ninety and in perfect health, she limped into the council offices and obtained a disabled parking ticket, and on Shrove Tuesday was booked by a traffic warden for then parking her car on double yellow lines on Torquay sea front and running in the over-50s pancake race. Cannoning into a car from behind, she was delighted to find a sticker in the back window reading 'Christians forgive one another' and traded on it hard. Her local butcher, enraged, once threw a pork chop at her. She rarely read a book but she loved her garden and the sea and was never, until she was 94, without a dog. In her various residential homes – and having been finally persuaded to leave her cottage and give up driving she worked her way through seven of them – she would build up a mountain of cushions opposite her bed so that, waking in the night, she and the dog might have immediate eye-contact.

I loved her dearly, but because of her emotional demands my love was often mixed with anger and resentment, until her world contracted more and more into the tiny world of her own room and my resentment shrivelled, to be replaced with the compassion I should have experienced long before. For here was the one who had, in the only way she knew, tried to teach me the early steps of the dance of love. I did not understand until too late how much her own traumas had taken their toll: losing her father at seven, her first husband from suicide, her second from a burst aorta, her third (a wonderfully happy too-brief marriage in old age) from cancer. She tried to shut her eyes to the pain, wanted life to be simpler and more perfect than it is, and spent her days searching for an emotional love which matched her own. She had always needed a man in her life, and in those times between marriages and in extreme old age she looked to me as her only living blood relative to fill the roles of son, father, husband and priest. Time and again, and perhaps inevitably, I failed her. The emotional ties were too close, the baggage of the years too complex. Like many of us I am better at giving comfort to friends, or even strangers. In the end perhaps only her succession of dogs gave her that unconditional affection she so craved.

I was left wondering afresh at the complexity of the dance. It is not simply only sons and only daughters who are vulnerable to the potential conflict, not least when they are married, between the duty owed to a parent and the primary duty and loyalty to their own family, though only children carry a greater burden. It is a conflict that can give you bad dreams, and sometimes a lasting sense of remorse, for few of us get it dead right. But how to atone? Dr Johnson famously stood for an hour in the market-place in his native

Lichfield to atone for his behaviour toward his father when he was alive.

Yet the failures in this most complex of relationships are rarely one-sided, and nowhere does that degree of love we call forgiveness have more potent force. Even the best parents know that they sometimes fail their children, not because they do not love them but because they love them with what can be a suffocating, too-protective love; and children in their proper adult independence may fail their parents in innumerable ways. When the poet Rilke was a child his mother, who had longed for a daughter, dressed him as a girl and treated him as if he were a doll. Significantly, in his version of the story of the Prodigal Son, the younger brother leaves home because he cannot bear the weight of a love which feels to him like the constraint of those who would shape him in their own confining image. Each sometimes needs to ask forgiveness of the other for mishandling the dance, for nothing is ultimately beyond redemption, even when death intervenes with the healing words unsaid. When all is understood, all is forgiven; and as my awareness of my mother's yearning has grown, so has my ability and desire to forgive her. In her eyes I could do no wrong. That was part of the problem; but I knew better, and now in asking her forgiveness the lingering anger and guilt are resolved. Sometimes only in retrospect do you master the movements of this most complicated dance.

No one knows who wrote that loveliest of medieval poems that begins:

> I sing of a maiden
>> That is makeles [matchless],
> King of all kinges
>> To her sone sche ches [chose].

and which ends:

> Moder [mother] and maiden
>> Was never non but sche;

26

Well may swich a lady
  Godes moder be.

Endless theological tomes dealing with the central Christian belief in the incarnation gather dust in countless libraries, and many writers and artists illuminate the role of Mary in making possible the enfleshing of the Word, the birth of the child who was to reveal God narrowed to the slender thread of her bewildered 'yes'. Yet much less has been written of Mary's unique role as mother, with all that word implies. It is not simply that she loved her child. She (with Joseph) did for him what no one else could have done: she taught him the language of love, taught him by her own example that love must be generous, self-giving, non-possessive, and that always in the end it is costly. No doubt it was as hard for her as it is for every parent. She too learned to walk the knife-edge between giving her son the security of un-conditional love and setting him free. Which was good training for the coming days when, as Simeon had fore-cast, the 'sword pierced [her] own heart', as she and Joseph anxiously searched for him when the 12-year-old was already about his Father's business, or found herself excluded from his company when he claimed that 'whoever does the will of my heavenly Father is my brother and sister and mother'; or, finally, as she stood weeping at the foot of the cross. If he was the Lord of the Dance, she taught him not a few of the steps.

I buried my mother on a perfect May day in the idyllic Devon country churchyard where she had once lived and where my two stepfathers also lie. The young gravedigger sat on a wall on the far side of the churchyard. His sheepdog lay at his feet. When the short service ended the dog got up, walked over to the grave, sniffed around and left his mark. My mother would have liked that.

# The Stillness
# at the Dance's Centre

At the still point of the turning world . . .
Neither from nor towards; at the still point, there
the dance is.

*T. S. Eliot*[1]

Nothing in all creation is so like God as stillness.
*Meister Eckhart*

In calm detachment lies your safety, your strength
in quiet trust.

*Isaiah 30:15*

The poet Edward Thomas imagined the 'speculating rooks'
seeing

> from elm-tops, delicate as flowers of grass,
> What we below could not see, Winter pass.[2]

On mild days the bees are stirring. The grass on footpaths is
sprouting and buds breaking: horse chestnut buds are shedding their sticky brown scales. Long-tailed tits are building
their nests, and great tits noisily proclaim the coming of
spring from the high branches. Goldfinch, greenfinch and
siskin, come daily to the bird-feeder. Primroses line the tall

Devon lanes of my childhood, and in the hedges the goat (or pussy) willow is flowering, the silver-grey male catkin buds which appeared last month now turning yellow-gold; once they were known as 'goslings', because their texture resembled that of newly hatched geese. Those 'spring messengers', the butter-coloured lesser celandine, are in full flower, opening and closing their petals according to the degree of light and warmth of the day; it was Wordsworth's favourite flower and he wrote three poems in its honour. Late in the month at Kempley, on the Gloucestershire–Herefordshire border, the wild daffodils known as Lent lilies stand in wondrous profusion round the Norman church, with its barrel roof and Romanesque frescoes, and carpet the churchyard.

In the Flemish calendar from the sixteenth-century Book of Hours, the March occupation is gardening, with the emphasis on **pruning**. An aproned gardener dressed in blue, interrupted in his digging, is doffing his hat to the lady of the manor in a pink surcoat with fur cuffs; in the background another is pruning fruit trees; while in a panel at the foot, five plump men are playing a curious game with rattles.

In *Burnt Norton*, Eliot writes that

> At the still point of the turning world . . .
> . . . there the dance is . . .
> . . . Except for the point, the still point,
> There would be no dance, and there is only the dance.[3]

After looking back at the personal, and before looking out at the cosmos, I want to pause and look within. Gardeners shape their plants by pruning, and each type of shrub responds to different degrees of pruning if it is not to outgrow its strength, run to seed or smother its neighbour. A life with no space, no still point, at its centre may be in need of some hard pruning if it is to grow to its own proper shape. The physicist David Bohm has written of how in

Latin the root of the word 'whole' means both 'to cure' and also 'to measure', and he relates it to the Platonic notion that every being, every thing, has its *right inward measure*; that a beech tree or a rose has its own quality of wholeness that gives it its proper shape; that each human being has a right inward measure, too, when everything is balanced and physiologically homeostatic.[4] There must be a balance, a proper tension, in my body between my public life and my inner space; the fusion of my inner and outer worlds. To be a person is to know at your centre an inviolable and unique personal space: it is what gives us our own integrity, a sense of our own reality. Each of us is called to grow (in the company of others) to our own right inward measure. If I am to do so, I must explore that kind of inner stillness which leads to harmony and enables me to do two things: to respond to God, who is both the source of my being and my ultimate destiny; and to recognise that on the journey each person and each object I set eyes on challenges me to recognise their right inward measure as well. The only way of doing so is by learning how to give them proper attention, as a way of recognising their proper space and learning to love them.

There is a house in Cambridge called Kettle's Yard, a house full of light and space. Twenty years ago its owner, Jim Ede, left the house and its contents to the University and each afternoon it is open to all. Here are paintings and sculpture, pottery and glass, books and plates and furniture, together with stones picked up on beaches and feathers picked up in fields. Ede was an inspired contemplative, able to create just the right space and light for each object to be seen in its own right; yet somehow each one is also related to all the rest. They stand, it has been said, 'as if entranced with each other'; and I know no domestic interior that creates in you such a sense of stillness, symmetry and pleasure.

There are certain people in whom you sense this inner harmony: they are centred, at one with themselves, poised to be attentive to whoever or whatever claims their attention, yet at ease – if need be – with their own solitude, that solitude which is the private source of memory and imagination. 'That man's silence is wonderful to listen to,' says Elias Spinks of Geoffrey Day in Hardy's *Under the Greenwood Tree*.[5] Such people are not scared of silence, but have learned to recognise it as something the spirit needs from time to time if it is to flourish in a world where noise invades our lives at every point. For it is sound which, when pitted against sight, wins out every time. I can block out those beside me on the train by burying myself in a book, but not this girl's invasive rap-beat leaking from her Walkman or the sound of that man noisily trading on his mobile. The ear is less easily stilled: noise mocks our privacy as light and colour on the retina never can.

Henry Thoreau, who built a wooden hut in the woods on the edge of Walden Pond in Massachusetts and produced one of the seminal books of the nineteenth century, wrote, 'I love a wide margin to my life', and reflected on the space necessary for contemplation, or 'the forming of a self'. He believed that the mass of people 'lead lives of quiet desperation'. Not that he escaped from the world like some desert mystic: from his hut he could hear 'the rattle of railroad cars, now dying away and then reviving like the beat of a partridge'. On his deathbed he asked that he might be lifted up in order to catch through the window a glimpse of one more spring. The Trappist monk, Thomas Merton, had read Thoreau's *Walden* in 1950, at exactly the moment when, in the setting of the wooded hills of his monastery in the mountains at Gethsemani, he made the most important discovery of his life: his vocation to solitude. From time to time, over the next 18 years, he escaped to his tiny hermitage, a hut in the woods where he explored that solitude he called 'a deepening of the present', and in which he not only grew in his awareness of God but also in his passionate love of the natural world. The Irish Augustinian poet, Padraig J. Daly, writes in his poem, 'Thomas Merton':

What is to be said about silence
Except that it is;
And you sought it out diligently in your woods,
Living alone with your books,
In the company of birds;

Walking to morning prayer on a snow carpet,
Nothing there before you
But the marks of the monastery cat
On the white ground;

Or the form where deer slept
Close to your window,
Rhythmically heaving with your sleep's heaving?

And there is little you can send us out of your silence
Except to say that it is;
And it cries out louder than our clamour.[6]

The fourteenth-century German mystic Meister Eckhart claimed that 'nothing in all creation is so like God as stillness', words which hung on my study wall at Westminster; enveloped as I was by the noise and bustle of that spinning city and high-profile place, they were a daily reminder of the truth about where our search for God must begin. At my own centre, and in the moment that is 'now'. For Eckhart also says, 'People who dwell in God dwell in the eternal Now.'[7] In Westminster Abbey, in the heart of that busy, crowded church, many found that stillness in the prayer-soaked walls of St Faith's Chapel, womb-like behind its thick oak door; and I have fed on such stillness in ancient village churches, or in deep woods, or at sunset on a Hebridean island, a stillness made all the more profound by the distant sound of sheep or a tractor or a barking dog. For most of us, the search for that tranquillity of spirit which lies at the dance's centre does not require Merton's solitude or a total absence of noise. That's a rare luxury. There can be a deep corporate stillness in the audience in a concert hall or a theatre, a calm created by the magic of music or the seductive dance of words. 'I think', said Saul Bellow, 'that art has something to do with the achievement of stillness in the midst of chaos. A stillness which characterises prayer too, and the eye of the storm.'[8] And Chekhov once wrote that he celebrated 'the private silence in which we live, and which enables us to endure our own solitude'.[9]

'At the still point of the turning world . . . /There the dance is.' If time is the dance and we are caught up in this 'dance to the music of time', yet at the heart of the dance, at the centre of *my* turning world in the moment that is *now*, I can discover a still point. A ballet dancer knows that without the still point there can be no dance. Over two millennia ago, Lao Tse, in the *Tao-te-ching*, wrote:

> Thirty spokes share the wheel's hub;
> but it is the centre hole which makes it useful.
> Shape clay into a vessel,
> but it is the space within that makes it useful.

Isaiah and Jeremiah liken God to a potter moulding clay. To complement these days of writing I am learning pottery at the local arts centre. Surrounded by women throwing immaculate teapots and elegant vases, I toil away undaunted at a pottery Eeyore for my granddaughter, remembering to make the space within its head and body and a hole in the tail, for else it will explode in the kiln. To be human is to be shaped by God with a space at our centre. The mystics of all traditions speak of what Thomas Merton calls 'a point of nothingness at the centre of our being that belongs entirely to God'. He is voicing one side of a strong tradition.

There have always been those who speak of God as Wholly Other, inconceivable and remote and utterly unlike our abortive attempts to picture him in our own image. Others have come to see God as the Reality present in all things, the true ground of our being. Here is the paradox of God transcendent and God immanent, God beyond and God within, two approaches which seem mutually exclusive, yet which speak both of my undeniable sense of awe and longing, my knowing and not-knowing, yet an encounter deep within myself. 'God' writes Harry Williams, 'is both other than I am and also the same . . . the source from which I continually flow. In my deep union with the mystery of another person and in the mystery of my own being, what I find is God.'[10]

'Our whole business in life', writes St Augustine, 'is to restore to health the eye of the heart whereby God may be seen.' 'In every soul, even the greatest sinner in the world,' writes St John of the Cross, 'God dwells, and is substantially present.' 'We are not forced to take wings to find God,' writes St Teresa of Avila,'but have only to seek solitude and look within ourselves'; and in the eighteenth century William Law wrote, 'Though God be present everywhere, yet he is present to thee in the deepest and most central part of the soul.' That is the only possible place in the universe where I may find him, and it echoes words of Meister Eckhart, that if we seek God in the world about us we shall find him nowhere, but if we first find him within we shall begin to find him everywhere. So for me, the 'still point of the dancing world . . . /[where] the dance is' can only be at that still point that lies at my own centre. I find God here, or I do not find him at all.

> I know this happiness
> is provisional:
>
>> the looming presences –
>> great suffering, great fear –
>>
>> withdraw only
>> into peripheral vision:
>
> but ineluctable this shimmering
> of wind in the blue leaves:

this flood of stillness
widening the lake of sky:

this need to dance,
this need to kneel:
            this mystery.[11]

So writes Denise Levertov. Silence, however, when applied to God, is an equivocal word. Herman Melville once wrote, 'Silence is the only Voice of our God.' That cuts both ways. It can imply absence or presence; a vacant emptiness or a Mystery which is infinitely beyond anything we can know or name. Melville's words might serve equally as a motto for the Humanist Society or for the Society of Friends; and in their positive sense they could be claimed by all those who have searched for the elusive God, from Isaiah ('Truly thou art a God who hidest thyself'[12]) to R. S. Thomas: He is

such a fast
God, always before us and
leaving as we arrive.[13]

For many, it is God's strange and haunting echo that draws them, rather than his calculable presence. Not-knowing is part of our encounter with the holy, and if we are honest, when all the dusty theological words are ended, we are left with the words with which Wittgenstein ends his great work on philosophy: 'Whereof one cannot speak, therein one must remain silent.'[14].

But there is much of which we can speak and nothing witnesses more convincingly to the godlikeness of the human spirit than the creative dance of language. In that most poetic and truthful of myths, the creation story in Genesis, God speaks the Word out of his eternal silence. He 'speaks' the land and sky and sea, the sun and moon and stars; he 'speaks' the plants and birds and fish; he 'speaks' the animals and he 'speaks' us; and finally, in the fullness of time (no longer mythical time but true, historical time) he 'speaks' (in his Word made flesh) as much of himself as we can understand in the startling form of one who is both like and unlike us: like us in the whole familiar feel of this man's birth and life and pain and dying, unlike us in the integrity of a life of trust and undefeated, self-giving love. Alan Ecclestone once said that 'the work of Jesus Christ consisted in his obedience to, his unswerving trust in, the Silence he called Father'. But it was not the silence of absence or emptiness: it was the silence of a creative, sustaining Love that held him; a Love that speaks in the moment that is now and to those who recognise his language. A language that lies beyond words: one that is learned in a spirit of 'obedience and unswerving trust'. So R. S. Thomas writes of kneeling in a small church in summer

> waiting for the God
> To speak: the air a staircase
> For silence . . .

yet knowing the importance of waiting:

> Prompt me, God,
> But not yet. When I speak
> Though it be you who speak
> Through me, something is lost.
> The meaning is in the waiting.[15]

That is a clear echo of some of Eliot's familiar lines, of how we so often hope for, and love, the wrong things, and of how

> the faith and the love and the hope are all in the waiting.
> Wait without thought, for you are not ready for thought:
> So the darkness shall be the light, and the stillness the
>     dancing.[16]

Prayer takes many forms, but I have come to understand the heart of it as a disciplined taking of time to remind ourselves of who we are and whose we are, in which the one necessary element is stillness. Which is why this simple contemplation is often so demanding, constantly at war with our spinning thoughts, this waiting quietly on the God who is the dynamic stillness at the heart of the universe, and therefore at the heart of the dance.

At the still point, there the dance is,
But neither arrest nor movement.

It is the stillness (which in our spiritual lives may well embrace times of darkness and barrenness), the passive, receptive, giving of attention which in the end feeds us best.

The Chinese sages wrote that the man in whom the child's heart and mind had died is no better than a dead man, yet when it comes to giving attention a child's and an adult's sensibility are very different. Children observe the world more nakedly, freshly, unconditionally, spontaneously; in Rilke's words:

A child may
wander there for hours, through the timeless
stillness[17]

absorbed by what lies before their eyes. Ted Hughes writes of how we lose the child's way of seeing:

Preconceptions are already pressing, but they have not yet closed down, like a space helmet, over the entire head and face, with the proved, established adjustments of security . . . We lose in readiness to change, in curiosity, in perception, in the original, wild, no-holds-barred approach . . . Picasso knew what he was doing when he expended his tremendous energy to strip himself back to that child nakedness.[18]

Hughes is right, but the recovery of that vision in maturity or old age is of a different kind. Victor Klemperer, from his diary written in wartime Dresden on 1 January 1942, writes:

It is said children still have a sense of wonder, later one becomes blunted. Nonsense. A child takes for granted, and most people get no further; only an old person, who thinks, is aware of the wondrous.[19]

Children see with new-minted eyes, old people (if they are wise) with wonder; but it is artists, like mystics, who have always witnessed to the creative power of silence and recognised that if we would search for meaning then it is to both the inner and the outer landscapes of our lives that we must look, allowing the eye, that most remarkable function of the brain, all the time it needs. 'Let us not . . . go hurrying about and collecting honey,' wrote Keats, 'bee-like buzzing here and there impatiently for a knowledge of what is to be aimed at; but let us open our leaves like a flower and be passive and receptive.'[20] Ronald Blythe tells of how the Orkney poet George Mackay Brown would spend time each afternoon sitting in front of a coal fire in order to 'interrogate silence'. No artist (or scientist) could report accurately on the world without this readiness to give attention to its constantly changing richness and mystery. Art, like music or poetry or any work of the imagination, is born out of contemplation, and that gives it the power to touch a deep, inner space within us.

Painting would seem the truest medium of passive reflection. I have written at length elsewhere[21] of how painters of landscape or the human portrait have given their absorbed attention to the mystery of the individuality of each object and person so that they may discover how (in Gerard Manley Hopkins' words) everything 'selves – goes itself; myself it speaks and spells,'[22] revealing what Hopkins calls its 'inscape', its 'thisness': that which makes it distinctively itself. John Ruskin, though Hopkins' contemporary, knew nothing of Hopkins' writing, but it was his lifelong desire to capture something of the truth and mystery of an object by observing not just its most minute detail but its inner construction, its rhythms and tensions, which are revealed to a steady, silent, penetrating gaze. Then, by drawing it, he grew to love it, and felt something of the silent force and great mystery of its existence; its *right inward measure.* Whether it was an ivy leaf or the curve of a building, Ruskin saw both as incarnations of God's activity. Others, Monet and Cézanne, painted again and again the same scenes in the changing, shifting light, seeking to capture a moment in time that would never quite be repeated. And painters require of us, in this give-and-take of seeing and sharing, that we bring to their paintings something of that same quality of stillness and attention, so that from time to time we may in our turn be enabled to see aspects of the world with fresh vision, and allow that moment to live again.

Sometimes a painting succeeds in capturing the quality of a profound stillness. Words are necessary when it comes to analysing and describing explicit experiences, but they are less effective tools when it comes to capturing those experiences that cannot be analysed or measured. For the language of the heart is of another kind: it requires images, symbols, dance, music and silence. When all the words end, when human concepts will go no further in rooting out the meaning of our lives, and especially in the face of what Christians dare to claim about how God has acted in his creation, we are reminded of the primacy of silence. In the greatest paintings of the Annunciation, the image of Mary face-to-face with the angel – those, say, of Duccio or Crivelli in London's National Gallery – there is a kind of frozen silence and stillness, a moment in time that rests somewhere between an ordinary day and eternity, perfectly captured in Edwin Muir's poem, 'The Annunciation':

> Outside the window footsteps fall
> Into the ordinary day
> And with the sun along the wall
> Pursue their unrelenting way.
> Sound's perpetual roundabout
> Rolls its numbered octaves out
> And hoarsely grinds its battered tune.

But through the endless afternoon
These neither speak nor movement make,
But stare into their deepening trance
As if their gaze would never break.[23]

That great Australian novelist, Patrick White, asked to list his pet loves and hates, placed 'silence with birdsong' top of the first category and 'harsh noises' top of the second, and struggles in his autobiography to describe what is ultimately indescribable, the sense of

an over-reaching grandeur, a daily wrestling-match with an opponent whose limbs never become material, whose blood and sweat are scattered on the pages of anything a serious writer writes, whose essence is contained *less in what is said than in the silences* [my italics]. In patterns on water. A gust of wind. A flower opening.[24]

His earlier namesake, Gilbert White, perpetual curate of Selborne, records the natural life of his village in meticulous detail, a swallow taking a fly 'like the noise of the shutting of a watch-case'. He teaches us how to look, with his silent vigils, getting up early and staying out late, as the natural world slowly releases to him its secrets. The naturalist Richard Jefferies was to say of him: 'It is in this quietness that the invisible becomes visible'. And it is in the natural world that the silence of anticipation or of recall can touch us, as in this stanza in Wallace Stevens' poem 'Thirteen Ways of Looking at a Blackbird':

I do not know which to prefer,
The beauty of inflections
Or the beauty of innuendoes,
The blackbird whistling
Or just after.[25]

Perhaps the secret of every true mystery is that it is both simple and profound, depending on the attention we pay to it. Like that familiar event: the birth of a child.

> There is no mystery on Earth
> Exceeds the mighty miracle of birth.
> Not all the fearful mystery of death
> Surpasses that first breaking into light
> And timid, fragile breath.[26]

Childbirth, or music. In Bernard MacLaverty's novel *Grace Notes*, Catherine, a young composer, is listening to her composition played in public for the first time:

> The music is simple. A simple idea – the way life is simple – a woman produces an egg and receives a man's seed into her womb and grows a baby and brings another person into the world. Utterly simple. Or so amazingly complex that it cannot be understood. So far beyond us that it is a mystery. And yet it happens every minute of every day. How can something be utterly simple and amazingly complex at the same time? Things are simple or complex according to how much attention is paid to them ... She has reached down into the tabernacle of herself for this music and feels something sacred in its performance.[27]

It is, if we have eyes to see or ears to hear, a kind of transfiguration of the commonplace, what Wordsworth called 'objects recognised /in flashes, and with glory not their own',[28] 'according to how much attention is paid to them'.

The wit Sidney Smith, one-time Canon of St Paul's, said of Lord Macaulay, 'He has occasional flashes of silence that make his conversation perfectly delightful.'[29] In that spirit I will stop this flow of words with what seems to me a perfect recipe if we would learn to recognise the still point at the dance's centre. It comes from Kierkegaard.

> But what does this mean, what have I to do, or what sort of effort is it that can be said to seek or pursue the Kingdom of God? Shall I try to get a job suitable to my talents and powers in order thereby to exert an influence? No, thou shalt first seek God's kingdom. Shall I then give all my fortune to the poor? No, thou shalt first seek God's kingdom. Shall I then

41

go out to proclaim this teaching to the world? No, thou shalt first seek God's kingdom. But then in a certain sense it is nothing I shall do. Yes, certainly, in a certain sense it is nothing: thou shalt in the deepest sense make thyself nothing, become nothing before God, learn to keep silent; in this silence is the beginning, which is, first to seek God's kingdom.[30]

# APRIL

## *The Dance of the Cosmos*

I danced in the morning when the world was begun,
And I danced in the moon and the stars and the
sun.

*Sydney Carter*

Man has weav'd out a net, and this net throwne
Upon the Heavens, and now they are his owne.

*John Donne*[1]

The Brain – is wider than the Sky –
For – put them side by side –
The one the other will contain
With ease – and You – beside.

*Emily Dickinson*[2]

Anyone informed that the universe is expanding
and contracting in pulsations of 80 billion years has
a right to ask, 'What's in it for me?'

*Peter de Vries*[3]

April is the month of the greening of the trees, and sudden
late frosts. In the woods the white wood anemone, the wind-
flower, is thick on the ground; known in parts of Derbyshire

as 'Moggie nightgown', it speaks of ancient woodland and only spreads by six feet every hundred years. Along the woodland paths the unscented dog violets are flowering, and around the woodland edges both wild cherry and black-thorn are in bloom; for John Clare the blackthorn in full flower 'that shines about the hedges' was 'like cloaths hung out to dry'. Willow warblers have arrived and are singing in the topmost branches; the rooks are building and the swallows are here and are looping and threading great pockets of sky: as a boy, W. G. Sebald would imagine that the world 'was held together by the courses they flew through the air'.[4] On the sandy cliffs at Hengistbury Head sand martins sweep in and out of their nests: some hundred holes, each two or three feet deep, are ranged like portholes along the clifftop. The new ferns begin to unfurl their crozier-like heads, the hedges are sprinkled with stitchwort and periwinkle; and the lawn needs cutting. At Clearbury Ring, by the end of the month, cowslips are covering the sloping chalky grassland round the copse; once they were as abundant as the but-tercup, and are now returning on the banks of motorways. Kingcups, or marsh-marigolds, one of our most ancient plants, are flowering in the dark mud of the creeks beside the Avon. There will be clumps of Shakespeare's 'bold oxlips' on the boulder clay around Cambridge; and on a small patch of heath near Royston the even rarer purple pasqueflower, the Passiontide anemone. Toads have emerged from their holes in the ground, where they have lain buried since the autumn, having (in the eyes of George Orwell) a very spiri-tual look after their long fast, 'like a strict Anglo-Catholic towards the end of Lent'. In Selborne, Gilbert White's famous tortoise, Timothy, would always come out of hiber-nation in mid-April, White sometimes shouting at him through a speaking-trumpet, which he ignored, perhaps because an eventual post-mortem found him to be female.

In Books of Hours the occupation for the month was again **gardening**; for the Bedford Hours it was planting trees and 'carrying branches', and beside a tree stump and lopped branches a gardener in a scarlet smock is carrying what looks like a young apple tree over his shoulder, his tools dangling at his side.

Milton writes of that other garden, planted by God in Eden, our first mythical home:

A Heaven on Earth: for blissful Paradise
Of God the Garden was, by him in the East
Of Eden planted . . .
              . . . in this pleasant soile . . .
Out of the fertil ground he caused to grow
All trees of noblest kind for sight, smell, taste;
And all among them stood the Tree of Life,
High eminent, blooming Ambrosial Fruit
Of vegetable Gold; and next to Life
Our Death the Tree of Knowledge grew fast by.[5]

But Eden was lost. The Genesis account of creation, perhaps the greatest of the creation myths, deeply buried in the collective unconscious and serving generations of poets and painters, has tugged at the heartstrings of all who grieve for a lost innocence, this sense that we still have what Edwin Muir calls 'one foot in Eden' and yearn for 'a new heaven and a new earth'. But what really happened?

'The first man of science', wrote Samuel Taylor Coleridge, 'was he who looked into a thing, not to learn whether it could furnish him with food, or shelter, or weapons, or tools, or ornaments, or *play-withs*, but who sought to know it for the gratification of knowing.'[6] I enter the world of science sharing W. H. Auden's nervousness, when finding himself in the company of scientists, of 'feeling like a shabby curate who has strayed by mistake into a drawing room full of dukes'.[7] But I take courage from Einstein's belief that 'Religion without science is blind: science without religion is lame'; and from the fact that the best scientists – those who, in Carlyle's phrase, 'have eyes behind their spectacles' – are drawn to science by a sense of wonder and mystery which, rather than diminishing, increases with each new discovery about the cosmic dance. Einstein spoke of it as a 'rapt amazement', and the humanist Professor of the Public Understanding of Science at Oxford, Richard Dawkins, sub-titled his last book 'The Appetite for Wonder' and writes:

> The feeling of awed wonder that science can give us is one of the highest experiences of which the human psyche is capable. It is a deep aesthetic passion to rank with the finest that music and poetry can deliver.[8]

(It has been claimed that Dawkins, who dismisses the claims of religion as a self-perpetuating mental virus, has had such a stimulating effect on believers in their dialogue with science that 'if [he] had not existed, the Christian church might have found it necessary to invent him'.[9] Only a sense of wonder unites us.)

The ancients believed that the earth was the back of an elephant that stood on a tortoise that swam in a bottomless sea. Today we see it as a spinning globe, with people on all sides of it, some of them the wrong way up. But it is in fact just as mysterious and extraordinary as that bizarre primitive picture. Four years ago, on a mountain top in North Caro-lina, I watched through field glasses the comet Hale-Bopp moving across a clear night sky, trailing its broad tail of gas. None who saw it will forget the sight, made all the more awesome by the knowledge that it was last seen in the time of Cleopatra and that it will not be seen again for 2400 years. The backdrop was a sky speckled with a myriad of stars such as I had never seen before: not only the familiar groupings of the Plough and Cassiopeia, but thousands upon thousands of pinpricks of light as far as my binoculared eyes could take me. What my brain told me, drawing deep on odd scraps of memory, was an unlikely truth: that the nearest fixed star was about 25 million million miles away; that six specks of dust in Waterloo Station represent the extent to which space is populated with stars; that, even so, there are more stars in the galaxies than there are grains of sand on all the beaches in the world; and that this planet on which I stood was just one of them. What my eyes saw reduced me to silence: a silence born of awe at the unimaginable scale of the creation.

Stay for a while on that isolated mountain top on this cloudless night powdered with stars and let those who study the heavens speak of the scale of this cosmic dance. With the naked eye you can see a couple of thousand stars. Above you is the Milky Way Galaxy, a disc-shaped island in space which is our home and which, therefore, we see from the inside. It is a sweeping band of light, turning in space like a great wheel, composed of 300,000 million stars. Each one shines because it is a furnace of raging gas held together by the force of gravity, and each shines as brightly as our sun, itself simply one of those thousands of millions of stars, but located much closer to the edge. Until a generation ago astronomers thought that this was the extent of the universe, and that was mind-boggling enough. But more powerful telescopes, together with research on the analysis of light from those fuzzy patches of brightness called the nebulae, revealed something strange: a subtle shift in the colours of the spectrum from the blue end to the red end, and this indicated that the distance between them and us was growing greater – rather as the siren of a police car or ambulance has a lower pitch the further it gets from us (the Doppler effect).

In 1990 the Hubble space telescope was finally ready to transmit images back to earth. It was named after Edwin Hubble, who in 1929 had proved that the universe is expanding. Fast. In the time it takes you to read this chapter it will have expanded some quarter of a million miles in all directions. The Hubble telescope was pointed at areas of sky which even to a small telescope looked blank. What the resulting photographs revealed was that what had previously been seen as unfocused blobs of light were galaxies in their own right, islands in space of which there are now thought to be at least 10,000 million, each home to some 100,000 million stars. I make that about 1,600 galaxies for every person on earth. Clusters contain two or three galaxies; superclusters contain thousands of them. Imagine looking back from somewhere out there among the myriad galaxies, seeing one dancing flake that is our Milky Way. No longer the centre of the universe, our own island in space is reduced to being no more than a snowflake floating in the air.

The astronomer John Gribbin reduces all this space to a more homely size by comparing the sun to an aspirin: on that scale the nearest star in the Milky Way would be 95 miles away; if we change the scale, so that the Milky Way Galaxy is itself the aspirin, the Andromeda Galaxy (our nearest galactic neighbour) becomes another aspirin just thirteen centimetres away from it, and three metres away there is a galactic supercluster of some 200 aspirins (each one representing a galaxy containing hundreds of billions of stars) in a swarm as big as a football.[10] The American space probe Pioneer 10, launched in 1972, is already 7 billion miles away, and is expected to reach the star Aldebaran in another 2 million years. Because of the speed of light we are looking back in time. If we look at Andromeda we see it as it was 2.3 million years ago. If I knew where to look in the Milky Way, I could find about 150 stars the light of which left them in the year I was born. The light that is shining through my skylight as I write left the sun eight minutes ago. But, writes Richard Dawkins, 'point a large telescope at the Sombrero galaxy and you behold a trillion suns as they were when your tailed ancestors peered shyly through the canopy and India collided with Asia to raise the Himalayas.'[11]

When the facts leave me spinning, I turn to the pictures. The images captured by the Hubble telescope are breath-taking. The planets in the solar system, with their respective moons dancing attendance, are revealed in the subtlest geo-chemical colours: rusty Mars, one of the brightest objects in the night sky; the storms raging around Jupiter, with its dark and light bands the colour of opal; Saturn, one of the 'gas giants', circled by its bright ochre rings and accompanied by its 18 moons. The star nebulae are startlingly beautiful. Very large, hot stars give out so much light that they push the surrounding gas away from them and the colour of the gas shows what kinds of atom are emitting light: hydrogen is green, oxygen blue and nitrogen red. The shape and patterns of the resulting columns of gas and star clusters, never seen on earth before, are awesome: great splashes of gold, orange, purple and green. The Cat's Eye Nebula, 3,000 light years away in the Draco constellation, is like an unfurling scarlet poppy; the Cartwheel Galaxy, 500 million light years distant in the constellation of Sculptor, like an image of the London Eye, its centre gold, its outer ring a clear cobalt blue.

In the face of this new awareness of the sheer scale of the cosmic dance, some have dismissed traditional ideas of God the Creator as pre-scientific and invalid; yet the Genesis story is a poetic, not a literal, account of the creation and our place within it. Science and religion are not competitive, but complementary, disciplines. Science tackles the *'How?'* and *'What?'*, theology the *'Why?'*, questions, in order to stammer out some answers to the mystery of our lives, each without the other (as Einstein said) blind and incomplete. Even so, 'the wonders of the Lord cannot be fathomed. When anyone finishes he is only just beginning, and when he stops he will still be at a loss'.[12] Thoughtful believers have always known that our concept of the Being of God and his creative power is absurdly inadequate, and stand with Sir Isaac Newton when he admits to being 'like a boy playing on the sea-shore and diverting myself now and then finding a smoother pebble or a prettier shell than ordinary, while the great ocean of truth lay all undiscovered before me'.[13] Ironically, as with the exploration of the heavens, the gaining of new knowledge always seems to reveal that the universe is more extraordinary than we thought. The answer to the questions of science ('How does this function?' and 'What happens if . . .?') open up a host of further questions, the 'Who?' and 'Why?' questions of religion ('Who is

God?' and 'Why are we here?'), which are no less complex or final in terms of once-for-all answers. The more we know, the less we know. The more we penetrate the mystery of the creation, the less our immature concept of the Creator will serve.

Especially when lying awake in the small hours of the night.

> I could not sleep for thinking of the sky,
> The unending sky, with all its million suns
> Which turn their planets everlastingly
> In nothing, where the fire-haired comet runs.[14]

Or, as the Psalmist puts it:

> When I consider the heavens, the work of your fingers,
> the moon and the stars you have set in their courses,
> What are mortals, that you should be mindful of them?
> mere human beings that you should seek them out?[15]

Many feel overwhelmed by the sheer, improbable size of it all: how can I matter, treading my measure on this familiar planet for all-too-brief a span if it is no more than another grain of sand in the vast and boundless galaxies in space? 'What is a human being, and what use is he? His span of life is at most a hundred years; compared with unending time, his few years are like one drop from the ocean or a single grain of sand.'[16] The only persuasive answer to that is one that goes back to St Augustine. He said that a single human mind is of greater worth than the whole inanimate creation, for you and I can do to the creation what the creation, for all its awesome size, cannot do to us: we can observe it, measure it, explore it and wonder at it. It is as if in us the universe becomes conscious of itself. Against its 100,000 million galaxies we can place in the scales a few pounds of meat, the human brain. As Bertrand Russell said: 'The stars are in one's brain.' We can carry the knowledge and the images of the galaxies in our heads, and that makes us pretty special. We can create a Hubble telescope with its deep field images, so that the universe then exists both out there and *in here*: we can create it in our mind's eye and, as we explore it, wonder what it means. In the words of one of the few poets to write about science, Alfred Noyes:

> Yet we, who are borne on one dark grain of dust
> Around one indistinguishable spark
> Of star-mist, lost in one lost feather of light,
> Can by the strength of our own thought, ascend
> Through universe after universe; trace their growth
> Through boundless time, their glory, their decay;
> And on the invisible road of law, more firm
> Than granite, range through all their length and breadth,
> Their height and depth, past, present, and to come.[17]

This telescope in space can photograph objects so distant that we see them as they were when the universe was only about a million years old. And balloon-borne detectors are now being used to measure with great accuracy how far the galaxies are apart today, and how fast they are separating, and soon it may be possible, working backwards, to discover at what point they began this expansion in that first fraction of a second of cosmic history which Genesis calls 'in the beginning' and the majority of scientists call the Big Bang.

When Edwin Hubble made his revolutionary discovery that the universe was expanding, it implied that all its enormous amount of mass-possessing energy would once have been packed into a single point, unimaginably hot and infinitely dense. Theologians speak of God creating *ex nihilo*, out of nothing, and most scientists agree: somewhere between ten and twenty billion years ago both space and time came into existence when that point of singularity exploded. The world is not made *in* time, but *with* time (as Augustine also said). Then, during a tiny fraction of a second, an inflation took place under the pressure of a momentarily reversed gravitational force: there was a violent expansion when everything raced apart. Slowly, over a million years, the universe began to cool. Electrons and nuclei began to form stable atoms. With atoms and molecules as building blocks, gravity allowed matter to be formed until, after about 1,000 million years, the first stars, planets and galaxies were formed. Stars contracted under the force of gravity, becoming hot enough for nuclear fusion to produce chemical elements; then, after another 10,000 million years, they began to die, some exploding with titanic force as supernovae, their elements embodied in a new generation of stars and planets, including the sun and the earth, and later the moon, in our galaxy of the Milky Way. In another 1,000 million years the earth was ready for the generation of life, and at some point over the next 3,000 million years some molecules became large and complex enough to make copies of themselves and become the first specks of life. The vital green chlorophyll pigments developed and life evolved, plants and animals and sea creatures. For billions of years this ball was spinning, with its sunrise and sunset, its mountains and its seas, but there was nothing alive to see it. 'I cannot help thinking with renewed wonder', writes Jacquetta Hawkes, 'how this luscious green spring has taken a thousand million years to attain its present singing youth, having been conceived in a dead, hoary world and passed through an old age of flowerless evergreen.'[18]

Then at last, just 300,000 years ago, there emerged *Homo sapiens*, who was gradually to become a quite new kind of creature, an ensouled body, who knew good and evil and the freedom to choose between them, who could think and laugh and weep, and fall in love and grieve, and imagine and create; stardust become persons. The writers of Genesis were not far off the mark when they pictured God forming the first human beings 'from the dust of the ground', for every atom of carbon in our bodies and every atom of iron in our blood, was created in the stars and broadcast by supernovae explosions before the earth was formed. The priest/scientist Arthur Peacocke presents a vivid illustration of the timescale in the Earth's estimated 4 billion years of existence:

If the earth was formed at midnight of the day before yesterday and each hour is equivalent to one hundred million years, then life first appeared during yesterday morning. Only at 6 p.m. today did calcareous (hard-shelled) fossils appear; at 6 to 7 p.m. on this second day, the seas filled with shelled creatures; at 8 p.m. fishes evolved; at 9 p.m. amphibia appeared on land; by 11.30 p.m. mammals and the first primates had spread across the globe; monkeys and apes evolved at 11.50 p.m.; in the past few minutes of this second day hominids arose, and only on the last stroke of tonight's midnight bell do we see tool-making *Homo sapiens*.[19]

In 1965 two American radio astronomers discovered the existence of background radiation, part of the residual heat from the Big Bang that still suffuses the cosmos. It is a dim wash of particles of the electro-magnetic force – observable as the snow on our television screens when no network is transmitting – and when this radiation was examined, it not only displayed exactly the intensity and spectrum consistent with the Big Bang, but more subtle high-density regions that echoed the clusters of galaxies that dominate the universe today. Astronomers at Berkeley dubbed this structure 'the handwriting of God', the lingering signature of creation. At that unimaginable moment when the universe came into being, of which this background radiation is the echo, everything was within the point of infinite density; everything within the explosion. Everything still is.

'Why does the universe go to all the bother of existing?' asks Stephen Hawking. 'What is it that breathes fire into the equations and makes a universe for them to describe?'[20] To believe that God is the source and ground of this stunning cosmic dance, moment by moment holding his universe in being, is to reject the once-popular concept of God as William Paley's divine watchmaker (who makes a staggeringly beautiful watch and leaves it to tick away), or that of the omnipotent but absentee landlord (who will appear for the final reckoning). It is rather to affirm God as a creator who is both omnipresent in his creative power and perpetually and lovingly involved with what he has made. And one of the more persuasive witnesses to the divine underpinning of all that exists is what scientists call the Anthropic Principle.

This principle starts with us, set in a world of the most exact proportions and elegant balance. It says that if the universe were any different then we should not be here. It speaks of the charge of the electron, the strength of the gravitational force, of the exact universal values of certain physical quantities, and it says that if these values had been marginally different life would have been impossible. If the universe had expanded faster, it would have been unfeasible for the stars and planets to be formed. If the forces that hold together the atomic nuclei had been just marginally weaker, the universe would have been composed of hydrogen; if marginally stronger, of oxygen. The astronomers John Gribbin and Martin Rees conclude: 'The conditions in our universe really do seem to be uniquely suitable for life forms like ourselves';[21] indeed Rees, the Astronomer Royal, explains how just six numbers defined the earliest moments of the Big Bang and the subsequent evolution of the universe. If you visualise the universe as a cake, the six numbers are the amount of each ingredient, or the oven settings, that decide its size and structure. At first, every atom was hydrogen: all the other elements (in that arrangement of elements according to their atomic numbers that chemists call the periodic table) were created only after a series of nuclear reactions. So, for example, as stars burn, hydrogen turns into helium. Tweak those numbers by a tiny percentage and carbon, the very stuff of life, could not be created.[22]

Another scientist, the cosmologist Paul Davies, writes:

> It is hard to resist the impression of something . . . possessing an overview of the entire cosmos at the instant of its creation, and manipulating all the causally disconnected parts to go

bang with almost exactly the same vigour at the same time, and yet not so exactly co-ordinated as to preclude the small-scale, slight irregularities that eventually formed the galaxies and us.[23]

And elsewhere he writes:

I belong to a group of scientists who do not subscribe to a conventional religion but nevertheless deny that the universe is a purposeless accident . . . There must be a deeper level of explanation. Whether one wishes to call that deeper level 'God' is a matter of taste and definition.[24]

Such remarkable fine tuning speaks of more than a mindless accident: it speaks of a Creator; and moreover, one whose delicate workmanship becomes the more apparent the more astronomers, biochemists, molecular biologists and geneticists unveil the timescale on which that Creator works. All this to produce a human baby, let alone a Mozart. Looking up at the heavens, looking back in time, and then turning to look within, it takes a poet to pinpoint the mystery of which science can only speak a part:

> For today let's pause
> At my first groping after the First Cause,
> Which led me to acknowledge (groping still)
> That if what once was called primeval slime
> (In current jargon, pre-biotic soup)
> Evolved in course of aeons to a group
> Playing Beethoven, it needed more than time
> And chance, it needed a creative will
> To foster that emergence, and express
> Amoeba as A Minor.[25]

The Talmudist writer, Joseph Soloveitchik, finds in chapters 1 and 2 of Genesis (which each describe creation in different terms) two human types, which he calls Adam I and Adam II. Adam I is commanded to 'fill the earth and subdue it': he is driven by a curiosity to know how the cosmos works, looking for empirical proof. His contemporary equivalent is the scientist, the mathematician, the technological wizard. Adam II is also bewitched by the cosmos, but is more intro- spective and intuitive: he 'looks for the image of God . . . in every beam of light, in every bud and blossom, in the morning breeze and the stillness of a starlit evening'.[26] His representative is the poet, the artist, the mystic. Any growth in our understanding of the world requires the energies of both Adams. The physicist/astronomist Chet Raymo writes:

> If the prodigious energy of the new scientific story of creation is to flow into religion, the story will need to be translated from the language of scientific discovery into the language of celebration. This is the work of theologians, philosophers, liturgists, poets, artists . . . Only when we are emotionally at home in the universe of the galaxies and the DNA will the new story invigorate our spiritual lives and be cause for authentic celebration. Knowing and believing will come together again at last.[27]

A poet like R. S. Thomas, for example, with his 'Blackbird':

> Its eye a dark pool
> in which Sirius glitters
> and never goes out.
> Its melody husky
> as though with suppressed tears.
> Its bill is the gold
> one quarries for amid
> evening shadows. Do not despair
> at the stars' distance. Listening
> to blackbird music is
> to bridge in a moment chasms
> of space-time, is to know
> that beyond the silence
> which terrified Pascal
> there is a presence whose language
> is not our language, but who has chosen

with peculiar clarity the feathered
creatures to convey the austerity
of his thought in song.[28]

The best scientists know that all parts of the universe are interconnected, a single undivided whole. Both animate and inanimate matter are inseparably interwoven in a universe which is, as it were, recreated and maintained moment by moment by an unbroken source of flowing energy. In modern physics matter has become a thing of amazing subtlety and potentiality, and as we probe its structure, writes Chet Raymo, 'we find ourselves awash in a sea of cosmic music – surging, billowing, animating, never at rest'.[29] Each of us, and every object in the universe, is part of a secret network of relationships, 'whose unceasing change, whether toward complexification or decay, appears to be like a Great Dance, harmoniously evolving in ever newer figures, following a mysterious suite of which our reason can grasp but a few themes'.[30]

Lucian, the Roman second-century poet, saw God as the 'unmoved Mover' round whom all creation dances, and spoke of 'the round dance of the stars . . . and the beautiful order and harmony in all the movements of the planets, [which] is a mirror of the original dance at the time of creation'. The physicist Max Born uses the same metaphor when he speaks of a restless universe, all of it 'rushing about and vibrating in a wild dance'. And in the musical language of the dance, order in *space* is the harmony, while order in *time* is the melody, 'indeed to the numberless melodies which are born and which may eventually fade away, thus signalling certain dancers that their parts are over'.[31]

Plato would have understood that. So would Shakespeare and the Elizabethans, but they would have taken the metaphor literally. They embrace the age-old idea of the Harmony of the World:

> . . . look how the floor of heaven
> Is thick inlaid with patines of bright gold:
> There's not the smallest orb which thou behold'st
> But in his motion like an angel sings,
> Still quiring to the young-eyed cherubins;
> Such harmony is in immortal souls;
> But, whil'st this muddy vesture of decay
> Doth grossly close it in, we cannot hear it.[32]

Lorenzo's words to Jessica reflect Shakespeare's belief in the Music of the Spheres. Pythagoras, when not pondering the square on the hypotenuse of a right-angled triangle, was working out a mathematical basis for music. He supposed the heavenly bodies to be divided by intervals according to the laws of musical harmony. Having discovered that the pitch of notes depends on how rapidly they vibrate, and also that the planets move at different rates, he concluded that each must make a different sound. Such early Greek philosophers saw creation as an act of music, and it was a commonplace from the early Middle Ages until the eighteenth century that the universe was in a state of music, that it was one ceaseless dance. So Dryden:

> From harmony, from heavenly harmony,
> > This universal frame began;
> > From harmony to harmony
> Through all the compass of the notes it ran,
> The diapason closing full in man.[33]

A hundred years earlier Johann Kepler, the scientist whose Laws formed the basis of Newton's work, discovered that the planets move in simple, elegant ellipses rather than circles. He exclaimed: 'O God, I am thinking thy thoughts after Thee,' and asked: 'Can I find God, whom I can almost grasp with my own hands in looking at the universe, also in myself?'[34] In his *De Harmonice Mundi*, Kepler studies the mathematical regularities of the dance of the celestial bodies and longs to hear the silent music of the divine composer.

In 1596, probably the year in which Shakespeare wrote *The Merchant of Venice*, a young student at the Inns of Court, John Davies, published his poem *Orchestra*.[35] It recounts how, one night at Ithaca, Antinous (suitor to Penelope) begs her to dance, to

> Imitate heaven, whose beauties excellent
> Are in continual motion day and night.

Penelope declines and they discuss the merits of dancing as a way of sharing in the cosmic harmony. Antinous argues that it was creative Love that persuaded the warring atoms to move in order and the stars to dance (cf. Dante's 'the Love that moves the sun and the other stars'[36]):

> The Fire, Air, Earth and Water did agree
> By Love's persuasion (nature's mighty King)
> To leave their first disordered combating;
> And, in a dance, such Measure to observe,
> As all the world their motion to preserve.

Love is the reason why all things

> Forward and backward rapt and whirled are
> According to the music of the spheres . . .
> Only the earth doth stand for ever still,
> Her rocks remove not nor her mountains meet . . .
> Yet, though the earth is ever stedfast seen,
> On her broad breast hath dancing ever been.

In the poem Davies then turns to Queen Elizabeth and her dancing court as an example of his profound belief that the cosmic dance is a symbol of the order and harmony that are to be the sign of a kingdom at peace with itself. The one who refuses to dance brings disorder to the world.

Just over a decade earlier, in 1541, in the village of East Coker, Sir John Elyot, one-time intimate of Sir Thomas More, had written *The Boke named The Governour*. Elyot describes dancing as both a symbol of marriage and of social and universal harmony. He writes of how in 'the association of

a man and a woman in daunsinge may be signified matrimonie'. He too speaks of the hierarchical order that governs
the universe, that 'Chain of Being' which stretches from the
foot of God's throne to the tiniest of inanimate objects, all
observing their proper order. Shakespeare knew that sense
of order as 'degree', and in *Troilus and Cressida* Ulysses warns,

> Take but degree away, untune that string,
> And hark, what discord follows.[37]

The dance, with its formal measure, is the basis of all
harmony as well as being the true expression of the Love
that must govern all things. Both Sir John Davies' *Orchestra*
and Elyot's *The Governour* have left their mark on Eliot's
musically named *Four Quartets*. Sir John Elyot's birthplace,
East Coker, becomes Eliot's setting for his second *Quartet*
where, at midnight in summer, you can

> see them dancing around the bonfire
> The association of man and woman
> In daunsinge, signifying matrimonie . . .
> . . . Keeping time,
> Keeping the rhythm in their dancing
> As in their living in the living seasons
> The time of the seasons and the constellations.

In so doing, they keep the rhythm of the cyclic seasons,
the rhythm of planting and harvesting, living and dying.
According to *Orchestra* it is also creative Love that 'dances
in your pulses and your veins', which finds its echo in Eliot's

> The dance along the artery
> The circulation of the lymph
> Are figured in the drift of stars.[38]

Today not only poets but a number of scientists are
resurrecting the metaphor of the 'cosmic dance' as a way of
unifying what is now known of evolution and the emergence of order and pattern, the laws of nature and the
genetic code, suggesting a view of the world in stark contrast

to a damaging retreat into greater and greater specialisation. In all sorts of areas, from astrophysics to ecology to medicine, there is a shift to holism, where everything is in a balanced relationship, an integrated and organic whole. The Dance is thus an image which hints at a wonderfully rich, continuously changing pattern of relations between the elements in this complex system we (significantly) call the *uni*verse. But let a novelist, Charles Williams, have the last word:

> Imagine that everything which exists takes part in the movement of a great dance – everything, all electrons, all growing and decaying things, all that seems alive and all that doesn't seem alive, men and beasts, stones and trees, everything that changes, and there is nothing anywhere that does not change. That change – that's what we know of the immortal dance; the law in the nature of things – that's the measure of the dance, why one thing changes swiftly and another slowly, why there is seeming accident and incalculable alteration, why men hate and love and grow hungry, and cities that have stood for a century fall in a week, why the smallest wheel and mightiest world revolve, why blood flows and the heart beats and the brain moves, why your body is poised on your ankle and the Himalayas are rooted in the earth – quick or slow, measurable or immeasurable, there is nothing at all anywhere but the dance.[39]

# MAY

## *The Dance of Nature*

---

Whence arises all that order and beauty we see in the world?

*Isaac Newton*

See, I am God. See! I am in everything. See! I never lift my hand off my works, nor will I ever. See! I lead everything toward the purpose for which I ordained it.

*Dame Julian of Norwich*[1]

Nature, Mr Allnutt, is what we are put into this world to rise above.

*Katherine Hepburn*[2]

The too-much-loved earth will always exceed our power to describe, or imagine, or understand it.

*A. S. Byatt*[3]

Wherever one looks twice there is some mystery.

*Elizabeth Bowen*[4]

---

'I have never seen anything more solemn and splendid than England in May,' wrote Katherine Mansfield after a train journey from Paddington to Cornwall. Sheets of bluebells, the wild hyacinth, carpet the woods at Vernditch Chase, while on both sides of the long eastern path are white ransoms, the wild garlic also known as 'Londoners' lilies'. Hopkins described the bluebells 'in falls of sky-colour washing the brows and slacks of the ground with vein-blue', with their 'faint honey smell and in the mouth the sweet gum when you bite them'. The hawthorn hedges, white and pink, mainly planted in the eighteenth century during the time of land enclosures, are in full flower. Horse chestnut trees are laden with their creamy candles, and great copper beeches have broken into leaf and are glistening in the sun. Each tree has its own singular beauty. Country roads are laced with cow parsley like white smoke, the Avon water-meadows are thick with buttercups, and in narrow West Country lanes leading down to the sea the yellow-green Alexanders stand shoulder-high. Introduced by the Romans as a spring vegetable and tonic, they would have been found in monastic herb gardens and cottage gardens, until in the early eighteenth century they were supplanted by celery. Grassland and woods are studded with the varying blues of speedwell, the purple and yellow of vetch and the pink of campion; and gardens are scented by lilac and laburnum. The first scythe-shaped swifts arrive, most winning of all the summer migrants, screaming as they hunt insects at dusk: country folk called them 'devil-birds'. Nightingales sing in the thick coppices on the heathland between Holt and Salt-house. Linnets and stonechats are nesting in the gorse at White Nothe on the Dorset coast. Nearer home, dabchicks build their nests and baby ducks are launched on the Avon, where the kingfisher, a flash of iridescent turquoise and copper, dives and perches. According to Dorothy Words-worth, on 14 May 1802, in a wood near Dove Cottage, 'William tired himself with seeking an epithet for the cuckoo'.

In medieval Books of Hours the occupation for the month was **hawking and hunting**. The gentry spent much of their lives hunting deer with horse and hound, or flying hawks at pheasant, partridge, duck and heron, and poaching was a universal passion. A fourteenth-century poem, a poacher's account of dawn in the woods as he waits for the deer, shows that those who lived their whole lives in the country were not always blinded by familiarity to the loveliness around them.

> In May, when airs are soft, I went to the wood to take my luck . . . I stayed on a bank beside a brook where the grass was green and starred with flowers – primroses, periwinkles, and the rich pennyroyal. The dew dappled the daisies most beautifully, and also the buds, blossoms and branches, while around me the soft mists began to fall. Both the cuckoo and the pigeon were singing loudly, and the throstles in the bankside eagerly poured out their songs . . . Harts and hinds betake themselves to the hills; the fox and polecat seek their earths; the hare squats by the hedges, hurries and hastens thither to her forme and prepares to lurk there.[5]

In a Book of Hours presented to Queen Mary in 1553 there is a May hawking scene in which two women are riding astride their horses, a man on foot is trying to recall the hawk with his lure, and the bird has settled on a flattened-looking duck. Hunting, hawking, poaching: all occupations that bring together the natural world, with its beauty and its pain, its evolution and its laws; and our proper stewardship of it.

There is in Westminster Abbey a much-damaged thirteenth-century retable measuring ten foot wide and three foot deep. Almost certainly it stood above the high altar in Henry III's newly-built Abbey. What remains of the painting is exquisite, delicately coloured, and full of character. In the centre stands Christ, holding with great tenderness a globe, his right hand above it, his left hand supporting it – an image almost unique in contemporary English art. On the globe is painted a miniature Eden: a garden with a river, a boat with a man fishing, sheep and birds, trees and clouds, the sun, the moon and the stars. The challenge we face is how to fuse this ever-potent image of the garden with that of a modern scientific view of how the world works. How can:

> You are worthy of our thanks and praise
> Lord God of truth,
> for by the breath of your mouth
> you have spoken your Word,
> And all things have come into being.
> You fashioned us in your image
> and placed us in the garden of your delight[6]

keep company with theories of chaos, unpredictability and chance?

Science is the only possible starting-point. Science is the search for laws, and no scientist could proceed unless it is true that there is a hidden order in nature, an order that is mathematical in form and which can be investigated and uncovered. Pythagoras found a basic relation between mathematics and musical harmony, and taught that numbers are nature's language. A single stretched string, when it vibrates as a whole, produces a ground note, and the notes that sound harmonious with it are produced only if the string is divided into an exact number of parts: two, three or four. If the still point on the string is not at one of these exact points, the sound is discordant. Plato and, following him, St Augustine argued powerfully for the mathematical order of the whole universe; Galileo wrote that 'The Book of Nature is written in mathematical characters', and the laws of physics, the enquiry into the structure and properties of matter, where some of the greatest scientific advances have been made, confirms it. The great modern physicist Richard Feynman said that giving any idea of what modern science means to those who cannot imagine higher mathematics was like trying to explain music to the deaf. 'The cosmic order is underpinned', writes Paul Davies, 'by definite mathematical laws that interweave with each other to form a subtle and harmonious unity. [These] laws are of an elegant simplicity.'[7] He claims that the job of the physicist is to reveal the patterns in nature and seek to fit them into simple mathematical schemes, although he adds that the question *why* there are such patterns and mathematical schemes 'belongs to metaphysics'. Questions of meaning, and of moral, aesthetic or social import that cannot be expressed in equations must be looked at with quite different eyes. 'Have you visited the storehouses of the snow?' asks God of Job. 'Can you bind the cluster of the Pleiades or loose Orion's belt?'[8] And Job is silenced.

When the temperature begins to freeze, the swarming millions of molecules of water vapour that fill the air are drawn together by their magnetism and form delicate shapes of snow crystals of amazing symmetry. And while no two flakes are the same, yet each has a six-pointed harmony. The mathematical patterns, the geometrical shapes and consistent rhythms that we find in nature and in the orbits and motions of the planets, as well as within the atomic and subatomic world – the perfect ellipse of a planet, the hexagonal design within the beehive and the perfect spiral of a shell – clearly point to laws. The question is: do we live in a universe which, with its rational, elegant laws undergirding its simplest and also its most complex structures, is shot through with signs of *mind* – which for the theist is the mind of God? Is it grounded in some reality other than itself which both holds it in being and is the source of its existence? If we dismiss any idea of divine underpinning from the equation, how can these laws be explained? For it is not that we are reading into the dance figures and patterns which *we* have invented: it is nature itself that is disclosing the presence of such laws. 'We discover that the universe shows evidence of a designing or controlling power', wrote the astronomer Sir James Jeans, 'that has something in common with our own individual minds . . . the tendency to think in the way which, for want of a better word, we describe as mathematical.'[9]

It is the discovery in nature of persistent, uniform sets of equations which (to a mathematician's eye) possess an elegant and harmonious beauty, that has made possible such things as the exploration of space, the development of nuclear power, and the invention of electric light. When scientists speak of such laws, they mean laws that govern how things work and how they change – or are prevented from changing. Darwin has shown just how radical have been the mutations and developments over time, but not the underlying primal *laws* of nature (such as the law of gravity) which govern such changes. And this gives the observable world a reliable and reassuring stability. The world is rational and ordered: the sun rises on cue; if I drop my book it hits the floor; if I plant my beans in early May they will be ready to eat in August. Cause and effect: take away that pattern and there would be chaos. Almost daily for ten years, I walked past Isaac Newton's imposing tomb in the Abbey; it was his laws which were the classic description of the *mechanical* view of nature. They assumed the reign of universal order in the heavens: they took for granted the strict causation of '*If . . . then*', that every physical process could be measured with precise accuracy; and that each event can be described in one and only one way, upon which all observers everywhere could agree. No more. In 1905 and 1915 Einstein put forward his two theories of relativity, which altered our concept of the *relative*, rather than the absolute, nature of time and space, and the law of gravity. He showed that our measurements of position, momentum, time and space are not unvarying, but depend in some way on the observer; that an object squashes up as it moves faster and increases in weight.

Then in 1927 the quantum physicist Werner Heisenberg produced his 'uncertainty principle', the discovery that all measurable quantities are subject to unpredictable fluctuations, and hence to *uncertainty* in their values; and the discovery of quantum mechanics (which deals with atoms and elementary particles) in the 1920s proved that atoms, electrons and other subatomic particles obey the rules of chance. Physicists can no longer pin them down: in the puzzling, quixotic world of quantum mechanics you can measure the *position* of an atom, and you can plot the exact *motion* of the atom, but not both at the same time. If you get one right, you get the other wrong. It seems that the world cannot be separated from our perception of it: it shifts as we look at it and interacts with us. Bizarrely, you cannot find out *both* where a particle is *and* the speed and direction of its movement, and physicists have still not come up with a theory that makes sense of the paradox.

The importance of this shift from Newton's absolutes of time and space to Einstein and relativity, Niels Bohr and quantum mechanics, reminds us that mystery is not the theologian's sole prerogative: scientists' accounts of how things are may also be incomplete and provisional. It seems that our view of the universe will be affected by the scientific procedures through which we seek to observe or measure it, and that this is always likely to be so. We can only know it through our theories, models and equations. Annie Dillard writes of science working the way a tightrope walker works: 'by not looking at its feet. As soon as it looks at its feet, it realises it is operating in mid-air.'[10] Science declares that the view of the observer affects the observed, that we may not necessarily see what is there but what our eyes tell us is there. After all, who would ever guess that a stone or a chair was not solid, but a constantly teeming dance of atoms, millions of little boxes in which electric charges are spinning, electrons circling round the nucleus at an unimaginable speed, attracted to the nucleus rather as the earth is attracted to the sun? Step through the gateway of the atom and we are in a world in which things are put together in a way we cannot know or easily imagine. Different kinds of atom combine as molecules to make different kinds of things: two atoms of hydrogen join with one of oxygen and we have water; a more complex combination of atoms produces a jellyfish or Napoleon. When atoms are bunched up in sufficient numbers to show us something solid we see them, but the atoms that make up our brains find it hard to accept that everything is constantly in motion, as if it all consisted of uncountable numbers of swarming insects. 'Things that look quiet and still,' writes the physicist Richard Feynham, 'like a glass of water with a covered top that has been sitting for several days are active all the time; the atoms are leaving the surface, bouncing round inside, and coming back. What looks still to our crude eyes is a wild and dynamic dance.'[11]

So even 'at the still point of the turning world' there is constant movement: the dance of (and within) the atoms. Professor E. N. de C. Andrade worked it out that if 1,000 men started to count the atoms in a single bubble of gas on the side of a glass of carbonated water, each one counting 300 atoms a minute, 12 hours a day, it would take them 1 million years. Physicists have come to understand that whatever fundamental units the world is put together from, 'they are more delicate, more fugitive, more startling than we catch in the butterfly net of our senses'.[12] This new-mined knowledge, which no previous age could have guessed at, can invite from theists and atheists alike a response of deep wonder. For the beauty of the rose lies not just in its shape, colour and scent, but also in the wild dance of the subatomic particles that makes the rose what it is.

Causality (the confident-making 'if . . . then' of things) is not expunged by the quantum theory: the Newtonian mechanics still work well enough on an everyday scale (my book will always hit the floor, not the ceiling, unless I'm in non-gravitational space), but in terms of both the cosmos and the atom, the huge and the infinitely small, things will never look quite the same again. Determinism is no longer the flavour of the day: within the consistency of the under-lying laws there is a creative freedom. Scientists talk of randomness, chaos and chance as ingredients of a somewhat less predictable world, no longer rigidly fixed in a pre-determined straitjacket, each event entirely determined by other, earlier events. Less and less do scientists believe that once they have discovered all the laws they will be able to predict and control the future. In Tom Stoppard's play, *Arcadia*, Valentine and his young sister Chloe are discussing whether this is a 'closed' or 'open' universe:

CHLOE: The future is all programmed like a computer – that's a proper theory, isn't it?

VALENTINE: The deterministic universe, yes.

CHLOE: Right. Because everything including us is just a lot of atoms bouncing off each other like billiard balls.

VALENTINE: Yes. There was someone, forget his name, nineteenth century, who pointed out that from Newton's laws you could predict everything to come – I mean, you'd need a computer as big as the universe but the formula would exist.

CHLOE: But it doesn't work, does it?

VALENTINE: No. It turns out the maths is different.

Later in the play, Valentine is rejoicing in unpredictability and randomness, seeing it as restoring mystery to ordinary life:

The unpredictable and the predetermined unfold together to make everything the way it is. It's how nature creates itself, on every scale, the snowflake and the snowstorm. It makes me so happy. To be at the beginning again, knowing almost nothing. People were talking about the end of physics. Relativity and quantum looked as if they were going to clean out the whole problem between them. A theory of everything. But they only explained the very big and the very small. The universe, the elementary particles. The ordinary-sized stuff which is our lives, the things people write poetry about – clouds – daffodils – waterfalls – and what happens in a cup of coffee when the cream goes in – these things are full of mystery, as mysterious to us as the heavens were to the Greeks.[13]

In the view of Queen Elizabeth I, the church of St Mary

Redcliffe in Bristol was 'the fairest, goodliest and most famous parish church in England'. She would have been fascinated by its Chaotic Pendulum. This device, driven by a flow of recycled water, is an icon of our modern understanding of the world, for while it obeys simple physical laws, it is unpredictable in its behaviour. It consists of a cross with a semi-circular steel rod attached to, and hanging beneath, each end of the horizontal arm, and a vertical, freely moving beam attached to the cross's centre – like the needle of a compass. Water slowly flows into the centre of the cross beam, which then tips to let it out. What is unpredictable is which way it will tip.

This is what scientists call chaos theory. Not only do the subatomic particles fail to move along predictable paths, but perversely, they may sometimes behave as *waves* (like the ripples on a pond) and sometimes as *particles* (the tennis ball floating on it). Sometimes the quanta of light, for example, appear to behave as waves and particles *at the same time*. The waves that make light are varying electric and magnetic fields, intertwined in a dance. Yet light can also behave as a particle, and it is this particle/wave duality that lies at the heart of the mysterious quantum world that is modern physics. Richard Feynman has described how, if you shine a lamp on a window, in every 100 particles of light 96 pass through the glass and 4 are bounced back by the electrons in the glass, and it is these which cause us to see the lamp's reflection. No one can predict the course of the photon (the messenger particle in an electromagnetic force). We don't know how a photon 'decides' which direction to follow: scientists can only work out the percentage probability. Like everything that seems ordinary, it is extraordinary, and even the swing of that simple pendulum becomes random and chaotic.

If such a paradox offends our sense of logic, then we need to ask three questions: whether everything in creation needs to be expressed in language which takes the form of logical 'If . . . then' statements; why we should demand that

71

God must work as a logician rather than as an artist; and why we assume that creation will ever be fully understandable even by our wondrous, but limited, brains.[14] For, despite the unpredictable, often chaotic behaviour of atoms, there is evidence of a Mind behind the laws. 'Chance' does not mean arbitrariness, life somehow emerging from the interplay of haphazard forces. Yet neither is the cosmic dance that of a clockwork music box with figures performing their set pieces, their tunes laid down from the beginning of time. The best analogy for God is that of the creative artist, who makes a universe whose laws allow an element of chance, freedom, randomness and choice which enable the Creator to control, and to interact with (though not to intervene in) a creation that is a truly *open* system, and one full of almost limitless potential. My pottery classes have reached the stage of attempting to throw the clay on the wheel: at the moment I am aiming at standard mug-shapes (though the clay has a mind of its own, and I get very small pencil-holders), but later I shall hope to be less rigid and more improvisatory, for the best potters set up possibilities and allow shapes to appear.

If chaos science introduces the notion of randomness, it is the randomness of British weather; of the way the sea is driven by a storm, or river water flows round a rock; of the way smoke from burning leaves curls and twists on a still evening; the way terns and fulmars are buffeted by a strong gust of wind. Here is a delicate balance between order and chaos. For there is also, in nature, the most mysterious, satisfying pattern and structure. We live in a world of patterns. Nightly the stars move in a circle round the sky; the perfectly shaped spiral of a nautilus shell echoes the spiral of the curling, breaking wave; the patterns in the desert sand point to the laws governing the flow of sand and air. Once again we are in the world of mathematics, the way we recognise and classify the patterns that lie all about us. And nothing is more intriguing than the mathematical equations that link leaf and flower patterns with the exact proportions the Greeks used in their architecture.

Leonardo Fibonacci was born in Pisa in about 1170. When he was twenty he went to Algeria, where he learned Arabic methods of calculation. He wrote on number theory and recreational mathematics. His most famous discovery was what is known as the 'Fibonacci sequence', in which each number is the sum of the two previous ones: hence 1, 2, 3, 5, 8, 13, 21, 34, 55, 89, 144 . . . and these turn out to be the numbers that dominate the natural world. The number of petals on most plants is a Fibonacci number: for example, 3 petals on lilies and iris, 5 on buttercups and the wild rose, 8 on delphiniums, 13 on ragwort and corn marigold, 21 on asters, 34, 55 or 89 on most members of the daisy family. More strikingly, the Fibonacci sequence is found in the spiralling seed-heads of sunflowers, where the clockwise spirals will always be 34, 55 or 89, and the counter-clockwise spiral 55, 89 or 144; on the diamond-shaped scales of pineapples, with 8 rows sloping to the left, 13 to the right; and on the spiralling base of pine cones, or the spiralling florets of a cauliflower. If genetics can give a sunflower any number of seeds it likes, a daisy any number of petals, or a pine cone any number of scales, why is there such a dominance of Fibonacci numbers? The answer almost certainly lies with the dynamics of plant growth.

Now go one stage further: take the ratio of two successive Fibonacci numbers, starting with 5, and divide each by the number before it: $5/3 = 1.666$, $8/5 = 1.6$, $13/8 = 1.625$, $21/13 = 1.61538$. The ratio settles down to a particular value, 1.618, and this is known as the Golden Number or the Golden Mean, the ideal proportion used by the ancient Greeks in building: an oblong with the proportion 1 to 1.618 found to be particularly pleasing to the human eye. At the time of the Renaissance this proportion was seen to be the secret of what we find beautiful in the human face and body: in a well-proportioned body $1/1.618$ is the ratio from the top of the head to the navel, and from the navel to the ground, as it is of the finger (measuring the length of the knuckle to the end of the first joint against that of the middle joint) or that of the middle joint against the finger tip; as it is also if you measure the width of the mouth against that of the nose, or the width of the incisor against that of the adjoining tooth. There is in mathematics what is known as the Logarithmic Spiral: if you draw within an oblong with these proportions further and ever-smaller oblongs, in which the shorter and longer sides are in this same 1/1.618 proportion, and then join the corners, the resulting spiral exactly matches that which is everywhere in nature: in the shell of the hermit crab, in the ammonite, the ram's horn, the breaking wave.

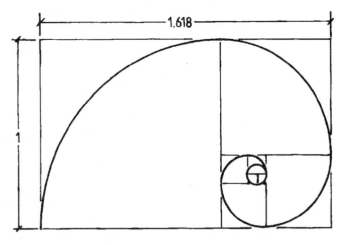

It doesn't stop there: 90 per cent of plants show the Fibonacci numbers in the arrangements of the leaves around their stems; and in a bee colony the number of female workers to male drones will be around the golden number of 1/1.618.

Another thing Sister Immaculata told them was about the Golden Mean and the Fibonacci series – how God's favourite ratio was 1 to 1.62 and how almost all growing things corresponded to this ... She made them measure the spirals of

74

chrysanthemum heads and the chambers of shells and the points where twigs emerged from branches. She shepherded their calculations and the class was amazed to discover the ratio was always the same. Then she asked them to measure where the horizon was in famous paintings. Catherine . . . volunteered to look at the climaxes in a Mozart piano sonata. The ratio was the same in every case: 1 to 1.62. How could this be?

'It's just that it's God's favourite number. A work of art is a prayer – and when artists create they instinctively offer back to their Maker things which are constructed in his favourite ratio.'[15]

There is a near-perfect symmetry, from whirlpools to honeycombs to ripples on a pond, which we find beautiful. But there are also in nature many examples of broken or imperfect symmetry, irregular geometrical shapes which scientists call 'fractals', which we find equally beautiful: the edge of a leaf, the outline of a tree, clouds and coastlines, even the human face. So that within the dance of nature we find a general tendency to the symmetry of circles, ellipses, spirals, cones and spheres, but also the unexpected asymmetry, a mixture of order and chaos, pattern and randomness, that science has shown to exist side by side.

What is known as 'natural theology' asks what can be known about God simply by observing the natural world in the light of what science now reveals and with the aid of reason. It claims that theism makes more sense of the world and our experience of it than atheism does; that we cannot escape the sense of a Mind behind the laws of the universe; that, however unpredictable the laws turn out to be, nowhere have we discovered mindlessness. It witnesses to the ancient idea that nature is the book in which a transcendent God writes his presence. When it considers how the universe has organised itself into galaxies, stars and planets, ecosystems, animals and human beings, it asks why the laws are so finely tuned to the possibility of human life, and why the universe is so special and this planet that we call home so constantly surprising and so absurdly beautiful. Which brings me to Stephen Hawking's question:

> What is it that breathes fire into the equations and makes a universe for them to describe? The usual approach of science of constructing a mathematical model cannot answer the question of why there should be a universe for the model to describe.[16]

If God is responsible for the laws of physics then he must have selected our world from an infinite number of possible alternatives (whether or not uniquely is another matter). If, as the Anthropic Principle suggests, all the conditions had to be exactly right for human life to evolve and we are meant to be here, then there must be an ultimate purpose to justify so much waste and account for so much splendour. What clues do we have that the dance makes sense? We have natural beauty; we have creation's rich and complex variety; and we have its undoubted interdependence. And we have the beauty of the equations. The mathematical physicist Roger Penrose writes that beauty is a guiding principle in much of his work, and Paul Davies writes,

> It is widely believed among scientists that beauty is a reliable guide to truth, and many advances in theoretical physics have been made by the theorist demanding mathematical elegance of a new theory.[17]

Nature is not shy of seducing us with the rich variety of its wares, the breathtaking colour even on birds and fish our eyes never see, the complexity of a mosquito's eye or the 330,000 kinds of beetle so far classified. (When the biologist J. B. S. Haldane was asked by a churchman to describe his concept of God, he replied: 'He is inordinately fond of beetles.') Geneticists now tell us that the number of plants and animals is far higher than experts once thought, that perhaps we have as yet only succeeded in describing one living species in a hundred, that the gut of a housefly contains thousands of microbes unknown to science, that 11 of the 80 known kinds of whales and dolphins were discovered in the twentieth century, that of some 5,000 known mammals, 3,000 more may be waiting in the wings.[18] It is the intricacy that astounds, the seemingly unnecessary detail. It is what silences Annie Dillard when she stands in Tinker's Creek, as she remembers that there are 228 separate and distinct muscles in the head of an ordinary caterpillar, and realises that all she sees is wholly gratuitous, as she is herself,

> not in any real sense necessary per se to the world or to its creator . . . If the world is gratuitous, then the fringe of a gold-fish's fin is a million times more so . . . I affix my attention to the intricacy of the world's spotted and speckled detail.[19]

The reductionism that has inhibited much modern science, the failure to see that the whole may be greater than its parts, has now been challenged by a growing recognition that the universe (while it may present itself to us in parts) is a single system which behaves as an organic whole, that what happens in one place is related to what happens in another, however distant. The global communications network has made us more aware of an ecological network and of the nature of the cosmic dance, an understanding that in a profound sense 'everything is in everything'. The growth of demonstrations worldwide at ecological confer-ences challenges our stewardship of the creation. There are some words printed in the shape of a globe, though I cannot trace their source:

If the Earth
were only a few feet in
diameter, floating a few feet above
a field somewhere, people would come
from everywhere to marvel at it. People would
walk around it, marvelling at its big pools of water,
its little pools, and the water flowing between the pools.
People would marvel at the bumps on it, and the holes in it,
and they would marvel at the very thin layer of gas surrounding
it and the water suspended in the gas. The people would
marvel at all the creatures walking around the surface of the ball,
and at the creatures in the water. The people would declare it as
sacred because it was the only one, and they would protect it
so that it would not be hurt. The ball would be the greatest
wonder known, and  people would come to be healed, to
gain knowledge, to know beauty and to wonder how it
could be. People would come to love it and defend it
with their lives, because they would somehow know
that their own lives, their own roundness,
could be nothing without it. If
the Earth were only a few
feet in diameter.

It was the image in space of the beautiful coloured ball of
the earth, hanging motionless in the black lunar sky (in the
words of a member of the Apollo 15 crew) 'like a brilliant
blue and white Christmas tree decoration' that from the
moon's Sea of Rains they could 'hold' between finger and
thumb, that drew the British chemist James Lovelock to
develop his concept of Gaia. The novelist William Golding,
Lovelock's neighbour in the Wiltshire village of Bowerchalke, suggested the name of Gaia, the Greek Goddess of
the Earth, to describe his theory that the whole earth is a
single living, breathing organism, just like a tiger or a bee;
that organisms adapt to their environment; that while life
is self-regulating and self-maintaining, it does much more
than adapt to the earth: it manipulates it to suit its needs.
'Evolution is a tight-coupled dance with life and the material
environment as partners, and from the dance emerges the
entity Gaia.'[20] The presence of life on earth has dramatically

changed conditions on its surface, and Gaia has enabled them to remain stable, yet 'Gaia is stern and tough, always keeping the world warm and comfortable for those who obey the rules, but ruthless in her destruction of those who transgress'.[21]

And we have transgressed. 'U.N. delivers apocalyptic warning on climate' is the headline in this morning's *Independent*. We have hugely damaged the earth by practices which pollute the atmosphere and reduce biodiversity. We belong to the earth, yet we have ceased to listen to the harmony of the whole creation, forgetting that nothing that exists can be excepted from the dance. Delicate, self-regulating mechanisms have kept the oxygen content of the earth's atmosphere and the saltiness of its seas almost constant for hundreds of millions of years, yet we have cut down the forests, polluted the seas (the Black Sea is now as good as dead, its 156 species of fish reduced to five, its monk seals extinct), and ravaged and exploited the earth's finite resources. Imperialism brought in its wake ecological exploitation, and that is not unconnected to starvation and bloodshed today in Africa. At least a thousand species a year are disappearing from the tropical rainforests. Of all fish species, 70 per cent are now being fished faster than they can replace themselves. The ozone layer, that protective lining which filters out the lethal ultraviolet rays from the sun, is shrinking, and the ice caps are melting. In Britain, the heedless over-intensification of agriculture, with margins pared to the bone to produce cheap food against foreign competition, has driven small farmers to the wall and led to the loss of two-thirds of our farms in 50 years. Artificial fertilisers have affected the natural habitat. BSE was caused by the unnatural practice of recycling cattle carcasses as cattle feed. It's a familiar list. And the Gaia theory tells us that our self-regulating planet can and does compensate within itself for change or damage, so as to keep the whole in equilibrium. But it warns us that if we go too far (in destroying the ozone layer, for instance) then the necessary homeostasis, the dynamic balance between us and our environment, will be damaged and the biosphere could shift to a new steady state – perhaps one incompatible with our survival. And we shall have deserved it.

Yet it is from within this delicately balanced, vulnerable, living ecosystem that we have emerged, created 'in the image of God', to be co-creators with God in a wise stewarding of the earth and the animal creation. We are both masters and servants of nature:

> We are even cousins to the wheat of the field from which we bake our daily bread; ancestral enzymes in each of us proves the point. The interplay of law and chance has woven both the wild scabious in the August hedgerow and the brain of the nuclear physicist.[22]

The best nature writers have shown both the kindredness and the otherness of the natural world, that forum for

> diarists and potterers and dedicated enthusiasts; a world where priests and farm-workers, teachers and postmen have found inspiration, relief and sometimes even a passion that was not always obvious in their professional lives.[23]

To have 'dominion' over the world of nature does not mean to dominate it, but to stand as the Creator's representatives in his creation: to respect and nurture it. Ecological insight not only demands that we closely observe the lives of animals, plants and streams and stones, but use our imaginations to enter into, and learn to empathise with, forms of life quite different from our own: mysteriously other than we are, but not alien to us. This is not to fall into what John Ruskin calls 'pathetic fallacies', attributing human feelings to nature. It is rather to do what Wordsworth saw to be the poet's task: to 'see into the life of things'. For Rilke, earth

> apparently needs us, this fleeting world, which in some
> strange way
> keeps calling to us.[24]

There was a subheading to that headline in this morning's paper: it reads 'To save the earth, human nature must change'. We must learn to see with new eyes.

For nature is actually on our side. Despite a world 'seared with trade; bleared, smeared with toil', one that 'wears our smudge' and 'shares our smell' and in which 'the soil is bare now', there remains 'the dearest freshness deep down things'.[25] To see nature as sacred and interconnected is one of the great insights of the Celtic understanding of the creation. It celebrates its essential goodness. 'Seeing with the eyes of the heart' is the familiar Celtic phrase. It recognises the thinness of the veil between the material and the spiritual realms, the eternal seeping through the physical, the interweaving of the human and the heavenly. It rejoices in a world which in its cosmic dance gives ceaseless praise to its creator in the delight of the kestrel riding the wind, the instinct of salmon to return to their own birth-waters to spawn, and the exact pattern on a dragon-fly's wings. 'If men were as much men as lizards are lizards,' wrote D. H. Lawrence, 'they'd be worth looking at.'[26] We are called to be attentive, wrote Alexander Scott, to 'the fathomless mystery involved in the mere existence of a pebble'.[27] In the best nature writing the emphasis is on the holistic, the organised, self-contained look of each living creature: its proper inward measure. John Stewart Collis, never sufficiently valued as a great nature writer and teacher, gazes as a single forglove and sees its unique perfection, its sheer *thisness*:

> It is quite obvious that the foxglove cannot be *improved* ...
> The fact is that we get perfection in this form and that form ...
> Just as there will never be a better foxglove so there will never
> be a better Shakespeare.[28]

The only question is: do I give proper attention to what lies before my eyes, and learn to see what the poet Douglas Dunn calls the 'transfigured common-place'? As children may, and artists must. William Blake saw the body lit by the five windows of the senses: 'If the doors of perception were cleansed everything would appear to man as it is, infinite'.[29] It was said of Blake that, like Thomas Traherne, he 'perceived the world as directly and freshly as if he had been Adam looking round Eden on the day of his creation'; and of the Dorset writer Llewellyn Powys, that 'nothing was too small to escape his notice; in every pebble he saw a miracle, in every flower a sacred mystery'. With cleansed eyes I can turn from the night sky to contemplate my own hand, and know that it is holy. I can begin to sense the meaning of Blake's words about seeing

> a World in a Grain of Sand
> And a Heaven in a Wild Flower.[30]

I can observe the flux and clarity of light and the subtle gradations of colour. ('It is strange how deeply colours seem to penetrate one, like scent,' says Dorothea in *Middlemarch*.[31]) I can echo St Augustine's words:

> I asked the earth, I asked the sea and the deeps, among the living animals the things that creep. I asked the winds that blow, I asked the heavens, the sun, the moon, the stars . . . My question was the gaze I turned to them. Their answer was their beauty.[32]

You do not have to believe in God to be aware of the harmony and sacred nature of the natural world. The sacred has been defined as that to which we have access but which is not at our disposal; a definition which the most unspiritual of environmentalists might accept. But for those prepared to attend to the daily miracle, to the prodigality, the variety, the ridiculous detail, of the world about them, and be astonished even at the commonplace, only the presence of a sustaining Creator will answer. As St Paul almost said: 'It is in him that [the whole creation] lives, and moves and has its being.' To believe in creation *ex nihilo* is to say that there is nothing other than God from which the universe was made, that while the world is other than God, it is nevertheless wholly dependent on him. All things in God: God in all things. This is not pantheism, the identification of God with nature, for that would be to deny that divine otherness we call transcendence. It is what is termed *panentheism*, the belief that the Being of God includes and pervades the whole universe, that every part of it exists and is (moment-by-moment) sustained by him, that he contains the world but transcends it – a little like the mystery of my self within my body. In the words of Martin Buber: 'To look away from the world, or to stare at it, does not help a man to reach God; but he who sees the world in Him stands in his presence.'[33] This is to celebrate the immanence of God, the in-dwelling of a God who constantly creates in and through the processes of nature. Arthur Peacocke draws attention to St Augustine's vision of the whole creation as if it were

> some sponge, huge, but bounded . . . filled with that unmeasurable sea [of God], environing and penetrating it through every way infinite . . . everywhere and on every side.[34]

Coleridge wrote that Wordsworth's Lyrical Ballads served the purpose of

> awakening the mind's attention from the lethargy of custom and directing it to the loveliness and the wonders of the world about us . . . There have been times when looking up beneath the shelt'ring Trees, I could Invest every Leaf with Awe.[35]

And it is awe (what Lawrence called 'the sixth sense, the natural religious sense'), that sense of reverential wonder, that best describes our response to the endless dance of nature. The mystery is not only *how* it is but *that* it is, a mystery that may not be so much expressed in approximate, inadequate words as felt. In which case a poet, who best understands the fusion of words and feelings, must have the last word. The Scottish poet D. M. Black wrote 'Kew Gardens' in memory of his father, a scientist:

> Distinguished scientist, to whom I greatly defer
> (old man, moreover, whom I dearly love),

I walk today in Kew Gardens, in sunlight the colour of honey
which flows from the cold autumnal blue of the heavens to
    light these tans and golds,
these ripe corn and leather and sunset colours of the East
    Asian liriodendrons,
of the beeches and maples and plum-trees and the stubborn
    green banks of the holly hedges –
and you walk always beside me, you with your knowledge of
    names
and your clairvoyant gaze, in what for me is sheer panorama
seeing the net or web of connectedness. But today it is I who
    speak
(and you are long dead, but it is to you I say it):

'The leaves are green in summer because of chlorophyll
and the flowers are bright to lure the pollinators,
and without remainder' (so you have often told me)
these marvellous things that shock the heart the head can
    account for;
but I want to sing an excess which is not so simply
    explainable.
To say that the beauty of the autumn is a redundant beauty,
that the sky has no need to be this particular shade of blue,
nor the maple to die in flames of this particular yellow,
nor the heart to respond with an ecstasy that does not beget
    children.
I want to say that I do not believe your science
although I believe every word of it, and intend to
    understand it
that although I rate that unwavering gaze higher than almost
    everything
there is another sense, a hearing, to which I more deeply
    attend.
Thus I withstand and contradict you, I, your child,
who have inherited from you the passion which causes me
    to oppose you.'[36]

# JUNE

## *The Dance of DNA*

Men go abroad to wonder at the height of mountains, at the huge waves of the sea, at the long course of the rivers, at the vast compass of the ocean, at the circular motion of the stars; and they pass by themselves without wondering.

*St Augustine*[1]

Little boys lie still, awake,
Wondering, wondering,
Delicate little boxes of dust.

*James Wright*[2]

The human mind and heart are a mystery.

*Psalm 64:7*

There are more molecules in a glass of water than there are glasses of water in the sea. There are also . . . more cells in one finger than there are people in the world.

*Lewis Wolpert*[3]

how should tasting touching hearing seeing
breathing any – lifted from the no
of all nothing – human merely being
doubt unimaginable You

*e. e. cummings*[4]

That engaging man William Cobbett – farmer, traveller, journalist, politician – writes of the glory of a Hertfordshire meadow in June 1822, as he rides down the broad grassy path on the edge of the cornfields:

> The hedges are now full of the shepherd's rose, honeysuckle, and all sorts of wild flowers; so that you are upon a grass walk, with the most beautiful of all flower gardens . . . on one hand, and with the corn on the other . . . What, that man ever invented, under the name of pleasure-grounds, can equal these fields.[5]

From a single meadow near Homington I pluck 12 different grasses, from the coarse cocksfoot to the delicate tufted hair grass, meadow fescue and wild oats. Grassy places are thick with red and white clover, the white flowers of the latter sometimes known as 'bee-bread' for the bead of honey that may be sipped when they are pulled out of the head. Wild roses scent the hedges. A field at Lopcombe Corner is a blaze of scarlet poppies, mixed with the white and gold of ox-eye daisies; on 15 June 1873, in Wiltshire, Francis Kilvert watched people crossing the Common 'through the golden sea of buttercups which will soon be the silver sea of ox-eyes'. On the Avon a great-crested grebe swims with its young on its back: when it dives the young is left bobbing on the surface like a plastic toy. Dragonflies and damselflies are on the wing, as they have been for the past 300 million years. In the hedges the creamy-coloured flowers of the elder (once thought to be the tree on which Judas hanged himself and to be a charm against warts and vermin) are ripe for picking. The garden is fragrant with the scent of syringa and roses. In the long June days the sun, writes Thomas Hardy in Dorset, 'seems reluctant to take leave of the trees . . . the shine climbing up the trunks, reappearing higher, and still fondly grasping the tree-tops till long after'. By the month's end, the wide grass verges where Cobbett rode would have been cut for hay, that hay-making so often delayed by the summer storms: in 1791 Horace Walpole at Strawberry Hill wrote that for him 'the contents of an English June are hay and ice, orange-flowers and rheumatism'.

It is **hay-making** that is the June occupation in all the Books of Hours, men and women with scythes and pitch-forks amid the tall grass. Fifty years ago I spent six weeks hay-making on a croft on the western coast of Iona. There was no hay-baler. We worked a 12-hour day, cutting the long grass and then turning endless rows of hay in the long Valley of the Glen again and again, using scythes and pitchforks almost identical to their medieval forerunners. When the hay was finally dry, we made it into triangular stooks known as 'prappocks', before the eventual loading onto hay-carts. It was tiring, back-breaking work, and even on a horsehair couch in the cowshed I nightly slept the sleep of the dead. Each day was interrupted only by a brief picnic of robust sandwiches – and by the occasional relief of hours of fine Scottish rain:

> Iona, an indecipherable
> blur, a slosh of boots and oilskins,
>
> once landed on, is even wetter.
> Not that it always rains: tomorrow
> everything will be as diaphanous
>
> as the penumbra of a jellyfish:
> I'll ride to Staffa over tourmaline
> and amethyst without a wrinkle.[6]

For me, those weeks saw the start of a lifetime's love affair with an island that, in all its moods, answers to an inner hunger for natural beauty that goes very deep. But they did more: working close to the earth – turning the hay, fetching every drop of water used in the house in buckets from the burn, dipping the sheep and watching the shearing – gave me a deep empathy for the island, its crofters, and the unrelenting demands of the changing seasons. When I left, I felt physically fit and spiritually refreshed; my body had gradually learned to function like the smoothest and most efficient of machines, co-ordinating – in the swing of the scythe and the lifting of the hay – muscle and nerve, hand and arm and shoulder and eye. And I didn't give the fact a second's thought. But what I took for granted, others were analysing and questioning.

Early in the morning of 15 April 1882 a funeral car arrived at Westminster Abbey. It had been driven from the Kentish village of Downe and contained the body of Charles Darwin. The coffin was placed in St Faith's Chapel. He had died on the previous Sunday. The papers were warm in their tributes, the *Daily News* sure that 'Darwin's doctrine is in no wise inconsistent with strong religious faith and hope'; the *Manchester Guardian* reassuring its readers that they should have no fears 'lest the sacred pavement of the Abbey should cover a secret enemy of the Faith', for the burial in the Abbey was 'a happy trophy of the reconciliation between Faith and Science'. (A little wishful thinking there. While Darwin was loath publicly to jettison his traditional faith, he found that his benign theism was gravely shaken. But the fact that his body lies close to that of Isaac Newton suggests that the ruffling of Victorian theological feathers had not been as great as is sometimes thought.)

The following day, in a gloomy, gaslit Abbey, the funeral service was held. Distinguished men (few women appear in the engraving) from the arts and sciences gathered in the nave. The Abbey organist, Frederick Bridge, had composed an anthem for the occasion: 'Happy is the man that findeth wisdom and getteth understanding'. At 12 noon the coffin was borne to the grave to the accompaniment of Beethoven's *Funeral March*, and the funeral service was sung to settings by Croft and Purcell, ending with Handel's anthem: 'His body is buried in peace, but his name liveth evermore'. On the following day there was a letter in *The Times* from Admiral J. Lort Stokes:

> Darwin and I worked together for several years at the same table in the poop cabin of the Beagle . . . he with his microscope and myself at the charts . . . My old friend suffered greatly from seasickness. After perhaps an hour's work he would say to me, 'Old fellow, I must take the horizontal for it' . . . a stretch out on one side of the table would enable him to resume his labours for a while, when he had again to lie down. It was distressing to witness the early sacrifice of Mr Darwin's health, who ever afterwards seriously felt the ill-effects of the Beagle's voyage.

The word evolution means an unfolding, a gradual development. By a strange chance, two scientists working independently – Darwin and Alfred Russel Wallace, who was to be a pall-bearer at his funeral – arrived at the theory of evolution by natural selection at the same time, but Darwin was the first to publish. When his theory of evolution appeared in 1859 in the book that became popularly known as *The Origin of Species* the complete run of 1,200 copies sold in a single day. It tackles the poet's question of just how did 'Amoeba become A Minor'? In doing so, Darwin appeared to deliver a body blow to traditional religious belief in a controlling, supernatural designer. Gone was the idea of original perfection, that seven-day wonder in Eden, its place taken by an inconceivably long history of experiment, of painful and seemingly arbitrary trial and error, of failures, accidents and extinctions; but also of growth and spectacular achievements. Life creates itself, claimed Darwin; it has evolved according to the ability of creatures to adapt themselves to their environment by mutations which arise by blind chance: 'I have called this principle,' he writes in *The Origin of Species*, 'by which each slight variation, if useful, is preserved, by the term of Natural Selection, [although] . . . the expression used by Mr Herbert Spencer of the Survival of the Fittest is more accurate.' And 'survival' is the word. There have been universal and near-fatal disruptions: the most serious were 250 million years ago, when a massive eruption of volcanic lava and dust covered huge areas of the world and some 85–90 per cent of life was destroyed; and some 65 million years ago, when it would seem that a meteorite hit the earth creating a huge fireball, so that the sun was obliterated for years and the dinosaurs (which had been the dominant group for 170 million years) became extinct. Even so, as Arthur Peacocke observes, the phrase 'the survival of the fittest' may have been an unwise borrowing on Darwin's part, for

> the depiction of this process as 'nature, red in tooth and claw' is a caricature . . . For . . . natural selection is not even in a figurative sense the outcome of struggle as such . . . It involves . . . better integration with the ecological environment, more efficient utilisation of available food, better care of the young, more cooperative social organisation and better capacity to survive such struggles as do occur – remembering that it is in the interest of any predator that their prey survives as a species.[7]

Many scientists have seized on the wastefulness and cruelty in nature, together with what seems a haphazard and purposeless creation, to reject any idea of a divine creator, let alone the Judaeo-Christian concept of a good and loving one. Yet, revolutionary as the discoveries of science have been, nothing can satisfactorily explain that delicate weaving of the web of life which has resulted in thinking, self-aware human beings, with a knowledge of good and evil and a haunting sense of God. 'By what genius did the atoms which fell to earth from the sun and the stars', asks Adam Ford, 'weave themselves into such intricate patterns; a filigree of order and design?'[8] In A. S. Byatt's novel *A Biographer's Tale*, the central character reflects:

> I was, so to speak, metaphysically baffled by the bee orchid and the eyes on butterfly wings . . . *I understood the argument* that a resemblance could be perfected over millennia by a

flower, or the scales on a wing, by natural selection – but I couldn't really *believe* it. It still had a quality of designed poetry that left me baffled.[9]

However I got here, whatever it cost in wastage, the fact of the 'designed poetry' won't go away; the fact that *I am here* in this beautiful and absorbing creation, and I need accounting for. In the words of Leontes, as the statue of the wife he believed to be carved in stone begins to stir:

There is an air comes from her. What fine chisel
Could ever yet cut breath?[10]

When the writers of Genesis spoke of the creation they were seeking to convey a mystery so profound (the Creator's relationship with his creation) that only a mythical story could hope to bear the weight of it, so they told of a garden made in seven wonder-working days. Scientists tell a quite different kind of story: of how, from the first primeval molecules that were able to reproduce themselves, and over hundreds of millions of years, simple organisms have developed into more complex ones, each better adapted than its predecessor to prevailing conditions. Susan Greenfield, writing of the development of consciousness 'from octopuses to Van Gogh', suggests the analogy of a dimmer switch being gradually turned up, varying 'from almost imperceptible light, say, the consciousness of invertebrates, to the floodlit brilliance of adult human consciousness'.[11] Muslims reject the theory of evolution as it denies their belief in a 'special creation' of human beings, a *discontinuity*, rather than the Darwinian *continuity* from the evolution of the first primitive cells, through the algae and the sea urchins, the trilobites and sea scorpions; the first reptiles and winged insects, the primitive birds and dinosaurs; and finally, through the primates to the earliest human beings. Literal-minded Christians, who cannot accept that there is more than one way of telling a truth, continue to wring their hands at what seems a rejection of Genesis.

Creationists – who in the southern United States seem as dominant as the dinosaurs once were – reject it because of their fundamentalist view of the Bible. They hold stubbornly to a concept of God as the great Architect, who acts once, at the beginning of time, and in a way that contravenes all we now know of the laws of nature, rather than an artist whose design gradually emerges over unimaginable epochs of time. Yet those who believe that the major findings of science and the fundamental concepts of religious faith can be combined with integrity see Darwinian theories of evolution as liberating in that they free us to think of God in a more mature way. A God who, despite being all-powerful, relinquishes control over the creation and allows creation to be self-creative. In short, one who writes freedom deep into its structure.

But there are still laws. The chemistry doesn't vary. As we saw, every atom in our bodies (excluding only the primordial hydrogen atoms) was fashioned in stars that formed and eventually violently exploded before the Sun and the Earth were formed. All life has been governed by a very few molecules, those that form the four bases in DNA. From those first primeval molecules that were able to reproduce themselves over 3 million years ago, has come (by some millions of steps) the blood in my veins. For the *one unchanging thing* in evolution is the structure of the molecule: whether in the stars or in our human bodies their properties remain the same. Significantly, beside Charles Darwin's grave in Westminster Abbey are those of the English astronomer John Heschel, and the Scot, James Clerk Maxwell, who were both his contemporaries. Clerk Maxwell wrote of how

> none of the processes of Nature . . . have produced the slightest difference in any molecule. We are therefore unable to ascribe either the existence of the molecules or the identity of their properties . . . to any of the causes which we call natural.[12]

He agreed with Heschel's view that the exact equality of each molecule to all others of the same kind 'gives it the essential character of a manufactured article, and precludes the idea of its being eternal and self-existent'. Both found the fact that molecules continue as they were created at the start of time a forceful argument for the existence of a Creator.

But could that Creator not have accomplished his creation in a less costly way? There are some questions which ultimately defeat us, for they inhabit that tantalising realm where logical thought is left beating its fists on the closed doors of mystery. We can understand that new life only emerges through the death of the old. We can understand the role of pain in warning us of danger or disease, but faced with the arbitrary pain and suffering in nature – the type of wasp, say, that lays its larvae in the body of a caterpillar which is then eaten alive from the inside – our brains only take us so far, and not as far as our hearts would like to go. (I'll come back to the even more tantalising question of our own arbitrary pain and suffering in August.) Yet we know that at the absolute heart of every good law and every good action lies the concept of freedom. I claimed in the last chapter that chance does not mean arbitrariness, life managing to emerge from the interplay of purely haphazard forces, and that certain primary laws of nature are powerful evidence of a Mind behind the laws; after all, disorder is only recognised as such when viewed against a background of order. Yet, at the same time, the creation is a truly *open* system full of almost limitless potential. If laws ultimately control the form of the dance, yet those laws allow for the dance to be interpreted with novelty and creativity. Where freedom is part of the package, that must imply choice – and thus randomness and chance. The law of gravity means I can walk to the window with safety, but I am then free to choose whether to admire the view or jump out. The fixed law of gravity is blind and impersonal, not deliberately cruel. Take away freedom and we are faced with an inflexible, programmed world, a kind of puppet theatre where any free activity or response – whether natural selection, or a lion stalking its prey, or a foot-and-mouth virus spreading among cattle and sheep, or a freely-entered-into relationship of love – would no longer exist.

We understand the logic of that. What we find it hard to grasp (because our emotions get involved) is that there is a consistency running throughout nature, that every living thing is capable of responding in one of two ways: healthy cells or cancerous ones, a flourishing or a blighted crop; from maggots consuming a corpse to the hawk swooping on its prey, the natural creation is controlled by the (to our eyes) harsh law of the jungle. Not only does the food chain depend on such hunting and killing, but the alternative would be bizarre. Take the codfish: a female codfish lays 9 million eggs a year. Alexandre Dumas wrote:

> It has been calculated that if no accident prevented the hatching of the eggs and each egg reached maturity, it would take only three years to fill the sea so that you could walk across the Atlantic dryshod on the backs of cod.[13]

To accept all the implications of evolution is to accept that God is responsible for ordering the world by allowing it freedom (thus guaranteeing its openness and indeterminism), and by creating it in such a way as to provide the various choices and potentialities which the world is then created to realise. Blind alleys, waste and pain are part of the price to be paid. 'The role of chance', writes the priest/scientist John Polkinghorne, 'can be seen as a signal of the Creator's allowing the creation to make itself.'[14] Yet, he goes on, the Creator participates in the creative process by 'encouraging a trend toward good'. Traces of such subtle influence may be seen in the long saga of evolution, in the ordered dance of the stars, in the rhythm of the seasons, the natural adaptation of creatures to their environment; and in the tendency of the universe to organise itself into

> a richer variety of ever more complex forms ... My own inclination is to suppose that qualities such as ingenuity,

94

economy, beauty . . . have a genuine transcendent reality . . . and that these qualities are reflected in the structure of the natural world.[15]

What Darwinism destroyed was not Christianity but eighteenth-century Deism (God as the expert Watchmaker, the Absentee Landlord) rather than the Creator omnipresent in his creative power and immanent in his creation, the evolution of which is still taking place. Arthur Peacocke writes:

> God is still creating in, with, and under the processes of the natural world. God . . . is continuously creating . . . exploring and actualising the potentialities of creation, achieving ends flexibly without laying down determinate lines in advance. God is improvising rather as did J. S. Bach before the King of Prussia, or . . . like an extemporising New Orleans jazz player in Preservation Hall. Creation is the act of God the composer at work.[16]

The theologian Hans Küng also contends that evolutionary theory now makes possible a deeper and more subtle understanding of God – one who is in the midst of the creation as it evolves, holding it in being at every instant; as well as a more profound understanding of creation, not as contrary to but as making evolution possible; and a richer understanding of ourselves as organically related to the entire cosmos.[17] A God who acts on a timescale that is almost beyond our imagining; and one who uses the process of evolution and the ground rules by which it works to invite the creation to express itself in increasingly novel and diverse ways. He establishes a system which most scientists accept must in the end produce self-conscious (if not God-conscious) beings. And with the gradual evolving of this creature with free will, self-awareness and a sense of right and wrong, one who can learn from the past and plot the future and ask 'how?' and 'why?', a quantum leap has been made. Which brings me back to me.

There is no mystery on Earth
Exceeds the mighty miracle of birth.
Not all the fearful mystery of death
Surpasses that first breaking into light
And timid, fragile breath.[18]

In mid-December 1928, my mother became pregnant. Here again the combination of law and chance took effect: the law dictates that male sperm fertilise female eggs, while chance allows just one sperm (out of 300 million or more) finally to reach and invade the ovum, some 85,000 times its own size. Around each one of us hover the shades of a million other lives that were not destined to be born. By early January a distinct tube-like structure had been formed in my mother's womb: it would become my heart, and it was already beating. By early February the early forms of all my internal organs were present, though the embryo that was potentially me was only a little more than an inch long and weighed less than one-fifth of an ounce. Already my genetic make-up had been determined. The genome (that sequence of genes which carries instructions for the manufacture of proteins) was directing the two hundred or more types of cells of which we are composed to their various ultimate locations in order to generate the necessary systems (skeletal, muscular, circulatory, reproductive, digestive, urinary, respiratory): to my lymphatic system which would fight disease; to my immune system whose role would be to distinguish friend and foe, what belonged to my body and what did not; and to my autonomic nervous system, that widespread web of nerve-cells, circuitry and chemicals with the task of preserving within my body both equilibrium and constancy. In a few more days tiny arms and legs could have been seen, the hands and feet still paddle-like, with web-like bits between the fingers and toes, and faintly detectable ears and eye sockets. ('In the absence of any other proof,' said Sir Isaac Newton, 'the thumb alone would convince me of

God's existence.') My central nervous system and muscles had formed sufficiently to respond to gentle stimuli. Every movement and change was now being choreographed by the genetic code, various cell groupings uniting to

> migrate, twist, turn, glide, fold, bend, lengthen, branch, fuse, split, thicken, thin, dilate, constrict, hollow out, form pockets, pinch off, adhere, separate . . . Hundreds of millions of dancers appear and they all participate, forming themselves into the shapes of various tissues and organs.[19]

I had become a foetus, and it was all systems go.

By the middle of March my head was still enormous in comparison with my body. Fingernails and eyelids had formed, plus lips and an enormous nose. My ribs and vertebrae had become cartilage. By the middle of April my body was catching up with my head: I was some nine inches long and my mother could begin to feel me kicking. By the end of May (approaching the maximum point at which abortions in Britain are legally allowed), with an ear to the womb you could have heard my heartbeat, and I was beginning to show signs of an individual personality, establishing patterns of sleep and wakefulness. I was even growing eyelashes. By Midsummer Day my eyes were complete and I could both hear and cry. Finally, on 10 September (the day on which Virginia Woolf sat down and started to write *The Waves*, Noël Coward's *Bitter Sweet* had just opened in the West End and Clara Bow was hitting London with her first 'all-talking sensation', the film *Dangerous Curves*) I was born. And already there was enough information capacity in every single cell in my body to fill some dozen copies of the *Encyclopaedia Britannica*.

Twenty-three years later, in early 1953, I was at Cambridge, living in college lodgings in Bene't Street just above the *Eagle* pub. Round the corner, in the Cavendish Laboratory, Francis Crick and James Watson were working on what was to be one of the most revolutionary and far-reaching discoveries of the century: the structure of DNA. One day at lunchtime

Francis Crick arrived in the *Eagle* to tell everyone within hearing that he and Watson had found the secret of life. Not long afterwards, Watson was invited to address the Hardy Club. Crick was present, and describes how the Club's practice was to ply the speaker with a fair amount of drink before the lecture. He recalls that an unsteady Watson did well for a while 'but when he came to sum up he was quite overcome and at a loss for words. He gazed at the model, slightly bleary-eyed. All he could manage to say was "It's so beautiful, you see, so beautiful!" ' 'But then, of course,' adds Crick, 'it was.'

And so it is: this wondrous double spiral in which we are trapped all our days. Within our bodies are something like 50 trillion different cells, all inter-relating to keep us alive and healthy, functioning like many millions of mouths greedily feasting on the ingredients carried to them in the bloodstream. Our blood consists of red cells (which supply the body with oxygen) and white cells (which attack potentially harmful microbes and bacteria). All these cells constantly die, their lifespan between three weeks and three months, and are at once replaced. Each cell is a kind of spherical sac packed with atoms and molecules, with the nucleus at its heart. Within that nucleus are the 23 pairs of chromosomes, dark-staining filaments which can be seen in the nucleus when cells divide. One pair of those chromosomes will have determined our sex. Strung out along the length of the chromosomes are the elementary units of heredity, the genes; these are molecules in the form of deoxyribonucleic acid, more modestly known as DNA. This nucleic acid is life's way of remembering how to perpetuate itself over our whole lives, and rather longer than that, for it carries the chemical messages of inheritance from generation to generation, and does so in a language of stunning simplicity. It is shaped like a spiral staircase, a twisting double helix, the side rails of which are made of molecules of sugars and phosphates; the stairs (with a turn of exactly 36 degrees between each) are paired molecules, in two of which the atoms are arranged in a hexagon, and in two in the form of a hexagon plus a pentagon joined together. For convenience these molecular bases are known as A, G, C and T. A always partners T, while G always partners C, in a constantly changing dance sequence. The stairs of the spiral staircase are a code which tell the cell step by step how to make the proteins necessary to life. Life has a strict time-table, and it is the DNA spiral that instructs the body's cells in the sequence in which that timetable must go. As my tiny body grew in the womb, the cells specialised into their different functions because they accepted the DNA instructions appropriate for the functioning of nerve cells or blood cells or the cells in my backbone and my toes.

Each cell in my body carries the instruction book for 100,000 genes. Scientists are attempting to analyse the contents of that book, yet all that information sits comfortably in a single cell in the tip of every surviving hair on my head. If I pull out a single hair I find at the end of it a tiny white root of living tissue. What I then have between my fingers is the complete recipe for making another me. Each one of the microscopic cells contains a complete book of what it takes to make a human being, written in the language of the genes, and it is the dance of the genes that partly dictates the kind of person I am. But not entirely; for my upbringing and environment, experience and culture, have also been hugely influential, and it is the combination of these other factors interacting with our genes that will always make the identical cloning of human beings an impossibility. It is these that makes me uniquely me and you uniquely you, such is the almost infinite variety of our experience and of the mix achieved by the DNA. Richard Dawkins asserts that the number of people who would have to be born for an identical Isaac Newton to be created is more than the number of atoms in the universe. The genetic code also celebrates and guarantees the interconnectedness of life, for it is our genes, inherited from our parents, that will survive through countless generations.

So the DNA double helix works by replication, a kind of constant unzipping down the middle and rebuilding a new strand. Each time my body makes a new cell, a copy of the replicated DNA moves to each side of the cell and the cell divides. This is an operation of startling complexity, for genes in themselves are inert molecules only activated through their constant dynamic exchange with their surrounding cells. At every moment replication of cells is taking place at hundreds of different sites, at precisely defined moments in the cell's reproductive cycle, and billions of chemical units in the DNA must be copied with absolute precision in this living organism of the body, in which it is (in the words of Steven Rose) 'both the weaver and the pattern it weaves, the choreographer and the dance that is danced'.[20] Because the DNA in a single cell is close-packed into 46 chromosomes, if you could stretch out the DNA in just one cell it would measure about six feet, but do the same with the DNA in the body's trillions of cells and it would stretch from the sun to the earth and back several times. An analogy may help. Imagine that each of your 50 trillion cells is the size of a large bedroom. In one corner stands a modest chest-of-drawers: that is the cell's nucleus. Stuffed into the drawers are several miles of cotton thread coiled up into 46 bundles: that is the DNA molecule of a single chromosome.

Yet such facts and figures may be less telling than the story of one migrating bird. In April 2000 I stood on a beach in South Carolina where hundreds of sandpipers feed on the shore and flocks of brown pelicans skim the waves, and watched a flock of red knots stabbing the wet sand. Each year these sandpipers travel from the southern tip of South America to the frozen islands of northern Canada and back again, stopping en route on the east coast beaches.

> I couldn't imagine the maps
> by which they travelled:
> miles of surface

etched into the brain's
wet geometry.[21]

Each year they know exactly where to find food, leaving the sunny beaches of the south and timing their flight north just as horseshoe crabs are laying millions of eggs. Over a few weeks a single bird will eat over 100,000 such eggs; then, plump and re-energised, they continue the nonstop flight north. Here they mate and breed. By mid-July, the female adults head south again, followed a month later by the adult males. But only at the very end of August do the young red knots start the 9,000 mile journey south, and without adult guides find their way along the old migration route, instinctively knowing at what points to stop for the best feeding grounds, before rejoining their parents for the summer. And they do it because of their genetic inheritance: because of the A, the G, the C and the T, the dance of the DNA. Chet Raymo writes of this phenomenon:

Each bird began life as a single fertilised cell. Already, that microscopic cell contains the biological equivalent of a set of charts, a compass, a sextant, and maybe even something akin to a satellite navigational system . . . Part of the red knot's brain comes already wired with a map of the globe and a navigator's skills.[22]

'There is nothing', wrote John Donne in one of his sermons, 'that God hath established in a constant course of nature, and which therefore is done every day, but would seem a miracle, and exercise our admiration, if it were done but once.'[23]

The discovery that the whole of life (with rare exceptions) is connected by this simple, masterly chemical messenger has led to the Human Genome Project, which early in 2000 had already completed the first 'rough draft' of the human genetic blueprint. That enabled President Clinton to echo the cosmologists' earlier claim to have read in space 'the handwriting of God' and speak of us 'learning the language in which God created life'. It is an astonishing time to be alive. 'Think of the human genome as the Book of Life,' says the Director of the Sanger Institute in Cambridge. 'We are about to read the first chapter, as important an accomplishment as discovering that the Earth goes round the Sun, or that we are descended from apes.' Then on 12 February 2001 scientists announced that they had successfully completed the reading of the correct order or sequence of the 3 billion 'letters' of the DNA code, more than 90 per cent of it; and that human beings have some 30,000 genes. It is not the gene itself that matters, but what it is the gene's job to make: that essential organic compound, the *protein*. These are the master molecules of life and the most diverse. Proteins regulate the chemical reactions by which cells keep healthy, grow and divide, and in each protein there is a 20-letter sequence of 20 different amino acids which must be very precise. These amino acids are the building blocks in the protein molecule, and small differences in proteins account for the evolutionary distance between human and animal. For instance, whereas a tiny plant called the thale cress has an impressive 26,000 different genes compared to our 30,000, there is just one difference in an amino acid between me and a chimpanzee, so clearly the qualitative difference between us lies in the proteins, not the genes. When scientists break the code of a particular gene, they discover which sequence of genes produces which protein. So it is not simply the *genome* that scientists are challenged to plot but the *proteone*, the complete mapping of the 250,000 proteins that the 30,000 genes are able to make.

None of this gets us much nearer understanding what it is to be human: that mystery still challenges us. It is more like assembling a list of ingredients which help us to understand how the body works, and it has huge implications for medicine. Many illnesses – heart disease, cancer, senile dementia – have a strong genetic component. We humans are more than 99.9 per cent identical in terms of our DNA, yet some tiny difference may cause one person to succumb to cancer or heart disease. Then there are the genetically inherited diseases like cystic fibrosis, and this new genetic knowledge will enable scientists to predict inherited predispositions to such diseases and develop tailor-made new drugs. But there are wider ethical implications. As with the splitting of the atom half a century ago, the potential for benefit or harm come in equal measure. The choice lies between a significant step in the ongoing story of the prevention and treatment of disease, not least in underdeveloped nations; and a dangerous new weapon in the yearning for human perfectibility, with the lurking fear of children being designed to order in whatever style catches our fancy, genetic manipulation for purely selfish reasons. And not only selfish, but unnatural. Cloning is the stabilisation of a single form, and that runs contrary to the whole current of nature. Thirty years ago, in his epic television series, *The Ascent of Man*, Dr Jacob Bronowski, said:

> Evolution is founded in variety and creates diversity; and of all animals, man is most creative because he . . . expresses the largest store of variety. Every attempt to make us uniform, biologically, emotionally, or intellectually, is a betrayal of the evolutionary thrust that has made man its apex.[24]

But cloned human *embryos* are another matter, and Britain quickly became the first nation to allow the use of them for the extraction of embryonic stem cells. The hope is that such cells might be grown in the laboratory into kidney, liver, heart or even brain tissue in order to mend the defective organs of the patient who supplied the clone. Cloning human embryos – by injecting the nucleus from the cell of an adult into an unfertilised egg with its own nucleus removed – means that stem cells can be created and turned into transplantable tissue that does not run the risk of tissue rejection. The way is open for us to use our new knowledge responsibly or irresponsibly. All ethical systems rest on whether we see ourselves as masters or stewards of creation, and on the value we place on human beings. 'To treat the genetic core of a person as a manipulable object', says John Habgood, 'is to compromise individual otherness at its very root.'

'Anyone who claims to be totally uninterested in any sort of spiritual response to the ache of life is little more than a narrow-headed thug.' Far too blunt to be my words, they are those of the playwright, the late Dennis Potter. There is a form of fundamentalism in some natural scientists which is as damaging to the human search for truth as that of any Bible literalist, a blinkered belief that their own specialised understanding is the only gospel that will prevail, an inability to look at people from any angle other than the scientific one. To the question 'Who am I?' they will say that we are staggeringly complex electrochemical machines. But there is no ghost in the machine, no clinically observable soul or spirit that exists independently of the body, so there can be no self that will survive the body's disintegration. And to the question 'Why are we here?' they will reply that we are here to make copies of our genes, thereby ensuring the continuance of our species. They forecast the day when artistic creativity as well as religious belief are explicable in terms of purely biochemical activity in the brain. Yet, when they have itemised all our physico-chemical processes, assessed our stakes in the genetic lottery, and even reduced the brain to its various particles, informing us that we are purely mind-machines and gene-machines, we (and they) are left with some mystery remaining. For being human does not *feel* like that. It feels more like what the Psalmist hints at when he says that we are 'fearfully and wonderfully made': that we love and dream and dance; that we value good and abhor evil; that we have a sense of beauty and can arrange words in a pattern or notes on a manuscript or shapes and colours on a canvas so as to create poetry and novels and music and art that has a universal and timeless value. That we can feel compassion, show mercy, exercise forgiveness, respond to that transcendent dimension we call

God, and even be prepared to sacrifice our lives for those we love. Is all this simply to be reduced to the expert interaction of molecules?

So what of our inner life and the baffling question of *consciousness*? Here the sciences generally invoked, writes Mary Midgley,

> are neurology and the study of evolution. This means [studying people] by looking at them either through a microscope or through the wrong end of a telescope – the telescope of evolutionary time. These are both useful methods. But it is a little odd to give them this kind of priority.[25]

She suggests that to choose these particular studies speaks more of their success in other fields than the likelihood of them illuminating the mystery of consciousness and the human brain, and likens it to the man looking for his keys under a street lamp and being asked if that is where he dropped them. 'No,' he replies, 'but it's much the easiest place to look.' For knowing how that sea-horse-shaped bit of the brain called the hippocampus works will not help me fit together the strange relationship of my inner and outer life. 'As soon as a system,' writes Susan Greenfield, 'be it a symphony or a curry or a whole human body or a brain, is reduced to its tiniest components, something special is lost.' It is as absurd as defining Strauss's *Four Last Songs* wholly in terms of its biological and physical make-up: black notes on a manuscript, modulations of the human voice and vibrations in the inner ear; or Rembrandt's Kenwood House self-portrait simply in terms of pigment and canvas. The indefinable core, the heart and spirit of the work, that allows it to live afresh at each viewing or hearing, has been lost. Whether we explore the heavens or the subatomic world of nuclei and genes, or whether we seek to analyse a work of art or the inner world of the artist, the mysterious whole must always be greater than the sum of its mysterious parts. And nowhere is this more true than with regard to this intimate stranger I call 'me'.

'In the human head', writes the American brain surgeon Roger Sperry, 'there are forces within forces, as in no other cubic half-foot of the universe that we know.'[26] So just what's in there? A kind of jungle: one brain, weighing some 3lbs and containing about 15 billion nerve cells, or *neurons*. Together with about 100 billion nerve cell connections, or *synapses*, which is more than the total number of humans who have ever lived, and as plentiful as the stars in a thousand galaxies. There are about fifty different types of neuron in the brain and within each type no two cells are alike, and each neuron has treelike projections called *dendrites*. In the brain stem there are a few thousand neurons which send out the finest conceivable cobweb-like hairnet to cover all the different parts of the brain, and has the power to influence millions of synapses all over the nervous system. The number of possible neural circuits in my head is 10 followed by a million zeros and in no two brains are the connections exact, as they would be in even the most advanced computer. The neurons work through electrical signalling, and through chemicals known as neurotransmitters and neuromodulators; they bind to different receptors and act on various biochemical pathways.

Stored in here is memory, inexplicable, arbitrary and immediate. All the people I have known and loved, all the places I have ever been, all the experiences of my life, are contained in parts of this 3lb miracle, and a word or a scent or a piece of music may bring the past flooding back into the present. What no neurologist yet knows is just how my (increasingly dodgy) short-term memory is converted into my long-term memory, how it is that I can at this instant see and feel all the defining moments of my life; how part of me is still (inside) the child mourning for a lost father, still (and always will be) the man falling in love and discovering the wonder of fathering children, or spinning in an over-busy parish, or standing beside Nelson Mandela at the grave of the Unknown Warrior. Here, inside my brain, past and present come together and fuse as I find my integrity in the moment that is now.

While I cannot deny that if all the atoms, all the chemicals, in our bodies were removed there would be nothing left, yet the ongoing, consistent self I know myself to be must be more than my ever-changing physical body and brain. The Greek view was that each of us is an imprisoned spirit, the soul like a bird trapped in a cage. The quite different Old Testament view is that each of us is an animated body, a psychosomatic unity, with physical, mental and spiritual potential. In the Greek New Testament the words for body, flesh, spirit and mind (*soma, sarx, psyche* and *nous*) do not refer to distinctive bits of me, that can be sorted and separated by the surgeon's scalpel, but always to the *indivisible* person that I am *seen from a particular angle*. I am a unity, with bodily, mental and spiritual functions: one whose essence is in *being*, not *having*; and always with some mystery remaining. Yet such a view has a chequered history. While Aristotle regarded body and mind as essentially inseparable, in the seventeenth century Descartes argued that mind and body are quite separate entities, united physically by the pineal gland. His thinking led to a damaging dualism that saw both mind and body in purely material terms and (among other things) dealt a blow to the psychosomatic understanding of illness from which we are only just recovering. Bodies need to have something added, and that something is an enlivening, activating breath or spirit in order that they may live. Evolutionists speak of the infinitely gradual emerging of a self-conscious being. In the more poetic Genesis account of creation the writers picture God breathing into Adam the breath of life (in Hebrew *nephesh*, which can mean interchangeably 'breath' or 'life', 'soul' or 'mind'), and 'man became a living soul'.

So, when I consider my own mystery, I find I need to say: 'I am *body*. I am matter, a physical organism, tall and pale and balding fast; and you can just about squeeze five of me into a Volkswagen Polo. But I am also *mind*, which is quite another sort of stuff. We use the word 'mind', says Mary Midgley, to indicate something quite different, 'ourselves as subjects, able to *mind* about things'.[27] I am me thinking, me with a unique collection of memories, me creating this book. The mind is an activity and the brain is its chief organ; but the brain is not its only organ, for what some in the forefront of medical research are now claiming is that every cell and molecule in the body is part of the mind – that, for example, the three major networks that make up the nervous system, the endocrine system and the immune system all interact. Candace Pert, formerly Chief of the Brain Chemistry Department at the American National Institute of Mental Health, has found that molecules called *neuropeptides* provide the vital connection between mind and body. Strung together like a string of pearls, they act as messengers which travel through every part of the body and link up with specific receptor molecules that are placed like millions of satellite dishes over each of our cells, as if guided by antennae tuned to the brain. Their activity and effectiveness varies according to our state of mind, translating our *invisible* emotions into *visible* bodily effects. So Pert is convinced that what we call the mind resides in the whole body, not just in the brain.[28]

Our problem is that the mind has nothing but itself with which to know itself. Certainly neurologists are defeated by the concept of consciousness. 'How do physical events that occur inside a fistful of gelatinous tissue give rise to a universe of conscious experience that contains everything we feel, everything we know, and everything we are?'[29] My own inner consciousness is for me, and in a profound sense, all there is. The mind's relationship to the body, is like nothing else encountered by science. German scientists have calculated that consciousness is made up of 12,000 different sensations; the Americans have trumped them and make it 40,000. Just how does the brain give rise to something so qualitatively different from itself – the ineffable *feel* of it all? I look out of my study window. Particles (waves?) of light strike the rods and cones in my eye and messages are sent via the optic nerve to the visual cortex in my brain for it to decode. It tells me the trees are green, that in the distance the tall spire of Salisbury Cathedral is pointing to the sky, which is the palest blue, and the sun through the glass is warm. Whenever I shut my eyes, that objective reality has become an invisible image in my brain and I see it afresh. A purely electrochemical reaction has changed into a visual picture; I see blue and I feel warmth. And, even in an age of brain imaging, EEGs and brain surgery, neurologists have still not resolved this enigma: some question if they ever will. We know how the prism divides light into its different wavelengths, but no scientific explanation will help us to know *what it feels like* to see blue. The seventeenth-century philosopher John Locke describes how a man blind from birth announced one day that he now knew what scarlet was. When challenged he replied: 'It is the sound of a trumpet.'

Descartes' concern was to prove that consciousness could not be a physical process: his mistake was to underestimate how intimately the mind (what I feel) is bound up with the life of the body (how I function physically). Physicists admit that, relativity and quantum mechanics having thrown a sizeable spanner in the works, they may know much more about the behaviour of matter but rather less about its nature. 'The time has come to admit candidly', writes the philosopher Colin McGinn, 'that we cannot solve the mystery. [We still have no idea] of how the water of the physical brain is turned into the wine of consciousness.'[30] What cannot be denied is that at the centre of my being is a unique core of memories that bring together my past and reach into my future and provide for each one of us an integrity, a continuity and a stability that says to the world: 'This is me.' And, if pressed further: 'Until I die I am an indivisible unity of body, mind or spirit: Blake's "human form divine". When I claim to be *spirit* or *soul*, I mean that there is in me an animating, uniting activity which has about it something God-given; a yearning for that which is beyond and other than I am. And my body's wholeness, the perfection of its tiniest parts, and that dynamism that enables each cell at once to respond to whatever threatens it – and which therefore threatens the whole organism – is a source of endless wonder.' It is this co-ordinated, unifying and dynamic activity, each part working in harmony, that (over two millennia ago) Aristotle identified as the soul. To watch for the first time beside a dying person, and to observe that moment when the last breath is exhaled and the spirit departs, is to realise with awe the immediate qualitative difference between a corpse and a body that is informed by this extraordinary thing we call life, and daily take for granted.

> The spirit is too blunt an instrument
> to have made this baby.
> Nothing so unskilful as human passions
> could have managed the intricate
> exacting particulars: the tiny
> blind bones with their manipulating tendons,
> the knee and the knucklebones, the resilient
>
> fine meshings of ganglia and vertebrae,
> the chain of difficult spine.
>
> Observe the distinct eyelashes and sharp crescent
> fingernails, the shell-like complexity
> of the ear, with its firm involutions
> concentric in miniature to minute
> ossicles. Imagine the
> infinitesimal capillaries, the flawless connections
> of the lungs, the invisible neural filaments
> through which the complicated body
> already answers to the brain.

Then name any passion or sentiment
possessed of the simplest accuracy.
No. No desire or affection could have done
with practice what habit
has done perfectly, indifferently,
through the body's ignorant precision.
It is left to the vagaries of the mind to invent
love and despair and anxiety
and their pain.[31]

But love, despair, anxiety and pain are for another day.

# The Dance of
# Words and Paint and Music

God created the arts in order that life might be held together by them, so that we should not separate ourselves from spiritual things.

*St John Chrysostom*

The world and being in it are such a mystery that the artist stands before it in a trance of bafflement, like an idiot at High Mass.

*Henry James*

The artist . . . speaks to our capacity for delight and wonder, to the sense of mystery surrounding our lives: to our sense of pity, and beauty, and pain.

*Joseph Conrad*[1]

[We are still faced with] the old verities and truths of the heart, the old universal truths lacking which any story is ephemeral and doomed – love and honour and pity and pride and compassion and suffering.

*William Faulkner*[2]

I hate all Boets and Bainters.

*George I*

Flora Thompson saw July as nature's breathing space, her pause between flower-time and fruit-time, and Henry James found 'summer afternoon' the two most beautiful words in the English language.[3] For a brief spell no birds migrate and birdsong is hushed: blackbirds will not sing again until February. On Laverstock Down the pyramidal orchids are in bloom; and the colourful burnet moths are feeding on the wild briars, their backs a bronze-green, with six scarlet spots on their wings: at the caterpillar stage they feed on trefoil and vetch, acquiring from them a form of prussic acid which the moth then exudes when attacked by birds, who only try it once. On Martin Down red admirals and peacock butter-flies are feeding on the fluffy strawberry-coloured hemp agrimony, and there are tiny common blues the colour of harebells. On the outskirts of the woods are the hedge browns known as gatekeepers, and if you go deeper you may find the first edible fungi: the saffron milk-cap, the dark yellow chanterelle, fawn-coloured fairy ring champignons and common puff-balls. On the marshes at Stiffkey the sea lavender will be flourishing, and patches of samphire, like very thin asparagus, used as a garnish for fish but much overrated. Bees are swarming, and the air is full of the sweet scent of limes. On 17 July in Hampshire, Gilbert White recorded that 'The jasmine is so sweet that I am obliged to quit my chamber'; and on 27 July his tortoise Timothy was in disgrace for eating the gooseberries. The strawberry fields and raspberry canes at Bake Farm are thick with fruit. The ferns are yellowing and the beech trees loaded with mast. The dusty country roadsides are pricked by the vivid, sky-blue of chicory, and Laverstock Down has patches of ragwort, which will cause horses and cattle cirrhosis of the liver, but which sheep eat with impunity and greatly enjoy. In many fields, some bearing those exotic corn circles which Wiltshire seems to attract, harvesting has begun.

In the sixteenth-century Flemish Book of Hours the occu-pations for July are falconry, chasing butterflies and **harvesting**; in the background peasants are furiously scything, in the foreground a falconer dressed all in blue is setting out on a scarlet-harnessed horse, a brown mongrel running alongside; and in the bottom frieze six plump men and women with nets in their hands are chasing butterflies the size of seagulls. All the Books of Hours feature harvesting – usually reaping the corn. And I now come to a different kind of harvest: the harvest of our creative imagination, the words and art and music that are an extraordinary, universal witness to the response of the human spirit to both the beauty and the pain which pierce our lives.

It was Coleridge who wrote that the antithesis of poetry is not prose, but science. For while, in general terms, a scientist's task is to look at the world and say, 'This is how things work' (even though, as we have seen, scientific 'models' are no more than ways of enabling us to think about the observable), the poet's task is to say 'This is what I love' or 'This is what it feels like to be human'. Artists give us an awareness of the ignored familiar or the 'transfigured commonplace'. In his poem *The Rock*, Eliot sees the artist's task as that of co-creator with God, drawing something out of nothing, giving shape to what is formless, making out of invisible thoughts and ideas objects that can move and even change us.

> The soul of Man must quicken to creation.
> Out of the formless stone, when the artist unites himself with stone,
> Spring always new forms of life, from the soul of man that is joined to the soul of stone;
> Out of the meaningless practical shapes of all that is living or lifeless
> Joined with the artist's eye, new life, new form, new colour.
> Out of the sea of sound the life of music,
> Out of the slimy mud of words, out of the sleet and hail of verbal imprecisions,

> Approximate thoughts and feelings, words that have taken
>      the place of thoughts and feelings,
> There spring the perfect order of speech, and the beauty of
>      incantation.[4]

Great works of art have to do with what Wordsworth called 'certain inherent and indestructible qualities of the human mind', the most mysterious of which is that of the creative imagination. The simplest definition of culture is 'that which makes life worth living', and to ask, 'What is art, or music, or poetry?' is merely another way of exploring what it is to be human. Forty years ago the theologian Howard Root wrote that 'the disengagement of theology from imagination is all but complete', and asked:

> Where do we look now for faithful, stimulating, profound accounts of what it is to be alive in the twentieth century? . . . We look to the poet or novelist or dramatist or film [director]. In creative works of art we see ourselves anew, come to understand ourselves better and come into touch with just those sources of imagination which should nourish efforts in natural theology.[5]

It is as if libraries, art galleries, museums, theatres, cinemas and concert halls are the DNA of civilisation.

Eliot's definition of good writing was of

> the common word exact without vulgarity,
> The formal word precise but not pedantic,
> The complete consort dancing together.[6]

And it is that dance of words that have been my lifelong delight: the magic of discovering what Seamus Heaney calls 'the world become word', and the writer Derek Jarman 'the word become goose-flesh', the power of certain writers to enable us to see the familiar in a different light, to tell a story that resonates with our stories, to find words that ring true to something we have known but never really grasped; to realise

> how ordinary
> extraordinary things are or
>
> how extraordinary ordinary
> things are, like the nature of the mind
> and the process of observing.[7]

We yearn to render the visible world in words. When human beings began to use language (perhaps some 50,000 years ago) our brain structure made its most significant evolutionary leap, making us a quite different kind of creature. Even though animals communicate – dolphins and whales, for instance, seeming to possess intricate signalling systems – they do not possess this miracle of conveying ideas to each other's minds by making sophisticated sounds. This is what sets us apart. It has enabled art and music and religious concepts to develop; and a sense of community, for the nearest we can come to sharing what it feels like to be another person, to sharing their consciousness, is through poetry, music and paintings. 'The presence of God in the human soul', writes the poet Ruth Padel, 'shines out of that uniquely human thing, language.'[8] Only with language can we reach deep within ourselves and discover how we connect and how we differ. But words are constantly cheapened and trivialised, and we read books or visit the theatre to rediscover their glory.

The theatre has given me some of the most unanticipated, and therefore magical, experiences of my life. I have known the spell of Ibsen ('Where do I find my plots? In the Bible and the newspaper.') and Chekhov, Sean O'Casey and Beckett, Pinter and Osborne, Peter Shaffer, Brian Friel and David Hare; and, as contemporary as any of them, Shakespeare, not least the RSC's stunning productions of the cycles of the *Histories*. I have admired the genius of Olivier's Oedipus, Othello, and Archie Rice; Judi Dench's Beatrice and Lady Macbeth and Cleopatra, Paul Scofield's and Ian Holm's Lear, Jean-Louis Barrault's Hamlet, Vanessa Redgrave's Rosalind. The memories crowd in: the matchless partnership of Gielgud and Richardson in David Storey's *Home* and Pinter's *No Man's Land*; Peggy Ashcroft as *The Heiress*, Noël Coward in his *Present Laughter* and Edith Evans in *Hay Fever*; Ruth Draper, Joyce Grenfell, Beatrice Lillie, Marlene Dietrich and Sammy Davis Jr; the original London productions of *West Side Story*, *Waiting for Godot*, *Look Back in Anger* and *Beyond the Fringe*; plus a myriad of half-remembered moments when actors and audience have transcended their surroundings in what Peter Brook calls 'holy theatre', 'the invisible made visible', briefly sharing some new awareness of the pain, the passion and the splendour that make us who we are.

The forming of alphabets and the telling of stories led to those epic works of literature which have lit up the peaks and valleys of the human journey. They may not be the books we would choose to take to our desert island (even if the Bible and Shakespeare do seem to come with the rations), for these will have a much more personal and homely significance. Yet where genius is at work, in the writer, the painter, the sculptor, the architect or the composer, what emerges will have not simply a universal but also a timeless, contemporary significance, and their insights are passed from one generation to another. Shakespeare said things about love and grief and jealousy and forgiveness that are as fresh and meaningful and true as the day he wrote them. It is this that gives great art not only an ever-present significance, but also (as Eliot said) its transcendence. It both goes *beyond* the limits of the concerns of any one age, but it also speaks of that indefinable and haunting *otherness* which is at once the deepest reality about us, and the hardest to analyse. In a telling phrase of the art critic Andrew Graham-Dixon, poets – and artists – can give us a sense of 'the instant elsewhere'; and another poet, Peter Jay, has written somewhere that 'we look to poetry for the thisness that it encapsulates, and the otherness that it evokes'. For me, it is the poets, painters and musicians who have most often unlocked this aspect of the world and made it sing. As

Seamus Heaney says, once poets have established their own personal voice, they may then go beyond themselves and 'take on the otherness of the world in works that remain [their] own yet offer rights of way to everybody else'.[9]

There is, of course, a depressing amount of self-indulgent art, sloppy writing and sentimental verse masquerading as poetry (with predictable subject-matter). The American poet William Matthews suggests four rubrics for much lyric poetry:

(i)   I went out into the woods today and it made me feel, you know, sort of religious.

(ii)  We're not getting any younger.

(iii) It sure is cold and lonely (a) without you, honey, or (b) with you, honey.

(iv)  Sadness seems but the other side of the coin of happiness, and vice versa, and in any case the coin is soon spent and on we know not what.[10]

Yet, increasingly, the gold is there to be found, not least among the Scottish and Irish poets, who have produced work which measures up to Robert Frost's reply, when asked if poetry might be defined as escapism, that 'poetry is a way of taking life by the throat'.

If we live in two worlds simultaneously, the outer world of the sciences and the inner world of the senses, then the challenge is to find a common language that speaks to them both. We may find it hard, even after a lifetime, to explore and give voice to this subjective inner world, this intimate, clamorous inner space of feelings, hopes, memories and desires. Some avoid the personal in life. 'The Wilcoxes did. It did not seem to them of supreme importance,' Forster writes in *Howard's End*. 'Or it may be . . . they realised its importance, but were afraid of it. Panic and emptiness.'[11] For many, the temptation is both to fear and to ignore it, always to sit looking out at the landscape beyond our eyes, focused on the outer world of work and wages, family and neighbours and the daily paper, *Big Brother* and *Who Wants*

*To Be A Millionaire?* We become passive observers of what is 'out there', often very intelligent and informed ones, yet (especially in the absence of any religious belief) increasingly disconnected with our inner world, starving the imagination, denying the spirit. And if we then catch ourselves feeling empty and strangely unsatisfied, it is because we lack the integrity of a vision which unites inner and outer, subjective and objective, the world of flesh and the world of spirit. Which is why the young, still touched by the spontaneous wonder of childhood and not attracted to what may seem an unimaginative church, are drawn to all manner of forms of spirituality with which the 'mind/body/spirit' shelves of Waterstones and Dillons are laden. It is also why the role of the creative artist within society matters so much.

Ted Hughes writes of how the principal human occupation, ever since we grew our enormous surplus of brain, has been to explore this inner universe of experience, this genuine self, and to do it we 'have invented art – music, painting, dancing, sculpture, and the activity that includes all these, which is poetry'. For just occasionally a poet may

> find something of the inaudible music that moves us along in our bodies from moment to moment like water in a river. Something of the spirit of the snowflake in the water of the river . . . And when words can manage something of this, and manage it in a moment of time, and in that same moment make out of it all the vital signature of a human being . . . we call it poetry.[12]

Poetry, at its most powerful, enables us to authenticate our inner promptings and, finding that the words are true to our inmost selves, say, 'Yes, that is how it is for me also.' At the end of David Malouf's novel *The Great World*, a eulogy is delivered at the funeral of Pa Warrender. Having run the family business for most of his working life, in his retirement he has turned to his private passion, writing poetry. The eulogist speaks of how poetry tells of what is deeply felt but might otherwise go unrecorded:

> All those unique and repeatable events, the little sacraments
> of daily existence, movements of the heart and intimations of
> the close but inexpressible grandeur and terror of things, that
> is our *other* history, the one that goes on in a quiet way under
> the noise and chatter of events and is the major part of what
> happens each day in the life of the planet, and has been from
> the very beginning. To find words for *that*; to make glow with
> significance what is usually unseen, and unspoken too – that,
> when it occurs, is what binds us all, since it speaks immediately
> out of the centre of each one of us; giving shape to what we
> too have experienced and did not till then have words for,
> though as soon as they are spoken we know them as our own.[13]

Poets help authenticate what we know most deeply by
appealing to our most creative faculty: imagination. It was
Samuel Butler who said that the true test of our imagination
is the ability to name a cat, and the first challenging test for
Adam was to find names for all the creatures. Yet teasing out
a child's creative imagination may not be the top priority in
our schools. Today the flavour of education, whether at the
secondary or tertiary level, is the imparting of objective
knowledge. In the nineteenth century John Henry Newman
and Matthew Arnold (who combined being a poet and an
inspector of schools) believed that the task of a university
was to familiarise the young with 'the best that has been
thought and said in the world'. They believed that this
would guarantee a future secure in the hands of those who
shared a common intellectual and cultural inheritance,
who knew their Greek myths, their Milton and their Shakespeare, and how the music of Bach differed from that of
Beethoven. When in 1892 the poet/scholar A. E. Housman
delivered his Inaugural Lecture as Professor of Latin in the
University of London, he differentiated between the task of
science to train people for the business of life, and that
of the humanities to expose them to the good and the
beautiful. He saw the purpose of study 'to transform our
inner nature by culture' and not to prepare people to earn

their livelihood, and he claimed that the most valuable knowledge is that which is 'properly and distinctively human', including 'the literature which contains the spirit of man' and which enables us to discriminate between what is excellent and what is not. He claimed that the craving for such knowledge 'is no less native to the being of man, no less universal through mankind, than the craving for food and drink, and that [when this craving is starved] part of [a man] dies, part of him starves to death . . . he walks lame to the end of his life.'[14] T. S. Eliot was to echo this plea when in 1940 he wrote of an education which had come to mean simply a training for the mind. He saw that as leading to scholarship, efficiency and worldly achievement and power, 'but not to wisdom'.

Such an elitist approach could not survive, and with the rise of the natural sciences and the rapid expansion of technology a quite new model was needed. From being custodians of the past, universities became places of research, of the discovery and codification of new knowledge, the need to train men and women for the kind of society on which the nation's welfare depended. So specialisation (which inevitably means fragmentation) becomes the order of the day, and a sense of an organic, holistic culture is increasingly remote. Schools are examination-centred, seeing this as the best way of preparing more and more children for further education. Government enquiries into the purposes of higher education (such as the Dearing Report of 1997) rightly put great emphasis on providing a well-trained workforce and the importance of funding research. Yet larger questions of education's ultimate purpose, which have to do with life in all its fullness, with culture, wisdom and the development of human imagination, are largely ignored.

Training in the sciences and in technology may help to guarantee that stream of professional and technological expertise needed in a competitive and globalised market, but if we are not to 'walk lame', if we are ever to join fully in the human dance, then a vital part of education is to introduce us, and encourage us to delight in, that which is intrinsically beautiful, true and of proven worth. Master-pieces in art or word or music from different cultures speak of things which are valuable for what they *are* rather than what they *do*. To discover Shakespeare's power to manipulate words that create an inner world with which we are familiar and at the same time turn those feelings into poetry; to glimpse the compassion and vulnerability in a Rembrandt portrait, his painted knowledge of what it is to live and to have to die; to learn how the sounds and shape in a Schubert sonata seem to forge 'the connection with the hidden crevices between . . . the Divine and the human';[15] is to expand our sense of the human and what gives value to our lives.

It is our imagination that enables us to see things whole (and holy). Auden writes of how to the imagination the sacred is self-evident, and Thomas Traherne, whose spiritual classic, *Centuries*, was discovered in a notebook picked up for a few pence on a London bookstall in 1896, had an almost sublime trust in the power of the imagination and writes of how 'God made you able to create worlds in your own mind which are more precious to him than those which He created'.[16] Those who have sought to meet this inner craving we all feel and to reconcile our inner and outer worlds, therefore meet a deep human need. The best of them contribute to that common body of knowledge that education should provide, which may have as much to do with myths and metaphors, dancing and dreaming, as with quarks and black holes, economics and deconstruction. If all is relative, if all judgements are transient and merely a matter of taste, then we are no longer fired with a sense of great minds worth encountering, great books worth indulging in and great paintings to experience and enjoy. But artists can do something more:

- they can show us what the world discloses once we learn to give it our *full attention*;

- they can remind us of the hidden power of the *transcendent*; and
- they can enable us, in Auden's phrase, to *'break bread with the dead'*.

*Giving attention.* No artist (or scientist) can report accurately on the world without this readiness to give attention to its constantly changing richness and mystery. Every work of the imagination is born out of contemplation, and it is this which in turn gives it the power to touch a deep, inner space within us. All art is born from what Simone Weil means by a way of looking which is 'attentive': 'suspending our thought, leaving it detached, empty and ready to be penetrated by the object',[17] setting aside the illusion that 'my eye' is the centre of the universe and attending to things as they are. We may use words either to analyse or to describe: the scientist does the first in breaking down objects into their basic components, while the poet seeks to describe the nature of people and things, using metaphor and analogy, image and symbol. So does the language of religious faith, which is the attempt to penetrate what may lie behind and beyond the mystery of the creation and its creatures. Only in contemplating what is before our eyes, seeking to feel what it means to *be* that thing, to honour its individual existence, can the mind (in the words of Austin Farrer)

> rise from the knowledge of creatures to the knowledge of their creator, but this . . . knowledge . . . comes from the appreciation of things which we have when we love them and fill our minds and senses with them, and feel something of the silent force and great mystery of their existence. For it is in this that the creative power is displayed of an existence higher and richer and more intense than all.[18]

The artist Cecil Collins also distinguishes between two necessary languages: that of our explicit experiences, those that can be analysed and described, and that for those implicit experiences which cannot be analysed or measured [or] described. This is the inner life of the soul, and the implicit language of the heart and the soul is poetry, the image, the symbol, dance, music and silence.[19]

'Art', writes R. S. Thomas, 'is recuperation from time.'[20] And Wittgenstein once wrote that works of art see objects under the aspect of eternity. Cézanne is the classic example of the painter who seeks to redeem time by capturing and preserving one moment, which then becomes eternal. A small epiphany, in time, yet transcending time, in which there is a kind of unveiling, when we grasp intuitively a deeper reality, momentarily aware of seeing a person or an object with the freshness of the eyes of childhood. Cézanne would ponder for hours before placing a single touch of colour, for he knew it would at once affect all the rest. A contemporary wrote of how for him 'each stroke must contain the air, the light, the object, the composition, the character, the outline and the style' in the attempt to restore to each object something of its true radiance. Constable said that the best lesson on art he ever had were the words: 'Remember: light and shadow never stand still.' 'Not since Moses', said Rilke of Cézanne's Mont St Victoire paintings, 'has anyone seen a mountain so greatly.' 'The landscape thinks itself in me,' wrote Cézanne. 'I am its consciousness.' It is as if he preempts the quantum physicists when he recognises that each of his brushstrokes affects all the others and that the appearance of objects change as the eye moves over and around them; the realisation that there is no such thing as an optically objective painting, which was to lead to Cubism and abstract art, with their new ways of representing things and seeing the world.

When Ted Hughes writes about how poetry is made, especially of how he seeks to capture the spirit of an animal or a bird, his advice is 'to imagine it, see it, live it, look at it, touch it, smell it, listen to it, turn yourself into it. When you do this, the words will look after themselves, like magic.'[21] In Saul Bellow's novel *Ravelstein* the novelist's task is described as

> to resist largely standardised categories . . . A face, a haunch, a pair of eyes, a foot, a set of ears . . . hold the key for the observer . . . But this is no longer observation, it is more akin to religion . . . We must continue to see as a child, straight into the Kingdom of heaven.[22]

The great Nobel Prize poet Czeslaw Milosz, in an almost mystical encounter on the Paris Metro, sits near a young woman whose face captivates him. He studies the face, 'dumbfounded', with its slightly snub nose, the high brow with sleekly brushed-back hair, the line of the chin.

> To absorb that face but to have it simultaneously against the background of all spring boughs, walls, waves, in its weeping, its laughter, moving it back fifteen years, or ahead thirty . . . Like a butterfly, a fish, the stem of a plant, only more mysterious. And so it befell me that, after so many attempts at naming the world, I am only able to repeat, harping on one string, the highest, the unique avowal beyond which no power can attain: *I am, she is.*[23]

*Tiepolo's Hound*, a long poem by the West Indian poet Derek Walcott, charts a quest to locate an absurd detail from a painting by a Venetian painter that has haunted the narrator's memory: the pink inner thigh of a white hound. But another dog is glimpsed here and there in the poem: a black mongrel. And in the end it is the mongrel that comes to matter more: not the lost and the exotic, but the living dog in this actual moment which unlocks the poet's compassion. A phrase running through the poem is 'the awe of the ordinary', and in her review of the book Paula Burnett wrote:

> The ordinary is the miracle . . . Walcott is drawn to the secular image – not heaven but a hound, not bravura but bread – yet to the possibility of beatitude in both. [This] is a book to read outside, breaking off to notice the light through a blade of

grass or a passing stranger's walk. Art's impetus is to return us to life, our eyes and hearts opened.[24]

Then there is 'the hidden power of the *transcendent*'. Seamus Heaney has spoken of poets who bring a poem alive by seeming to lift the reader's hand and 'put it on the bare wire of the present', and it is possible to relate to a painting in such a way that you feel a kind of expanding glow – like a current being passed through a filament. There is in the Tate Britain Gallery a painting by Jack Smith of a mother bathing her baby in a sink in a bare corner of her kitchen. It is painted entirely in colours of fawn, grey and white, yet there is a kind of luminosity about it. 'I wanted', said Smith, 'to make the ordinary miraculous.' The Scottish painter S. J. Peploe wrote: 'There is so much in mere objects, flowers, leaves, jugs – colours, form, relation. I can never see mystery coming to an end.' Painting expresses an artist's inner vision, and it is not only the great sweeping canvases of Rubens or Veronese that astonish. It is those of painters who paint the ordinary in such a way that it becomes extraordinary: Monet, obsessed with haystacks, Rouen Cathedral or a line of poplars, as these are transfigured by the changing light; Turner, experimenting with coloured veils of paint that seem to capture the very elements themselves; Cézanne's apples, Chardin's basket of wild strawberries, Van Gogh's yellow chair or golden sunflowers, Bonnard's daffodils in a green pot, Morandi's range of bottles and jars. Some may capture in one moving image the sadness and poignancy of life by painting its ordinary moments, like Sickert in his *Ennui*, the archetype of bored melancholia, a glassy-eyed husband, sitting with his cigar and empty beer glass, his wife leaning against a chest-of-drawers, turned away from each other and gazing into space; in Bonnard's words, 'investing people and things with a meaning and value that goes beyond literal representation'. It is that 'beyond', it is that 'instant elsewhere', that artists, as well as poets, seek: what Rilke described as his ambition to lift objects out of time and make them 'capable of eternity'.

For the truth (as Austin Farrer affirms when he speaks of 'the knowledge of creatures rising to the knowledge of their creator') is that art and poetry and music can mediate meaning and a sense of a 'higher, richer and more intense' existence, and the nearest we come to the holy and the numinous is through these signs and instruments of the divine. This is what it means to live in a sacramental world: that matter is one of God's languages; that it is indeed the bearer of spirit; that we can come to understand, if only we would learn to open our eyes and ears, that the creation mirrors the Creator. That there are not two worlds, for just as my spirit informs my physical cells and nerves and muscles and enables me to fall in love and respond to beauty, so we may find the holy in the ordinary at every level and there is nothing that exists that does not contain some mystery. Yet we know that perfection, like God, is always just beyond our grasp, and however moved we may be during a concert, at a play or art exhibition, even experiencing what George Steiner calls 'being possessed by that which one comes to possess',[25] we may emerge feeling vaguely dissatisfied, because it has awoken a hunger that (in this life) will never be fully satisfied. C. S. Lewis put this well:

> The books or the music in which we thought the beauty was located will betray us if we trust in them; it was not in them, it only came through them, and what came through them was longing . . . They are not the thing itself; they are only the scent of a flower we have not found, the echo of a tune we have not heard, news from a country we have never yet visited.[26]

And Oliver Soskice, a painter, also writes of the ultimate, elusive mystery to which all art points:

> Existence is received as the unreachable beckoning horizon within stones, the sky, brickwork rained upon, daylight, pools of reflecting water, apples in a bowl. A painter may spend a

lifetime trying to translate this strange, innermost utterance of visible things. Yet inexpressibly other is not the same as inexpressibly alien, because the unknown pole of everything is precisely what imposes our humanity upon us.[27]

Artists also enable us to *'break bread with the dead'*. Auden wrote that without such communion, such keeping faith with the past, a fully human life is not possible. Another writer, the fine American poet Stanley Kunitz (whose most recent volume is published in his ninetieth year: 'Who said', asked a reviewer, 'that old men cannot dance?') believes that in writing a poem 'you are in touch with the whole chain of being', always trying to get in touch 'not just with your most primal self, but with the whole history of the race'. Through the arts we conduct a dialogue with ancestors we never knew, for 'where is the history of the race inscribed if not in the human imagination? Poetry is . . . the telling of the stories of the soul.'[28] There are certain portraits by Holbein – that of Sir Thomas More in a luxurious velvet gown, black cap and great gold chain of office, his intellect conveyed through the set of the mouth and the gaze of the eyes, or that of More's friend Erasmus, with his gentle scholar's face, his delicate hands and fingernails deeply engrained with dirt – that are more revealing than the history books. George Orwell talked of the easy flushing of memories down the memory hole so that the history which those memories preserved could be freely rewritten, and of how it was the poet's job to preserve memory; and Czeslaw Milosz, who witnessed his Polish culture being destroyed in first the Nazi and then the Stalinist eras, speaks of how 'our planet gets smaller every year . . . and is characterised by a refusal to remember'. Politicians and journalists rarely have much sense of history, and the arts, by giving a sense of what has been called 'the livingness of the past', can help to give meaning to life. 'Things become more precious with the awareness that others have looked at them, thought about them, written about them,' writes Amy Clampitt. 'There is less originality than we think.'[29]

But such remembering has much more serious implications. In an important book, *The Song of the Earth*, Professor Jonathan Bate looks at the role of literature in ecology. He believes that the writer's role in an age obsessed by technology is nothing less than to restore to us the earth which is our home. He quotes widely from the works of Hardy, Wordsworth, Keats, John Clare and Ted Hughes, writers who celebrate our deep bond with what Wordsworth called 'the beautiful and permanent forms of nature', largely destroyed by urbanisation and industrialisation, with the pollution and ravaging of earth's natural resources these brought in their wake. When we commune with those forms of nature, argues Bate, we live with a peculiar intensity, but when we are alienated from them we are diminished, and he sees the poet as the guardian of language, able to celebrate and witness to the sacredness of the earth as values shift and times change. He claims that certain poems have the power to recycle from age to age the richest thoughts and feelings of a community about the earth; to engage imaginatively with the non-human; in Wordsworth's phrase 'to see into the life of things'; and to preserve, protect and secure that which is of lasting value. This chimes with some words of the Russian poet Joseph Brodsky, that it is wrong to label a poet as Elizabethan or Victorian, for the 'poet's appetite for the infinite' makes him one who has 'got to tell you something about your life no matter when and where he lived his'.[30] And it chimes with the words of Seamus Heaney at Ted Hughes' Memorial Service in Westminster Abbey, when he claimed that Hughes

> had singlehandedly *re-minded* England as it were, put the country and its culture in *mind* again of much that its land and its language entailed.

Even post-Holocaust, Hughes could still 'sing about the glory of creation'. So to the question 'What is a poet for?' Jonathan Bate asks:

> Could it be to remind the next few generations that it is we who have the power to determine whether the earth will sing or be silent? As earth's own poetry, symbolised for Keats in the grasshopper and the cricket, is drowned ever deeper – not merely by bulldozers in the forest, but more insidiously by the ubiquitous susurrus of cyberspace – so there will be an ever greater need to retain a place in culture, in the work of human imagining, for the song that names the earth.[31]

'Works of art, mostly poems,' writes Bate, 'may create for the mind the same kind of re-creational space that a park creates for the body.'[32] Poems like Keats' 'Ode to Autumn' or Wordsworth's *Prelude* or Coleridge's 'Frost at Midnight', and the paintings of Constable, Samuel Palmer or the English watercolourists, create powerful echoes in us, for our own stories are made up of memories of days when the skies were Constable's skies and the valleys Samuel Palmer's 'valley of vision' thick with corn, and the woods and water Cotman's woods and river estuaries; nature seen and loved in all the aggravating yet rewarding unpredictability of English weather. Theodor Adorno writes of days 'which seem to be waiting to be taken notice of'. We alone use language: we alone recognise that the clouds are lovely and find words and images in which to say so. When we are willing to look and listen to the world we discover we belong to it; we feel the same kind of sensations as all the generations that have loved this earth before us; and yet the beauty that moves us, like music, is hard to define and it is the poets and painters who have come closest.

But in our time some of them have served an equally important cause. Joseph Brodsky said that human beings are put on the earth to create civilisation, and Seamus Heaney asserts that poets have been true to that purpose, especially when civilisation is threatened by the forces of violence, injustice and oppression, when 'the question of transcendent values was plied and preserved most urgently in the lives and works of poets'.[33] Auden wrote his poem 'In Memory of W. B. Yeats' between Yeats' death in 1939 and the German invasion of Poland. It includes a line, often taken out of context, that 'poetry makes nothing happen', but the poem rebuts the phrase in its ending:

Follow, poet, follow right
To the bottom of the night,
With your unconstraining voice
Still persuade us to rejoice . . .

In the deserts of the heart
Let the healing fountain start,
In the prison of his days
Teach the free man how to praise.[34]

In the grimmest days of the twentieth century poets did just that. They kept alive the spirit of resistance. In face of formidable Stalinist repression, the poet Osip Mandelstam, first imprisoned and then exiled, continued to write lyric poetry deeply out of fashion with his Soviet masters, to be rewarded with a sentence of five years' hard labour (though he died of a heart attack on the way to the camp). Anna Akhmatova's devastating poems on the Stalinist terror led to her being singled out for attack, and Irina Ratushinskaya was imprisoned in a Siberian labour camp for her subversive poetry. In the post-war years in Eastern Europe, poets such as Milosz, Paul Celan and Zbigniew Herbert and prose-writers like Primo Levi, Elie Wiesel and Vaclev Havel, witness to human worth and dignity in the face of demeaning and repressive regimes; they draw attention to our responsibility to ensure that the good, the true and the beautiful survive.

'I am quite positive', said Brodsky when he made his acceptance speech on receiving the Nobel Prize for Literature, 'that a man who reads poetry is harder to prevail upon than one who doesn't.'[35] And Ted Hughes, writing of these

Mid-European poets who witnessed such suffering, saw them as recording,

> along with the suffering their inner creative transcendence of it ... Like men come back from the dead they have an improved perception, an unerring sense of what really counts in being alive.[36]

Faced with finding the means to resist the brutal assault of war and oppressive dictators, there is a sense in which Auden was both right and wrong. Poetry and the imaginative arts are not at first sight very effective weapons. And yet, writes Heaney,

> they verify our singularity, they strike and stake out the ore of self that lies at the base of every individuated life. In one sense the efficacy of poetry is nil – no lyric has ever stopped a tank. In another sense, it is unlimited. It is like [Jesus] writing in the sand in the face of which accusers and accused are left speechless and renewed.[37]

And then there is music. Among the arts it was the latest starter. We saw previously how Pythagoras believed that the universe had its own music, the 'music of the spheres'. There is a lovely conceit that Adam and Eve lost the capacity to hear this music when they fell from grace, until that night when a few shepherds tending their flocks in the fields of Bethlehem were momentarily able to hear it in the form of 'a multitude of the heavenly host' praising God. Plato, in the *Timaeus*, argues for what he calls a 'hidden affinity' between music and the soul. He taught that the structure of the soul is determined by ratios directly related to the ratios of intervals in music, and that exactly the same ratios governed the distances between the planets. But for the next 1,500 years most music was improvised and lost. Then, between 1000 and 1400, European musicians learned a whole new language of musical composition, thanks to Guido of Arezzo's invention of notation and counterpoint.

This moved the creation of music from the hands of the players to the pens of composers, and enabled it to be written down and preserved, and indeed transported without alteration to other times and other places, thus opening the way which led from Gregorian chant to Bach's Mass in B Minor and Louis Armstrong. As Shakespeare was writing *Twelfth Night*, opera was being born, and the composer Howard Goodall, in his recent survey of Western music, writes of how the Pythagorean concept of music representing the cosmic harmony of the spheres was giving way to a more modern concept of music as a vehicle for touching the human emotions of love, jealousy, anger or sadness (as in Orsino's 'If music be the food of love, play on;/ Give me excess of it that, surfeiting,/ The appetite may sicken, and so die'[38]).

Scientists mapping the activity of the brain have long known that our response to music is in part physiological, that we respond to a beat which echoes the natural pulse and rhythm of our bodies; perhaps there was some subtle programming in those months when we listened to the beat of a mother's heart. Changes of pulse communicate emotion and are deeply important to us. Brain research shows that discordant chords create erratic neuron firing patterns, while 'harmonic' chords give rise to even neuron firing, and which areas of the brain are brought into play when listening to, or performing, music. Scientists are exploring the phenomenon of a blind, autistic youth like Tony who cannot tie his own shoelaces but who is a brilliant jazz improvisor and has a memory for thousands of tunes, which he plays after a single hearing. And those suffering from Alzheimer's, who may lose their ability to recognise those closest to them, often retain their musical response. Keith Sutton's wife Jean suffered in this way in her early fifties, and in a recent radio programme[39] he spoke of how, though she had lost her ability to speak, she could still 'hum and sing along' to her favourite music, especially the moment in Beethoven's Pastoral Symphony where the raging storm is transformed into 'the glorious melody of the shepherds' hymn, and I'll always hear her singing it'.

Keith Sutton also spoke of hearing Alfred Brendel play the last three of Beethoven's piano sonatas (Opus 109, 110, 111), of how the audience demanded an encore, and of how Brendel played Busoni's transcription of Bach's chorale, 'Now comes the Saviour of the world'. Later, meeting Brendel, he asked him why he had chosen that piece, and Brendel told him he needed to play something that 'was pure in its absolute simplicity'. Sutton paraphrased that as meaning that whereas the Beethoven sonatas are an ascent to the divine, it is the simplicity of 'Now comes the divine to us', God coming to find us, that astonishes, and that it needs 'something of perfect simplicity to say it'.

'At the inner core of music', says the singer Dame Janet Baker, 'is the possibility that performing it can touch and change the human heart.'[40] For the mystery remains – and perhaps always will – of just how it is that music stands somewhere between matter and spirit and has the power to touch us so deeply, whether it echoes the pure, mathematical sounds, as in much of Bach, or reflects the richness and beauty of the universe, as in the Pastoral and Choral Symphonies of Beethoven. Howard Goodall ends by admitting that the power of great sacred and classical music is one of the few things we have left in our culture which cannot be explained:

> There are no easy answers to account for being moved to tears by notes on a page, or of being stirred to anger and action, or being comforted in our loneliness. It is a mystery how Rachmaninov's flowing melodies and ripe harmonies make people feel romantic and amorous . . . or how Shostakovich manages to express all Russia's Stalinist agony without losing the essentially unbreakable spirit of the people at the same time. It is a mystery . . . why Tippett's use of Negro spirituals in his 1945 secular oratorio *A Child of our Time* so perfectly captures the

desperation of the victims of Nazism in the Second World War.[41]

We do not know exactly what music is saying, but we know that it comes from beyond the frontiers of what we know and understand, and that it relates something essential about our humanity. It has been called 'the arithmetic of creation', a kind of divine mathematics that makes sense of what we are, and will perhaps comfort us when we come to die. Beethoven was comforted on his deathbed by Handel's *Messiah*; and in turn his last quartet comforted Schubert as he too lay dying in Vienna a year later. In Vikram Seth's novel *An Equal Music* the narrator is a member of a quintet. One night they play Beethoven's String Quintets in C Minor and E Flat Major:

> The quintet exists without us and yet cannot exist without us. It sings to us, we sing into it, and somehow, through these little black and white insects clustering along five thin lines, the man who deafly transfigured what he so many years earlier had hearingly composed speaks unto us across land and water and ten generations, and fills us here with sadness, here with amazed delight.[42]

As they play Haydn's Quartet Opus 20 ('If I had any advice to give,' says the pianist Sriatoslov Richter, 'it would be to listen to the Haydn quartets; they're such a pleasure that it wouldn't surprise me to learn that they're good for your health.'), he thinks with amazed wonder of the players' separateness and their coming together, in order to produce

> these complex vibrations that jog the inner ear, and through them the grey mass that says: joy; love; sorrow; beauty. And above us here in the apse the strange figure of a naked man surrounded by thorns and aspiring towards a grail of light, in front of us 540 half-seen beings intent on 540 different webs of sensation and cerebration and emotion, and through us the spirit of someone scribbling away in 1772 with the sharpened feather of a bird.[43]

It was the great Swiss theologian Karl Barth who said that when the angels play for God they play the music of Bach, but when they play for their own pleasure they play Mozart, and God eavesdrops. And St Augustine claimed that in heaven the variations on the 'alleluia' will be of such length and beauty that we shall never be bored. Well, maybe ... but in the meantime our lives are for the most part more humdrum and earthbound. There is a poem by John Press called 'After *Le Nozze di Figaro*':

> It did not last. Before the year was out,
> The Count was once again a slave to women,
> The Countess had a child by Cherubino,
> Susanna was untrue to Figaro,
> Young gallants went to bed with Barbarina.
> But for a moment, till the music faded,
> They all were ravished by a glimpse of heaven,
> Where everything is known and yet forgiven,
> And all that is not music is pure silence.[44]

Music can 'for a moment' expose us to a kind of beauty and hopefulness about the human race that cannot be expressed in any other terms, 'a glimpse of heaven,/ Where everything is known and yet forgiven'.

There is in the side chapel of the Church of San Zaccaria in Venice a painting of the Virgin and Child with saints. Giovanni Bellini painted it in 1505. In its colour, and the harmony of the composition, it is as beautiful as any picture I know, and in late afternoon it is irradiated by the sun from the west window. There is, at the start of the Adagio in Schubert's String Quintet in C Major, a passage of such aching stillness that you wish for it never to stop. It is at such moments, in the words of Bernard Levin, that we have an unmistakable understanding 'that [we], the work of art, and the artist are ... bound together like the particles of the atom, and that – like the atom – we are part of something which is vastly greater than ourselves, *and which makes sense'*.[45] 'All art, all creativity,' says David Hockney, 'comes from love.' Because artists and writers and musicians have looked at what is before their eyes with absorbed attention in order to learn to love them, we can, by watching where they plant their steps, do the same. They invite us to join in the dance of words and paint and music.

So I end with a poem and an image. The poem is by the 90-year-old Czeslaw Milosz:

> Pure beauty, benediction: you are all I gathered
> From a life that was bitter and confused,
> In which I learned about evil, my own and not my own.
> Wonder kept seizing me, and I recall only wonder,
> Risings of the sun over endless green, a universe
> Of grasses, and flowers opening to the first light,
> Blue outline of the mountain and a hosanna shout.
> I asked, how many times, is this the truth of the earth?
> How can laments and curses be turned into hymns?
> What makes you need to pretend, when you know better?
> But the lips praised on their own, on their own the feet ran
> The heart beat strongly; and the tongue proclaimed its
>     adoration.[46]

And the image? Henri Matisse painted three different versions of *Le Danse*. The first two are in Leningrad and New York. There was a round-dance popular in Provence, called the farandole, which expressed for Matisse the whole essence of rhythm and joie de vivre. In the 1909/10 versions his naked dancers, male and female, link hands and dance in an energetic clockwise circle, their arms stretched out to each other and linked. All except one. The nearest dancer is reaching out desperately to the hand of the dancer on her left, but there is a gap. But there is a quite different version of *Le Danse* in the three great murals Matisse was to paint over three years from 1931, and which were then lost for 60 years and rediscovered in a Paris warehouse. 'This dance,' said Matisse, 'I have had it inside me for so long.' For him, the dance is a symbol of being alive and content and in harmony with the creation, and in this final version the dancers, some whole, some fragmented, move and tumble across a field of blue. It is a kind of dream of perfection. And yet the dancers are on their own, and in the early versions, that stretched-out hand reveals that the circle is broken and incomplete. The dance will never be perfected, for perfection is always just out of reach. Indeed, the dance is more exhausting than it looks, for there are tears at the heart of things, and much heartbreak along the way.

# AUGUST

## *Dancing in the Dark*

---

I wept when I was born, and every day shows why.
*George Herbert*[1]

I was merely cursing, under my breath, God and
man, under my breath, and the wet Saturday afternoon of my conception.

*Samuel Beckett*[2]

I dance, for the joy of surviving,
on the edge of the road.

*Stanley Kunitz*[3]

There is beauty and there are the humiliated. Whatever the enterprise may present, I would like never
to be unfaithful either to the one or the other.

*Albert Camus*[4]

---

I love the English country scene
But sometimes think there's too much Hooker's green,
Especially in August, when the flowers that have lent a
Lightness, don't; being gamboge or magenta.[5]

'Gamboge' was new to me: my dictionary tells me it is a
'gum resin from various East Asian trees used as yellow

pigment and as purgative'. The yellows are hawkbit and hawkweed, fleabane and fennel, and the corn marigold, Shakespeare's

> marigold, that goes to bed wi' the sun,
> And with him rises weeping.[6]

On Iona the damp and meandering path that takes you (if your luck holds) to the Hermit's Cell will be thickly bordered by both ling and bell heather, and in the sea off the machair eider duck will be feeding. Nearer home, tortoiseshell butterflies feed off wild marjoram, and cover the long purple flowers of buddleia, finding a rich source of nectar in the shrub which has rampaged across the country since it was first sent home to Britain a century ago from the rocky scree of the foothills in Western China.

On the hottest days, with the countryside dusty and drained of colour, cattle seek the shade, thistledown floats in the air and wasps invade every picnic. On 14 August 1873, Gerard Manley Hopkins wrote of the bleached grass on the cliffs in the Isle of Man as being 'the same colour as the sheep', behind them 'a sleeve of liquid barley-field, then another slip of bleached grass, above that fleshy blue sky. Nearer at hand you see barley breathe and open and shut and take two colours and swim.' In August 1800, Dorothy Wordsworth walked round Grasmere and Rydal Water and gathered white foxglove seeds. On 15 August 1783, Gilbert White (having lost part of his gooseberry crop to Timothy the previous year) 'took by birdlime on the tips of hazel-twigs several hundred wasps that were devouring the gooseberries', noting with satisfaction that 'a little attention this way makes vast riddance'.

The Books of Hours are consistent in the task for August: it is **threshing**, separating the grain from the husks, and all show labourers working with a flail. The flail had a 4-foot-long handle, usually made of ash, attached to a beater rod (the swingle), made of crab apple or holly wood, the thong being made of eelskin. The beating was usually done in the barn, the beater whirling the swingle round his head and aiming to bring it down flat on the corn; but in the year that Gilbert White was eliminating his wasps, the flail received the kiss of death by the invention of the first threshing machine. Combine harvesters, which cut and thresh in a single operation in a very clinical sort of way, may have diminished the contemporary impact of Jesus of Nazareth's likening the kingdom of heaven to the final sifting of the grain from the chaff, the wheat from the tares, at the harvest, yet that remains a powerful image of a creation in which good and evil, darkness and light, go hand-in-hand. One which leaves us asking, with Job in his anguish: 'Why?' Or with Elie Wiesel, watching in his prison camp while a young boy takes half-an-hour to die on the end of a rope: 'Where is God now?'[7] Or with Christopher Leach, his 12-year-old son dead of asthma, crying out: 'Does my Creator weep?'[8] If we are to answer that most poignant of human cries, we must ask three questions:

- What sort of a world is it into which we are born?
- What sort of creatures are we, able to unlock the secrets of DNA, track the course of the atom, and compose *The Magic Flute*, yet at the mercy of earthquake, accident and cancer cell?
- What sort of a God might be the creator and sustainer of the creation and all its creatures?

What sort of a *world*? One that is shot through with match-less, constantly renewed beauty; and one that is witness to intolerable pain. Once again it is a question of finding an integrity that can be faithful to both without compromising truth. If we had 'a keen vision and feeling of all ordinary human life,' says George Eliot in *Middlemarch*, 'it would be like hearing the grass grow and the squirrel's heartbeat, and we should die of the roar which lies on the other side of silence. As it is, the quickest of us walk about well wadded with stupidity.'[9] Behind our concept of moral evil lies a physical evil, part of which is what some have called 'evolutionary evil', the 'roar which lies on the other side of silence', the suffering of creatures over more than a billion years: the survival of the fittest, the major extinctions of whole species, the blood on the hooked beak of the owl, the lion and the jackal hunting their prey. In 'June' (Chapter 6) I argued that the logic of God creating a world that is guaranteed both openness and indeterminism implies freedom. Freedom may seem cruel to those civilised enough to feel pity, yet only such freedom could guarantee the various choices and potentialities which the world is created to realise, and the emergence of a creature capable of feeling such pity and distinguishing right from wrong. Blind alleys, waste and pain are part of the price we pay for being here. While they challenge and disturb us (for they undoubtedly entail suffering and death), some would deny that they can be described as 'evil'. Moreover, if the existence of pain and suffering suggest that we live in a Godless and purposeless creation, the existence of human consciousness, tenderness and self-sacrifice then become infinitely harder to explain.

Then there are what the insurers call 'acts of God': an unhappy phrase, suggesting a primitive concept of a capricious God who, like Zeus, tosses down a few punitive thunderbolts, as if throwing his toys around. Yet in a world in which the laws of nature, the 'if . . . then' of cause and effect, are (thank God) so deeply ingrained and its people truly free, there will be floods, earthquakes and hurricanes, and none may claim divine protection. Often, where deaths occur, human carelessness or iniquity are to blame. An estimated 1.5 million people died in earthquakes in the twentieth century, the vast majority because 80 per cent of the buildings were so ill-designed that they collapsed, most of them put up without planning permission and built in violation of construction rules. During elections in poor countries politicians often grant amnesties for illegal buildings. Time and again international charities have called attention to the role poverty plays in such disasters. The poor can only afford badly built housing, and quakes such as the one that killed 23,000 people in Guatemala City in 1976 have been called 'class quakes' because of the accuracy with which they hit the poor. As do floods. Due to ecological blindness, in which river courses are straightened, forests are cut and hillsides denuded, those living in the low-lying sandbars of the coast of Bangladesh, or in the hillside slums of Rio de Janeiro, suffer terrible losses. There is no denying the terrifying power that lies coiled in the forces of nature, but if God has written into the creation the potential for a tectonic plate in the earth's crust to shift and the waters to rage, then equally he has written into us our matching potential to steward the earth with wisdom, and meet human need with compassion. That wisdom, and that compassion, are equally 'acts of God'.

So what sort of *creature* are we? One who is free to choose between good and evil. Sharing a common story, and vulnerable to suffering, we share too an empathy which enables us to enter into the experience of others. Good and evil were the warp and woof of our first state of consciousness, and they will be there to the bitter end. While they may be out of fashion, the terms 'original sin' and 'the Fall' are still useful shorthand theological terms to describe the power we have within us to create or to destroy our earth, our neighbour and even our own souls by the choices we make for light or darkness, that which builds up or that which destroys. They speak of the gap between what we are and what we long to be, although there are two contrasting approaches to the story. Augustine spoke of a primal innocence from which we fell away, and that view became the common currency of the Western Church. Yet everything we now know of evolution and human development denies it, and confirms the force of the second-century theologian Irenaeus' contrary argument in favour of a desperately slow climb towards a not-yet-attained maturity. In this view, we are created by Love in order to learn to love. We must therefore be free to make moral choices. Only in choosing good in a world where we can opt for evil, and where patience, caring and loyalty at whatever cost are possible, and one where we may accept or reject the concept of God, are we free spirits. The world of suffering is a necessary context for the growth towards God of such free spirits: any other kind would be one without moral values and without much point.

Faced with the problem of evil some have been tempted to take a dualistic view of the world: to see God and a personified force of evil (the Devil) locked in conflict. It is a tempting concept, but the danger of visualising Satan as the pantomime Demon King writ large is that of projecting onto some mythical figure a potential for evil that lies deep in the human heart. This is not to deny that there is a kind of demonic corporate evil that can infect large numbers of people to terrifying effect, as we witnessed in the Holocaust or the Rwandan massacre, where in a hundred days 800,000 people were massacred, most of them hacked to death; and as we see nightly, in less dramatic ways, on the news. We catch glimpses of the infective power of strong feelings, either for good or evil, at pop concerts or the Last Night of the Proms, or in the racist taunts and chanting in a football stadium. Yet even the Holocaust or Rwanda cannot persuade me that there is a personalised source of evil, or even that there are people who are totally, irredeemably evil. Not if the great world faiths of Judaism, Islam and Christianity are right in their root beliefs: that everything is made by God and that God is holy; and that we are all made in God's image: that is to say, that there is in each person, however deeply buried, that which is of God informing the human spirit.

In Hebrew the word for the Devil is 'Shitan', which means 'no response', he who cannot respond to God. Psychotic sadists feel nothing in the face of their victims' cries: they can no longer recognise a fellow human being, let alone the sacredness of human life. Yet those who work among 'lifers' who (in the more enlightened prisons) are taking part in group therapy – and where the collective pain may be intense – report that although such men and women may have committed terrible crimes it is hard not to see that their very anger is a cry to be recognised as human. In war, those conditioned to fight and to kill may quickly reach a point where they no longer see their victims as human, simply as the enemy: to the Nazis the Jews were 'pigs', to the Americans the Vietnamese were 'gooks'; the Hutus of Rwanda were urged to kill the Tutsi 'cockroaches'. An English newspaper can refer to asylum-seekers as 'human sewage'. By demonising enemies or strangers we open the way for actions – between Israeli and Palestinian, Hutu and Tutsi, Protestant and Catholic – which simply match evil with evil, and let loose the poison of mindless destruction. War has always been an evil, only morally justified as being the lesser of two evils if it meets certain strict conditions; for it plays to a kind of cancerous potential in human nature, and the development of ever more sophisticated weapons has not lessened the potential for inflicting the most inhumane of deaths on soldier and civilian alike. There have been reports that Britain is developing a 'vacuum bomb' which has been condemned by human rights groups as likely to cause devastating damage to civilians. It is a hi-tech urban warfare weapon: a shoulder-launched thermobaric weapon which sends out shockwaves, causing massive damage to the victim's internal organs, before enveloping them in a fireball. At the same time, the air is sucked out of their lungs by the pressure created by the blast.

'Man's capacity for evil', wrote Reinhold Niebuhr, 'makes democracy necessary and man's capacity for good makes democracy possible.'[10] And one of Robert Frost's poems begins: 'I have been one acquainted with the night', the darkness without and the darkness within which, writ large, spells out the whole catalogue of our evil deeds. We each have our 'shadow' side, the dark, unacceptable side of our personality. Our own potential for rage or lust or cruelty may be deeply repressed, surfacing only in manageable forms – bad temper, depression, unspoken desire or wounding words. Yet we know that in certain situations we cause others to suffer and do harm to ourselves. Further, much sickness is caused by how we neglect or abuse our bodies. Once again it is our freedom that is our Creator's most hazardous, but inevitable, gift to us. 'One would be loath to reject self-consciousness,' reflects a character in David Lodge's novel, *Thinks*,

> to return to the unreflective animal existence of pre-lapsarian hominids, swinging from the trees or loping through the broad savannahs . . .
>
> *for who would lose,*
> *Though full of pain, this intellectual being*
>
> as Milton put it. Satan speaking, of course. Or as John Stuart Mill said, 'better to be a dissatisfied man than a satisfied pig'.[11]

All that we can understand. Yet the anguished, niggling questions remain. The existence of pain and the unmerited suffering of the innocent seems either to limit God's power or to qualify his goodness. What sort of creature are we? One to whom terrible things may happen at any moment and on any day. Virginia Woolf records in her diary:

> London . . . is shot through with the accident I saw this morning and a woman crying Oh, oh, oh faintly, pinned against the railings with a motor car on top of her. All day I have heard her voice. I did not go to her help; but then the baker and the flower-seller did that. A great sense of the brutality and the wildness of the world remains with me – there was a woman in brown walking along the pavement – suddenly a red . . . car turns a somersault and lands on top of her, and one hears this Oh, oh, oh.[12]

It is the 'Oh, oh, oh' that looks for an answer. When my child dies of asthma, does my Creator weep?

No worst, there is none. Pitched past pitch of grief,
More pangs will, schooled at forepangs, wider wring.
Comforter, where, where is your comforting? . . .
O the mind, mind has mountains; cliffs of fall
Frightful, sheer, no-man-fathomed. Hold them cheap
May who ne'er hung there.[13]

If God weeps, why does he not act? Hardy's novel *Tess of the D'Urbervilles* ends with the narrator telling us that ' "Justice" was done, and the President of the Immortals, in Aeschylean phrase, had ended his sport with Tess'; which caused Edmund Gosse to ask why his friend Hardy should have 'shaken his fist at Providence'. 'Hardy depicts suffering which is not so much "innocent" as pointless,' writes A. N. Wilson.

> The reader finishes a novel of Hardy's knowing that stoicism is not its own reward; nor will it be rewarded by some sympathetic external agency. Many church Christians . . . must have tried to hide this from themselves when they read Hardy's novels, and seen his 'pessimism' as a distorting lens; they had to wait until they were exposed to the shrapnel and gunfire on the Western Front before their imaginations were exposed to such pitiless Homeric reality, which Hardy could see relentlessly at work in the country villages of Dorset.[14]

When John Keats was staying at Teignmouth in 1818, he wrote to a close friend of a world full of pain and heartbreak and of how 'we see not the balance of Good and evil' but only feel 'the burden of the mystery'. In a bleak poem, 'Complaint', the Augustinian poet Padraig Daly addresses God:

> I will tell you, Sir, about a woman of yours,
> Who suddenly had all her trust removed
> And turned to the wall and died.
>
> I remember how she would sing of your love,
> Rejoice in the tiniest favour;
> The scented jonquils,

> The flowering currant bush,
> The wet clay,
> Spoke to her unerringly of benevolence.

> I remind you, Sir, of how, brought low,
> She cowered like a tinker's dog,
> Her hope gone, her skin loose around her bones.

> Where were you, Sir, when she called out to you?
> And where was the love that height nor depth
> Nor any mortal thing can overcome?

> Does it please you, Sir, that your people's voice
> Is the voice of the hare torn between the hounds?[15]

In another poem, 'Ministers', Daly writes of how

> It is we who are kicked for your failures . . .
> When eyes cannot lift to see the sun,
> People ask us to explain; and we are dumb.
> When rage against you is a fierce sea
> We are the first rocks on the shore.[16]

Only such relentless honesty, rather than overconfident assertions, will serve in those who still affirm the goodness of God if they are to be taken seriously by those who cannot easily do the same.

So what sort of creature are we? One who suffers and is capable of asking hard questions of God as to why these things should be. At the heart of our dilemma we find ourselves both accusing God who, if omnipotent, could not desire the death of a single child, and appealing to God as the one who is loving and benevolent and on the side of justice. This is not the atheist's problem, but the Christian's, and the long saga of our attempts to make sense of this is in itself an act of faith. When Kierkegaard argued in *Works of Love* that the Christian preacher should not hesitate to preach *'in Christian sermons . . . AGAINST Christianity'* he was challenging the integrity and honesty of those who return soft answers to the hard questions, the bitter reality of suffering, cruelty and oppression. For suffering, while it may ennoble and prove creative, also degrades. Dostoevsky, himself a Christian, writes such a 'sermon' in *The Brothers Karamazov*, where Ivan says that he can never accept a God who deliberately brought about the suffering of a single child for the achievement of some higher good:

> If all have to suffer so as to buy . . . harmony by their suffering, what have children to do with it – tell me, please? . . . We cannot afford to pay so much for admission. And therefore I hasten to return my ticket . . . It's not God that I do not accept, Alyosha. I merely most respectfully return him the ticket.[17]

It is not hard to build up the case for the prosecution. In the Holocaust Museum in Washington there is a series of coloured paintings by children from the Theresienstadt Ghetto. In 1941, the eighteenth-century Czechoslovakian town of Terezin was made Hitler's 'model' ghetto for the Jews. It has since been described as 'the anteroom to hell'. One painting, by Eva Schurova, who was eight years old, is of a circle of girls holding hands and dancing in a circle. She was deported to Auschwitz in 1944. She did not survive. The Australian poet Les Murray asks ironically why such a powerful weapon as the Holocaust is not used more effectively by atheists:

> Higamus hogamus
> Western intellectuals
> never praise Auschwitz.
> Most ungenerous. Most odd.
> When they claim it's what finally
> won them their centuries'-
> long war against God.[18]

The Book of Job exists to assure us that we are meant to question God, to feel anger, hurt and bewilderment, to argue with God. Elie Wiesel, who saw his family fed into the gas

chambers and ovens of Auschwitz, wrote that such engage-
ment with God, pleading with him and challenging him on
moral grounds, is part of our task as human beings; that
even our shouts and our blasphemies in the face of such evil
are a form of prayer. For the horrors of the twentieth century
fly in the face of all meaning. The attempt by the Third
Reich to annihilate the Jewish race took twelve years; the
Stalinist purges of Jew and non-Jew lasted for seventy, and
the toll was almost five times higher. Such human purges,
which could be mirrored on varying scales in China, Cam-
bodia, Iran, Bosnia and parts of Africa, are off the scale of
our imagination and reduce us to an appalled silence.

But it is never simply the silence of despair, and it leads us
to ask with a new urgency: what sort of a *God* might be the
creator and sustainer of such a creation? If it is easy to argue
the case for the prosecution, it is not so hard to argue the
case for the defence, provided we remember two facts. The
first is that for theist and atheist alike these are puzzles to
which there are no solutions, mysteries which remain just
out of our range: there are only what Eliot called 'hints and
guesses'. The second is that suffering, whether in the loved
person beside us or in the starving child on the other side
of the globe, gives rise to that most Godlike (and otherwise
inexplicable) of our qualities: compassion. This is the key
that can unlock the logical impasse of God's omnipotence
versus God's love. Compassion means literally 'to suffer
alongside', and in what Christians call 'the incarnation' God
does just that. That is the mystery to cap all mysteries, the
bringing together in a single human life of the divine and
the human, revealing the ultimate power and meaning of
self-giving love; and it has the power to create light in the
darkness. It is the belief that we cannot solve the riddle of
undeserved suffering; that however hard we press into the
darkness God does not, indeed cannot, give us answers.
Instead, he does something infinitely more radical: he enters
with us into the questions.

He does so (though this is where words struggle and ultimately fail) in the only terms we can understand: in the shape of the man who lived and suffered and died as we do. The words and actions of Jesus, and most of all his death, came to be seen as the one authentic window into God. Near the end, he even enters into our questioning of God's absence, yet dies trusting in the Father's love. He teaches that much suffering is unmerited and undeserved; that bad things may happen to any of us and are not in any way a punishment for sin. His healings are signs of God's presence and power. His compassion can silence his enemies. When he tells the stories we call parables he is giving people an insight into the time when God's purposes will be truly known through the re-ordering of our lives in relation to each other and to God: he calls it the kingdom. Jesus is realistic about evil, knowing how we long for the good, yet constantly add to the world's pain. He reveals how such evil may be overcome, and on the cross lives out his conviction by meeting injustice and cruelty with the most powerful weapon of all: forgiveness. And when his followers look back at the events of Good Friday and that first Easter, it does not just bring them (predictably) to a new awareness of the love and forgiveness of Jesus, but (unexpectedly) of the love and forgiveness of God. They claim that after this life and death and rising everything must be newly defined. Starting with God.

There is a kind of parallel Darwinian evolution in our emerging understanding of the Divine. The Old Testament records the centuries-slow shift from the primitive worship of the local fertility gods of nature to the one true God of Israel, jealous and powerful. He is the creator God of Genesis, and he discloses himself to a particular people through a sequence of formative historical events (the call to Abraham, the leading out of slavery, the covenant). There is little attempt to penetrate what he is in himself, only guesses – some inspired, some less so – that may be deduced from the events. He remains Job's hidden God. For the most perceptive of the prophets he is stern but merciful, his justice matched by his loving-kindness; and there is the promise of a coming Messiah who will establish the kingdom in which God's sovereignty is affirmed. The New Testament records that coming: it speaks of 'the Word made flesh'. Jesus radically reinterprets the Messiah's role as that of the 'suffering servant', and makes known the loving, forgiving, compassionate nature of the one he calls 'Abba'. Gradually, as the implications of his birth, his teaching, his death and his rising become clear, they come to see that in Jesus they have been faced with the spirit and power of God himself, and there is the final great seismic shift to a belief that God is Christlike.

Faced by so powerful a claim, the church Fathers and theologians have quarried away at the mystery of suffering down the succeeding centuries, with all the flashes of insights and blind alleys you would expect. The floor has been largely dominated by those in the tradition of Augustine, looking to the past and emphasising the Fall, seeing suffering incurred as a divine punishment for sin; but a minority have always preferred the Irenaean view, looking to the future and believing that in the end good will be triumphantly brought out of evil (as it was on Good Friday), trusting that God's purpose will finally be vindicated, in the light of which all that has led up to it will be seen to be justified. If, as Christians claim, the cross stands at the still centre of the world, what is shown beyond the suffering is the definitive shape of costly, self-giving love; and for those who would draw near to the truth of God this is the only starting-point. It is what defined the life of the one who said: 'Whoever has seen me has seen the Father', not claiming to be the unimaginable God 'in whom we live and move and have our being', but to reveal the love of God in human terms. That is his whole purpose: not to placate an angry God, but to embody in words and actions (that are life-changing for those who accept them) the love of God for his creation, whatever the consequences.

My concept of God has shifted and changed with the years, but I now see him as deeply involved in the evolutionary process, suffering in and with his creation; not asking us to endure anything that he is not prepared to endure as well. Love can do no other: love affirms the beloved and is ready to be subject to the same forces that so puzzle and seek to damage us, all the pain and all the unpredictability of life. In recent decades, and not least in light of the Holocaust, there has been renewed emphasis on a God who suffers and yet is still God. Arthur Peacocke writes:

> The processes of creation are immensely costly to God in a way dimly shadowed by and reflected in the ordinary experience of the costliness of creativity in multiple aspects of human existence – whether it be in giving birth, in artistic creation, or in creating and maintaining human social structures. We are then seen not to be the mere playthings of God, but as sharing as co-creating creatures in the suffering of the creating God engaged in the self-offering, costly process of bringing forth the new.[19]

That is to say: God is not omnipotent in the sense that he is independent of the world and untouched by it. He does not by coercion force the world to do his will. He can only work in accord with his nature, which is love: in love, with love, through love. A remote and self-sufficient God could not be genuinely loving. Love is vulnerable, and exposes itself to hurt; so Jesus was vulnerable. He was affected by others, always inviting, never coercing, easily silenced, seemingly destroyed. So is God vulnerable, open to his world and affected by it, fully identified with us because love knows no other way: rejoicing with us and suffering with us too. And if the world is to be made in God's likeness, if at the end of the day all that is good and true and beautiful is to triumph, then it can only be by the way of costly love of which the cross has become the most potent and universal symbol. It is as if God is saying: 'This is how I have to work in the world. There is no other way'; as if the figure of the crucified is the most valid image of God the world has ever seen. Fifteen years after Julian of Norwich had a series of visions of Jesus suffering on the cross, she wrote:

> I desired often to know what was our Lord's meaning . . . and I was answered in inward understanding, saying, 'Would you know your Lord's meaning in this? Learn it well. Love was his meaning. Who showed it you? Love. What did he show you? Love. Why did he show you? For love. Hold fast to this, and you shall learn and know more about love, but you will never need to know or understand about anything else for ever.'[20]

Nor, if Calvary is a window into an eternal truth about God, is it simply an event *in* time, on a certain day in Palestine. In last year's 'Seeing Salvation' exhibition at the National Gallery, many found the most moving and disturbing image was a limestone sculpture from around 1500 entitled *Christ on the Cold Stone*. The near-life-sized figure of Christ, sitting on an outcrop of rock, is completely naked, stripped of his robe and awaiting crucifixion. Here is Christ as Everyman, abandoned, humiliated, his eyes downcast and vacant, looking on death. It speaks a universal language about life and death, pain, fear and compassion. Neil MacGregor, Director of the Gallery, described it as 'an image of inconsolable sorrow' calling to mind the words from Lamentations: 'All ye that pass by, behold and see if there be any sorrow like unto my sorrow', and reminding us:

> we have seen sorrow like this sorrow: we see it all the time. We see it in photographs of countries at war, we see it in the sufferers from flood and famine, we see it sitting on the cold stone of our own city streets and pavements . . . Sixteenth-century viewers would have recalled . . . [how] Christ reminds the disciples that all kindness shown to the naked, the hungry, the thirsty, is kindness shown to God, for God is in all suffering.[21]

In Helen Waddell's novel *Peter Abelard*, Abelard and his

friend Thibault release a rabbit screaming in pain in a trap. It dies in their arms. At once Abelard exclaims at the injustice of innocent suffering and asks why God does not stop it.

> 'I don't know,' said Thibault. 'Unless . . . it's like the Prodigal Son. I suppose the father could have kept him at home against his will. But what would have been the use? All this,' he stroked the limp body, 'is because of us. But all the time God suffers. More than we do.'
>
> Abelard looked at him, perplexed . . . 'Thibault, do you mean Calvary?'
>
> Thibault shook his head. 'That was only a piece of it – the piece that we saw – in time. Like that.' He pointed to a fallen tree beside them, sawn through the middle.
>
> 'That dark ring there, it goes up and down the whole length of the tree. But you only see it where it is cut across. That is what Christ's life was; the bit of God that we saw. And we think God is like that . . . kind, and forgiving sins and healing people. We think God is like that for ever . . . But not the pain. Not the agony at the last. We think that stopped.'
>
> Abelard looked at him . . . 'Then . . . you think that all this,' he looked down at the quiet little body in his arms, 'all the pain of the world, was Christ's cross?'
>
> 'God's cross,' said Thibault. 'And it goes on.'[22]

When the poet Jane Kenyon was dying of cancer five years ago, her husband Donald Hall writes of their painful vigil:

> When their minister,
> Alice Ling, brought communion to the house
> or the hospital bed,
> or when they held hands as Alice prayed,
> grace was evident
> but not the comfort of mercy or reprieve.
> The embodied figure
> on the cross still twisted under the sun.[23]

Two years ago I visited Dachau, the first of the Nazi concentration camps and still a place of desolation. It was the camp to which all the German priests and pastors who seemed a threat to the Third Reich were sent: nearly four thousand of them over the years, of whom a great many died for their faith. One day, collecting the camp refuse and emptying a bucket of swill belonging to one of the SS families, one of the priests saw a stub of wood sticking out of the mess of ashes and rotting potatoes. He pulled it out. It was an old crucifix. One of the arms was broken and the body covered in filth. He hid it under his jacket and placed it in the tiny room the priests used as a chapel. It was a reaffirmation of what they already knew: that Christ was in their midst.[24]

When Dietrich Bonhoeffer was imprisoned by the Nazis he wrote to a friend, a year before he was executed:

> God lets himself be pushed out of the world onto the cross. He is weak and powerless in the world, and that is precisely the way in which he is with us and helps us . . . The Bible directs man to God's powerlessness and suffering; for only the suffering God can help.[25]

Belief in a God who 'lets himself be pushed out of the world' does not imply one who is helpless and inactive; but it does mean a redefinition of what we mean by God's power and omnipotence. We define power as force and aggressive strength, the ability to inflict our will on others; often, in worldly terms, this will mean that the weak and suffering are despised. Yet this, writes Paul Fiddes (whose book *The Creative Suffering of God*[26] is a classic treatment of this theme),

> falls wide of the mark of true power, which is a matter of winning people's hearts and minds and changing their attitudes . . . This is the kind of allegiance a suffering God can inspire.

'Power', writes Paul to the church in Corinth, 'is most fully seen in weakness,' and again, 'The weakness of God is stronger than human strength'.[27] This weakness is the weakness of love. Austin Farrer asks:

Are not his making hands always upon us, do we draw a single breath but by his mercy, has he not given us one another and the world to delight in, and kindled our eyes with a divine intelligence? Yet all his dear and infinite kindness is lost behind the mask of power. Overwhelmed by omnipotence we miss the heart of love.[28]

Isaac Watts' hymn speaks of how Christ crucified reveals the nature of God:

Here his whole name appears complete;
nor wit can guess, nor reason prove
which of the letters best is writ,
the power, the wisdom, or the love.[29]

Over two centuries later W. H. Vanstone, in his Good Friday hymn, 'Love's endeavour, love's expense', writes:

Therefore he who shows us God
helpless hangs upon the tree;
and the nails and crown of thorns
tell of what God's love must be.

Here is God: no monarch he
throned in easy state to reign;
here is God, whose arms of love
aching, spent, the world sustain.[30]

The inmost nature of God is self-giving – or self-emptying – love, with all the winning authority and conviction that carries with it. Fiddes writes of how classical theologians have often shrunk from the thought of God as vulnerable, for to be affected by another's suffering is to be changed by that experience; yet he argues persuasively that when God chooses to engage with his creation, it is, like marriage or any deeply loving relationship, a journey into the unknown. 'It must be possible for the world to bring something new to God each morning in a real relationship.' Meister Eckhart sums it up in three words: 'God needs man', and centuries later Martin Buber was to write: 'You know always in your heart that you need God more than everything; but do you know too that God needs you?'.[31] This is surely, like the best of paradoxes, both false and also deeply true. God does not need us in the sense that he is self-sufficient and eternal; yet he has chosen to need us as an artist needs to create, and in creating to express his or her own nature. God needs us because love, with all its potential for suffering, is his very essence. Julian of Norwich wrote that there was in God 'a desire, longing and thirst from the beginning', and this longing is for fellowship with those who will engage with him in the give-and-take of love. This is what the long and painful process of evolution has been about: this is why we are here. God, if not loved, is somehow incomplete.

When the darkness engulfs us, none of us know how we shall respond. Whether we are called to face a terminal illness, the death of one we love more than life itself, the breakdown of a marriage or the desolation of an unrequited love, a parent with Alzheimer's or the loss of a job, dancing in the dark is the hardest dance, and many are defeated by it. Yet I have learned many times that suffering, when permeated by love, can have creative power. There is an anonymous first-century saying: 'When I light a candle at midnight, I say to the darkness: I beg to differ.' While the cross was evil in that it was a violent rejection of God's love as that was offered in Jesus, and a rebuff of all that we might be ('they know not what they do'), yet the spirit in which that death was faced challenged the darkness and turned the destructive power of evil into good. Many have drawn strength and courage from seeing their own Calvaries in this light. I think of just two.

One is Richard Coles, who in a broadcast six years ago told of his 30-year-old friend Hugo, who was seriously ill with AIDS. Richard had dabbled with the church, but had been deterred by what seemed to him its irrelevance to his needs. On the night Hugo lay dying in hospital and while he slept, Richard called to mind all the images of Christ and tried to find comfort in them:

> I went through Christ the Light of the world, but there was no light; Christ the King, but there was no kingly glory that I could see; Christ the Comforter, but I felt no sense of comfort; Christ the Healer . . . I thought of Christ the first-century social worker . . . promising to make everything better when nothing could make anything better, proclaiming that everything was all right when nothing was.
>
> I went out of the room for a cigarette and watched Hugo on the monitor set up in the ward. It was then that I saw another image of Christ before me – Christ crucified – Christ nailed on the cross, scourged, bleeding, ruined. And it wasn't difficult to make the connection . . . What did seeing the crucified Christ in Hugo mean? . . . What was in evidence that night [was] a dying man's suffering, his wit and strength, a group of friends around him, a gentle exchange, a taking leave. And it was in these things that Christ was truly revealed; through them came comfort and confidence and calm. Not a cheap, fingers-crossed wish against wish, but the grace of God; grace in the arms of catastrophe, unmistakable and overflowing. Hugo died the next afternoon.[32]

The second example is one of my dearest friends, Stewart Cross, who died of a decimating cancer while Bishop of Blackburn. A week before his death he agreed to be interviewed on Radio 4. He spoke of the tension between seeking to live one day at a time and the apprehension and anxiety about his approaching death.

> About a week ago I had a bout of extreme pain, and lying on the bathroom floor I couldn't help recalling our Lord's last words from the cross and saying out loud: 'Lord, Lord, why have you forsaken me?' But I also remembered his words in Gethsemane: 'Take away this cup . . . nevertheless not my will, but thine, be done'. And so I was able to say into the midst of it all: 'Father, into thy hands I commend my spirit.'

Stewart ended by affirming what for him was the unbreakable promise of the God he knew to be Christlike, summed up in Paul's words to the church in Rome: 'I am convinced that there is nothing in life or death . . . in the world as it is or the world as it shall be, in the forces of the universe, in heights or depths – nothing in all creation that can separate us from the love of God in Christ Jesus our Lord.'[33]

Nothing I have written explains the world's darkness. 'There can be no completely rational defence of God in a world of pain,' writes Paul Fiddes. 'If there could be, it would justify suffering on the one hand, and destroy faith on the other.'[34] Not all are able to make such affirmations as Richard Coles and Stewart Cross. But many of those who do believe that evil is ultimately defeated, not through strength but through the weakness of the cross, and that God in Christ is numbered with us among the victims, have witnessed to the fact that such a belief does three things: it consoles; it gives us a larger story of suffering that does possess a meaning that can help us find meaning in our own; and when we cry out in protest it reassures us that God does the same.

Herman Melville's *Moby Dick* is the story of Captain Ahab's obsession with a demonic God who for him is symbolised by the great white whale that has bitten off his leg, in pursuit of which his boat and crew are destroyed and only he is saved. In Auden's poem on Herman Melville is the discovery that

> Goodness existed: that was the new knowledge . . .
> . . . the truth was simple.
> Evil is spectacular and always human,
> And shares our bed and eats at our own table,
> And we are introduced to Goodness every day.[35]

When I read that, I remember the obituary of a young playwright, Roy McGregor, who died of cancer during the production of one of his plays: 'He had the grace of a man who, knowing all the bad, allows himself to be continually surprised by the good.' What is undeniable is that even in the dimmest corners of the kingdom of darkness flashes of light illuminate human beings, with their indomitable spirit and a refusal to surrender their humanity. Even in Auschwitz some of the Jews on the way to the death chamber could recite for themselves the Kaddish, the prayer for the dead: '*Yitgadal veyikadach shme raba* . . . ('May his name be blessed and magnified'). In Auschwitz, Elie Wiesel could not do so. He lost his faith in God and found no answers, yet he has gone on asking the questions. The teenaged Wiesel, seeing that young boy taking half-an-hour to hang, and hearing behind him someone ask 'Where is God now?' heard a voice within him answer: 'He is here. He is hanging here on the gallows'. 'Never shall I forget', he wrote, 'those moments which murdered my God and my soul and turned my dreams to dust. Never.'[36] For him God was dead. That with all my heart I understand and respect. And yet . . . may it not be that what for Wiesel proved the ultimate example of the absent God, unable to prevent this act of evil, was precisely the point at which others may see God to have been most present? Where is God? 'Here he is – he is hanging here on the gallows.' In my copy of Wiesel's *Night*, there is a foreword by the French novelist François Mauriac. He tells of Wiesel coming to see him soon after the war. And he writes this:

> I, who believe that God is love, what answer could I give my young questioner, whose dark eyes still held the reflection of that angelic sadness which had appeared one day upon the face of the hanged child? . . . Did I affirm that the stumbling-block to his faith was the cornerstone of mine, and that the conformity between the Cross and the suffering of human beings was in my eyes the key to that impenetrable mystery whereon the faith of his childhood had perished? This is what I should have told this Jewish child. But I could only embrace him, weeping.[37]

Some of us believe, writes Julian of Norwich,

that God is all powerful and may do everything; and that he is all wise and can do everything; but as for believing he is all love and will do everything, there we hold back. In my view nothing hinders God's lovers more than the failure to understand this.[38]

Dame Julian wrote those words in the fourteenth century, in the midst of the Black Death, the Hundred Years' War and the Peasants' Revolt; and despite all the darkness through which some of us have lived, it is a profound and unchanging truth. In the lifelong game of 'hints and guesses', I would stake my life on the fact that this is the truth of God as he has always been from the beginning, and will be to the end.

# SEPTEMBER

## *The Dance of Forgiveness*

---

Let them come up that hill. I don't care if it's an 80-year-old woman or a child of three. I'll open fire. We are prepared.

> *Yael-Ari-El, a Jewish woman in the*
> *Israeli-occupied West Bank*

Whoever opts for revenge should dig two graves.

> *Chinese proverb*

When thou dost ask me blessing, I'll kneel down, And ask of thee forgiveness.

> *King Lear*[1]

The Glory of Christianity is To Conquer by Forgiveness.

> *William Blake*[2]

---

By the end of the month the harvest is in, the last beans picked and the best blackberries gathered. An old saying suggests that the Devil spits on them on Michaelmas night, spoiling their flavour. Blackberry seeds have even been found in the stomachs of Neolithic people; gathering them, and returning home scratched and empurpled, gives even the most urbanised some sense of sharing in the harvest. Country church fonts and window sills are laden with apples, marrows and home-baked bread, and hedgerows are hung with the feathery seedheads of old-man's-beard the colour of cygnets: in the seventeenth century the naturalist John Gerard named it 'Traveller's-joy'. Spear thistles (otherwise known as Donkey's breakfast) attract flocks of goldfinch. By the Avon the scent of the Himalayan balsam, a rampant plant which has been known to hurl its seeds up to twelve yards, and known vulgarly in Somerset as 'Bee-bums', pervades the air. Great horse chestnut trees, first noted as growing in John Tradescant's garden in Lambeth in 1633, are shedding their conkers, and their ancient cousins, the oaks, their acorns. Gardens sport golden rod and Michaelmas daisies, the over-gaudy dahlia ('Hurrah! blister my kidneys!' exclaimed he in delight, 'it is a frost! – the dahlias are dead!'[3]), and the subtler chrysanthemum.

On the Norfolk coast the waders are at their most numerous, great flocks of dunlin turning from dark to light as they wheel in the air, knots and sanderlings muttering in a disgruntled sort of way as they work the sands. Swallows flock together in the skies, on roofs and telephone wires, where (observes John Clare on 10 September 1824) 'they twitter as if they were telling their young stories of their long journey to cheer and check fears'. Two weeks later, and forty years earlier, Gilbert White notes that 'red-breasts whistle agreeably on the tops of hop-poles . . . but are prognostic of autumn . . . Black snails lie out, and copulate. Vast swagging clouds.'

In some of the Books of Hours the September occupation is **treading grapes**. In the fifteenth-century Bedford Hours, a labourer dressed in a green smock and unsuitable white breeches is thigh-deep in a great wooden vat of purple grapes. Isaiah likens God's people to a vineyard: 'and he looked that it should bring forth grapes, and it brought forth wild grapes;'[4] and Jesus, so often drawing his images from nature, asks 'Can grapes be picked from briars, or figs

from thistles?' and adds, of the test of the validity of a
prophet, 'You will recognise them by their fruit';[5] which Paul
echoes in 'Everyone reaps what he sows'.[6] Nothing is more
fruitful in forming the person we are created to be, and
nothing more central to the life of the kingdom, than the
costly willingness to join in the dance of forgiveness.

On 1 April 1989 there was held in St Stephen's Cathedral,
Vienna, the funeral of the Empress Zita of Austria/Hungary,
the widow of the last Emperor Charles I, who had died 70
years before. She was 96. The service lasted two hours; 6,000
people attended; the setting was Mozart's *Requiem Mass*; at
the end the coffin was placed in a hearse drawn by six
black horses and accompanied by 600 Tyrolean militia to the
nearby Habsburg burial place, the church of the Capuchins.
When the cortège arrived the doors were closed. The
chamberlain knocked three times and one of the friars inside
called out: 'Who requests entry?' The reply was formidable
(and spoke of a vanished Europe): 'Her Majesty Zita, Empress
of Austria, crowned Queen of Hungary, Queen of Bohemia,
Dalmatia, Croatia, Slavonia, Galizia, Illyria, Queen of Jerusalem, Archduchess of Austria, Grand Duchess of Tuscany
and Cracow, Duchess of Lorraine, Salzburg, Carinthia,
Krain and Buconia, Grand Duchess of Transylvania, Marchioness of Moravia, Duchess of Upper and Lower Silesia, of
Modena, Parma, Piacenza, of Dubrovnik and Zara, princely
Countess of Habsburg and Tyrol, Duchess of Trent and
Brixen, Marchioness of Upper and Lower Lausitz and Istria,
Countess of Hohenembo, Ruler of Trieste, Great Princess of
Serbia, born Royal Princess of Bourbon, Princess of Parma';
there then followed her orders, which were not modest. The
friar replied: 'We do not know her. Who requires entry?'
'Her Majesty Zita, Empress of Austria, Queen of Hungary.'
Again the reply came: 'We do not know her. Who requires
entry?' This time the chamberlain replied: 'Our sister Zita, a
poor mortal sinner.' The gates were thrown open. Last May,

in Vienna to conduct a retreat, I stood beside her enormous tomb, where fresh flowers lay, and pondered.

A Buddhist monk, asked to define sin, told his questioner to open his hands wide and consider what he could do with them: he could offer his hand in friendship, embrace a loved one, create beauty, arrange flowers, break bread, tend the sick. He was then asked to close his hand, finger by finger. 'And what can you do now?' 'Hurt, injure, destroy, even kill.' 'Sin', writes Simone Weil, 'is not a distance [from God], it is a turning of our gaze in the wrong direction.'[7] Sin is a kind of blindness, both to God's goodness and to human worth. Recognising our own potential to cause others pain, even to take a perverse pleasure in doing so, we acknowledge the child within us, on whom once the whole world centred, and whom we never entirely leave behind; still a good manipulator of others, still expert in the art of self-justification, and still instinctively wanting to retaliate when hurt or offended. Or, for the sake of a quiet and uncompli-cated life, we may choose the lesser good or refuse to go the extra mile. Priests who hear confessions quickly learn how often and how deeply the words we are hearing find an echo in our own hearts, how trivial most of our offences seem, yet how damaging they can be. Solzhenitsyn's words are true:

> If only there were evil people somewhere insidiously commit-ting evil deeds, and it were necessary only to separate them from the rest of us and destroy them. But the line dividing good and evil cuts through the heart of every human being. And who is willing to destroy a piece of his own heart?[8]

A recent television documentary, fronted by the former hostage John McCarthy, examined the possibility of forgive-ness in the cases of four people who had been deeply wronged: a woman who, as a child, had been traumatised by witnessing her father's repeated violence against her mother; a Chilean who was tortured by Pinochet's henchmen, and whose fiancée 'disappeared'; a woman whose daughter was murdered by a man who in prison has never revealed where her body is buried; and a policeman shot in the face by a thief. The first woman, determined in mid-life that such memories should no longer have the power to damage her, had come to terms with her father's actions and had found a sense of liberation in writing to say that she forgave him. The second could not forgive his torturers, believing that to do so would be to condone their actions. The third was torn between believing that she had no right to forgive her daughter's killer – 'only my daughter had the right to do that' – and the feeling that 'if he showed remorse, that would be different'. The policeman said that, as a Christian, he had felt no anger, just a determination that justice should be done. His attacker, in prison, wrote to him from Broadmoor asking his forgiveness, which he at once gave; they have since met and regularly correspond. McCarthy himself still finds it impossible to forgive his kidnappers for one thing: that they showed no compassion for the fact that his mother was terminally ill and died during the years of his captivity, not knowing if he was alive or dead.

Forgiveness is complex and often painfully hard; if it were not, it would have no power to be life-changing. What does forgiveness mean in terms of the Palestinian/Israeli conflict ('They kill us; we kill them'); or of Northern Ireland, still carrying the terrible weight of the injustices of the past; or of the days of apartheid in South Africa? It means Gordon Wilson, Nelson Mandela, Desmond Tutu, and every other man or woman, unobserved and unheralded, who walks in their shadow. It does not mean forgetting. It matters to remember. We need to bring the perpetrators of evil to justice. But it introduces a wholly new concept, for it calls us to take a demanding journey of empathy, seeking to identify with the experience of others; seeking to understand the roots of past hurts and present anger, but to bring those involved into a new relationship. Memories are corporate as well as individual: reconciliation in the Middle East or Northern Ireland will only be achieved through facing the memory of offences on both sides, and not simply selective memories of sectarian groups. Forgiveness means affirming that there is another way to face the damage we do to each other, one that alone has the power to earth and neutralise its creeping poison. Forgiveness is a radically changed attitude to life and to others, one that looks not to the past but to the future. It means, for Christians, Jesus of Nazareth.

Forgiveness was not a new concept in itself. In the Old Testament it is used both of divine and human forgiveness. 'If anyone nurses anger against another, can one then demand compassion from the Lord?'[9] It is always conditional upon that change of mind and heart we call repentance. Sometimes it was accompanied by sacrifice. But there were limits. The Law of Moses, like that of Texas, strictly enforced the boundaries and allowed for revenge: an eye for an eye, a life for a life. Then Jesus comes to disclose something radically new: life in the kingdom, life solely conditioned by the twin commands of love of God and neighbour, where justice and mercy are paramount; and at once there is a different agenda. In an act of sheer grace (which is how God's love is expressed and how we experience it) Jesus reveals forgiveness as the key to the kingdom and lives and dies to prove it. St John writes that 'the Law was given by Moses, but grace and truth came by Jesus Christ'.[10] This is a radically new way of acting. Jesus tells Peter, who was to deny him three times and be three times forgiven, that his followers must forgive endlessly (the meaning of the Rabbinic phrase 'seventy times seven'); and forgive not just their friends but those who do them the greatest wrong.

That most compelling of stories, of the compassionate father and his prodigal son, is a story about coming home and discovering that 'home' is where the father is, awaiting to embrace him with joy; not so much a restored *place* as a restored *relationship*. Jesus places forgiveness at 'the still centre of the turning world, where the dance is' – and where the cross is too. For in his dying, Jesus acts out the deepest truth that is in him, with words of repeated forgiveness (that's how the Greek puts it: he *goes on saying* 'Father, forgive . . .') on his lips. If his life is a window into God, then the cross provides the deepest insight of all: if he comes to be God's love in our midst, then he must be God's forgiveness too. We can only conceive of forgiveness being a response to penitence, apology or remorse. The cross shows that this is not God's way. God forgives, period. It is his nature. There is no conditional clause, no added 'if . . .', and it is when we begin to grasp what it means to be so loved that we are set free to repent, and to receive that forgiveness. That is how we join the dance. In some words of Austin Farrer:

> God forgives me with the compassion of his eyes, but my back is turned to him. I have been told that he forgives me, but I will not turn and have the forgiveness, not though I feel the eyes on my back. God forgives me, for he takes my head between his hands and he turns my face to his to make me smile at him. And though I struggle and hurt those hands, for they are human, though divine – human and scarred by nails – though I hurt them, they do not let go until he has smiled me into smiling; and that is the forgiveness of God.[11]

There are some, and I am among them, who believe that one of the truths of the cross is that it is God's way of reconciling us to him by making amends to those who are unable to forgive him for the unwanted pain and suffering that life has delivered. Some years ago a primary school head, Brenda Dawson, was dying of cancer in St Christopher's Hospice, where she wrote this poem:

> God, you need to ask my forgiveness,
> Your world is full of mistakes.
> Some cells, like weeds in the garden
> Are growing in the wrong place.
> And we your children
> Have polluted our environment.

> Why did you let it happen, God?
> We prayed with faith, hope, love,
> We perceived no change in our bodies or environment,
> We are made sick by your world.
> God, you need to ask my forgiveness.
> Was this why you sent your Son?

So are there no conditions to God's forgiveness? Yes, there is one: that we, in our turn, forgive. That we reflect in generous, gracious and unlooked-for words or actions something of what we have received. In Northern Ireland a Christian peace movement recently rewrote the ending of the Lord's Prayer for St Patrick's Day:

> And forgive us our trespasses, as we have forgiven those who trespass against us. For if we haven't, there is no point in going any further. But if we have, then we dare to ask for two great favours: to be delivered from evil and to learn to live together in peace.

Forgiveness, like Haydn, is good for us. It is as if it were a necessary law of the human spirit, claims Laurens van der Post when he recalls the effect of atrocities perpetrated on prisoners-of-war in the Far East; it is as fundamental as the law of gravity. Break that law and you break your neck: break the law of forgiveness and you inflict a deep wound on your spirit, and become once again 'a member of the chain-gang of mere cause and effect from which life has laboured so long and so laboriously to escape'.[12] Eric Lomax, tortured in that same war, was finally enabled through wise counselling to come to terms with what had been done to him. He traced the former Japanese member of the secret police who had come to symbolise the torture he suffered, and upon whom he had long contemplated revenge. He went to meet his former enemy, who expressed deep sorrow, and was finally able to assure him of his complete forgiveness. He felt an immense sense of liberation: 'I had proved for myself that remembering is not enough, if it simply hardens hate . . . Sometime the hating has to stop.'[13] Recently I gave the address at the memorial service for Susan Cole-King, doctor and priest. On the Feast of the Transfiguration 1998, which is also Hiroshima Day, Susan preached at the eucharist held for the bishops gathered for the Lambeth Conference. She spoke of her father, Leonard Wilson, who as Bishop of Singapore was imprisoned and tortured in Changi jail. He tried to picture the Japanese guards who were beating him as they would have been as children and as they 'were capable of becoming, transformed by the love of Christ'. Contemplating Jesus' words of forgiveness on the cross, he was able to forgive them; after the war he returned to Singapore and baptised and confirmed one of his torturers. After her death the Primate of the Anglican Church in Japan told her family that her address had not only moved all who heard it, but that it had changed the whole mood of a rather troublesome Conference.

When Gordon Wilson and his daughter were trapped beneath a heap of rubble after the IRA bomb at Enniskillen on Remembrance Day, he held her hand as she died. He consistently refused to bear ill will, saying that this would not bring his daughter back, nor help the cause of peace. 'Those who have to account for this deed', he wrote, 'will have to face the judgment of God . . . but I do my best to show forgiveness.' His story is familiar: what is less known is the fact that he received sackloads of hate mail, and was ostracised and attacked by many in his own tradition for this refusal to condemn. When the President of Ireland, Mary McAleese, wrote of him she said:

> His words [of forgiveness] shamed us, caught us off guard. They sounded so different from what we expected and what we were used to . . . It was as if [his detractors had never heard] Christ's words, 'Father, forgive them . . . '. As one churchgoing critic said to me: 'Sure, the poor man must have been in shock', as

171

if to offer love and forgiveness is a sign of mental weakness instead of spiritual strength.[14]

After the Omagh bombing a CD was made which included a reading by Liam Neeson of a poem by Seamus Heaney. It includes these stanzas:

Human beings suffer,
They torture one another,
They get hurt and get hard.
No poem or play or song
Can fully right a wrong
Inflicted and endured . . .

History says, Don't hope
On this side of the grave.
But then, once in a lifetime
The longed for tidal wave
Of justice can rise up,
And hope and history rhyme.

So hope for a great sea-change
On the far side of revenge.
Believe that a further shore
Is reachable from here.
Believe in miracles
And cures and healing wells.[15]

There is a Jewish saying: 'We must meet extravagant and unreasonable hatred with extravagant and unreasonable love,' and the South African novelist Alan Paton writes: 'There is a hard law . . . that when an injury is done to us, we never recover until we forgive.' A dynamic illustration of that truth was the manner in which Nelson Mandela emerged from Robben Island. Whatever South Africa's continuing problems, few who witnessed the worst excesses of apartheid believed that the avoidance of civil war was possible. Mandela has shown how a nation's story may be rewritten when forgiveness is offered and reconciliation is achieved. When on Millennium Eve he stood with a child in his former prison cell and together they lit a candle of hope, it was an action more telling than all the fireworks and rivers of fire. As memorable as the action of the white pastor who, 30 years before, when expected to address a great crowd of black South Africans in a shanty town, had walked among them in silence, asking their forgiveness by inviting each one to make the sign of the cross on the palm of his hand. Or like the moment described by Solzhenitsyn after he was arrested when, travelling across the steppes of Russia to the prison camp, the train slowly passed a shabby peasant woman, tears streaming from her eyes, who 'lifted a small, work-calloused hand and blessed us with the sign of the cross, again and again . . . until she was lost to view'. Or the moment in Dostoevsky's *The Brothers Karamazov* when Jesus, returned to earth at the time of the Inquisition and standing in judgement before the Grand Inquisitor, responds to all his accusations by walking up to him and planting a kiss on his bloodless lips.

Whether on a world scale, or between two people, there are always two possible responses to hurt: to pass it on, in the form of negative retaliation, an upping of the stakes; or to 'absorb' it, not passively but with a deliberate breaking of the chain. There is a shift in the pattern of the dance. And this is true both of current hurts and past wounds – which can be much more damaging, for (like limpets) such hurts have held tight to the offence and gathered accretions. The Bible's view of memory is that when we remember something from the past, we actually make it present again, potent in our lives for good or evil, with the chance to wallow in it and recharge our anger, or to change it. Every nation needs to be a community of shared memories and shared forgetting; and where forgetting is impossible, then there must be a remembering and a moving on. It is never 'forgive and forget', but 'remember and forgive'. Such an act of creative remembering, this healing of memories that we call forgiving, enables us to relive the past and rewrite our history by giving it a different outcome. Only that vision and desire will mend a broken relationship, or (for example) enable there one day to be both security for the State of Israel and justice and equity for the Palestinian people.

Such acts are costly because they demand of me a journey of imagination and empathy, as I seek to stand in your shoes and understand why you acted in the way you did. Nothing quite like South Africa's Truth and Reconciliation Commission had been seen before. Chaired by Archbishop Desmond Tutu, it was a pioneering international experiment that sought to deal creatively with the past. To those who had committed gross violations of human rights, the Commission offered conditional amnesty in exchange for public disclosure of the truth about their crimes; and it offered to their victims the chance to be heard by those who had violated them and the promise of reparation. In Desmond Tutu's words: 'To be able to forgive one needs to know whom one is forgiving, and why.' When the Commission was attacked for providing some with an easy way out, he defended it on two grounds. He argued that it was wholly consistent with the African concept of *ubuntu*, a word which speaks of the very essence of being human:

> A person with *ubuntu* knows that he or she belongs in a greater whole and is humiliated when others are humiliated or diminished . . . tortured or oppressed, or treated as if they were less than who they are.

His other defence was that a refusal to forgive is dehumanising:

> Forgiveness gives people resilience, enabling them to survive and emerge still human despite all efforts to dehumanise them . . . Forgiving means abandoning your right to pay back the perpetrator in his own coin, but it is a loss which liberates the victim.[16]

Tutu writes time and again of black individuals who had

174

been victims of terrible violence and who spoke simply of their desire to forgive, a desire that only became practical and effective once the Court hearings had allowed them to meet up with those who had abused them and heard their remorse. No one pretended things were other than they were. The victims may not have got legal justice, but they had got moral justice, the recognition of who did what to whom. You cannot be reconciled without facing the truth of the pain, the abuse and the degradation, but if that is where you start you may end by being healed.

The sentence with which L. P. Hartley begins *The Go-Between*, 'The past is a foreign country: they do things differently there,' is only partly true. For the past still resonates with the present: in the words of the poet Michael Donaghy, 'it falls open anywhere'. It is not a wholly foreign country and, even if we have inherited from it what often seem intractable problems, there is a sense in which it can be relived and the ending rewritten. The Truth and Reconciliation Commission proved that an honest telling of a grim story, a facing of the pain and injustice, and a public apology such as that offered by the Dutch Reformed Church to their black fellow Christians in providing a theological justification for apartheid, can prove cathartic and turn the closed fist of resentment to the open hand of forgiveness. It may seem that to speak of forgiveness in the case of the worst excesses of oppressive evil is to betray the memory of those who were victimised. In one sense that is undeniable, especially as there is a growing practice of suspiciously easy apologies for momentous wrongs, a kind of forgiveness on the cheap. Yet there can be no peace at any level – national, racial, individual – while we live in the shadow and under the burden of past injustice. True penitence and forgiveness must come to terms with the past in the light of what we know now. Christians do well to ask forgiveness of Jews for much anti-Semitism over the centuries, not unconnected with making the Holocaust possible. But if we dare to apologise on behalf of the oppressors, we may hardly dare to forgive on behalf of the victims. Only they could do that.

Yet remorse leading to forgiveness may be only the starting point, especially where forgiveness is allied to social justice. In South Africa, for example, it is the terrible disparity between the (mainly white) rich and the (mainly black) poor, largely created by apartheid and which sustained it, which still threatens the reconciliation process. Until those things that the white population has taken for granted – decent housing, clean water, electricity, affordable health care – are available to all, reconciliation in the fullest sense will remain a pipe dream.

In the Chapter House of Salisbury Cathedral there is one of the four extant copies of Magna Charta, a single, closely written sheet of vellum which sets out the rights and liberties extorted from King John in 1215. 'To no man', it declares, 'will we sell, or deny, or delay, right and justice.' The men it had in mind were largely the bishops and the baronial classes, and we had to wait until 1945 for the broad sweep of the Universal Declaration of Human Rights. If I had to find one word to describe what it is that damages our world and destroys individuals and communities it would be hard to choose between 'poverty' and 'injustice'.

Those prophetic figures who in every age have shared a vision of a changed world have all had a concern for the poor and a passion for justice. For the most perceptive of the Old Testament prophets penitence/forgiveness is twinned with justice. Isaiah writes of how Israel is called to be the Servant of the Lord, whose task is to reveal to all nations God's will and establish his justice:

> Here is my servant, whom I uphold.
> I have put my spirit on him,
> He will establish justice among the nations . . .

> He will never falter or be crushed
> Until he sets justice on earth.[17]

'Let justice flow on like a river,' demands the God of Amos, 'and righteousness like a never-failing torrent.'[18] 'What the Lord requires of you', writes Micah, 'is to act justly, to love loyalty, and to walk humbly with your God.'[19] From Israel comes the Messiah (the Christ) in the form of Jesus, and it is Isaiah's words about justice that are on Jesus' lips when he first speaks in the synagogue of his home town: 'The spirit of the Lord is upon me . . . he has sent me to announce good news to the poor, to proclaim release for prisoners . . . to let the broken victims go free.'[20]

The proclaiming of God's concern for the poor and the marginalised seemed scandalous to leaders of church and state, who tried to silence those who did so. It does not deny God's equal love for all; it affirms how love for neighbour is exercised by the rich through a special concern for the poor. Unlikely as it is that the radical words of the Magnificat, which is a celebration of God's justice ('He has filled the hungry with good things, and the rich he has sent empty away'), were actually said by Mary, the fact that they were placed by the gospel writers in her mouth is their way of revealing that sense of justice which from childhood moti-vated her son, who in his adult life sought out the broken and ate with the outcasts. The Christian manifesto is rooted in Jesus' brief to his followers: 'Set your minds on God's kingdom and his *justice* before anything else and all the rest will come to you as well.'[21] God's kingdom, in the words of Hans Küng, 'is creation healed', and the love which is to be the measure by which that kingdom is known, is achieved in social and community terms as justice.

Justice is love in action; if forgiveness is the key to the kingdom, then justice is its fruit. So often the church has been mistaken for the *end* that Christians are to strive for, but the church is people (the means) and the end is the kingdom, and it is the kingdom that Jesus brought into being. This is the most far-reaching of those sudden shifts of understanding that can open your inner eyes. God's kingdom is not about time, but about *relationship*. It already exists alongside our earthly kingdoms, for it is created wherever people respond to the implications of the sovereignty of the God whose love and justice are revealed in Jesus. The task of the church is to worship God, and to be a foretaste or pledge of God's loving rule over his creation, with an irrefutable duty to care about the way society is ordered. Politics, therefore, the use of power to shape and direct the life of a nation, is not only its proper but its necessary concern. Not to enter into the trivia of party politics, nor to prescribe in fine detail what governments should do in matters where it has no expertise, but to point to the justice or injustice implicit in the conditions in which people live. That the Church of England, which I cling to with a mixture of lifelong affection, gratitude and exasperation, is so closely linked to the state, makes its intervention at once more fitting and more misunderstood and, often, resented. Fortunately, when it comes to moral questions of social justice, most Christian traditions are at one, and recent years have witnessed reports on homelessness, poverty, urban renewal and globalisation which speak with a common voice.

Justice means the recognition that all people are of equal worth in the sight of God. It implies the right to life, freedom of speech and worship, decent housing, good education, clean water, available health care, and the chance to work. Only we, their fellow human beings, can 'announce good news to the poor . . . proclaim release for prisoners . . . [and] let the broken victims go free'. So what are the facts? Nineteen out of twenty of all the deaths of children are in the Third World. Eleven million of them die each year from preventable diseases; 170 million are undernourished; 100 million never see a classroom; and 200 million are employed in appalling conditions, many of them producing goods we consume. Nike paid the sports star Michael Jordan $20 million to promote its shoes – more than the entire annual income of the Indonesian workers who make them. Thirty-five million of the world's poorest people – 25 million of them in sub-Saharan Africa – are facing death from AIDS, and by 2010 two-thirds of today's African teenagers may have died of it. In Malawi, for example, half its teachers and nurses will almost certainly die in the next seven years. Only 0.01 of them can afford Western drugs, and the legislation concerning patents prevents equally effective, infinitely cheaper, drugs from being imported. (As I write, the drugs companies have just lost an important round in South Africa's battle to use their own, far cheaper drugs.) One large British drugs company has just announced record profits of $8.1 billion.

'*Good news to the poor*'? In Britain one in four children lives below the poverty level, and the mortality rate among young children is five times greater in Class 5 than in Class 1. Between 1979 and 1991 living standards for the richest 10 per cent of the population rose by 62 per cent in real terms. The poorest 10 per cent suffered a loss of real income of 14 per cent.[22] In the United States there are 149 billion-aires, yet 36 million people live below the poverty line. Societies which break down into such unequal blocks are ripe for disaffection and crime. Globalisation means that, whereas in 1950 just 25 per cent of the world's population lived in cities, by 2010 75 per cent of it will be urban, millions moving from rural poverty to seek work and live in the urban slums; that the effect of the technological revolution, the worldwide web and the growth of unimaginably powerful transnational corporations (whose individual annual turnover may exceed that of a nation) is what increasingly dictates the economic policy of governments; that there is a burgeoning international arms trade; and that there is a culture of dominant values, where 'everything and everyone is reducible to a cash value ... [where] success is measured by its rate of productivity rather than its innate value ... [and where] knowledge means information rather than wisdom'.[23] But at last, in a world where well over a billion people live on less than $1 a day, there seems to be a Europe-based backlash against the effect of globalised capitalism, a real concern to offer the world's poor a way out of such crippling poverty. The demands of international debt have meant governments cutting back on spending on the provision of clean water, schools and primary health care. The (largely Christian-inspired) Jubilee 2000 campaign played a major part in an agreement to reduce Third-World debt and work towards international trade reform that would give more power to poor nations.

Even so, my paltry support of Oxfam, Amnesty International or Christian Aid seems a mere drop in the ocean, for the poor need more than our cash and our prayers. The systems that cause poverty need to be challenged and changed. Yet I still have a voice in my own land, where (while there is much to celebrate) there is much over which to feel shame: our policy with regard to prisons and asylum-seekers, to name but two. Prison is an example of what Aristotle called corrective justice, the needs of the refugee an example of what he called distributive justice. I commit a crime and am sentenced to ten years in jail: that is *corrective* justice. I live in the rich West enjoying the freedoms of a democracy, while you live in a repressive regime and face torture for defending human rights; I share some of what I have or I make you welcome in my land: that is *distributive* justice. Yet such a distinction may be too simplistic, for even the corrective justice of prison needs to be balanced by an attempt at reform and restoration.

'He has sent me to . . . *announce release for the prisoners* . . . '. When Jesus told one of the 'kingdom' stories containing the words, 'I was in prison and you visited me, I was a stranger and you took me into your home', he added, 'Anything you failed to do for one of these, however insignificant, you failed to do for me.'[24] In the fourth century Gregory of Nyssa wrote a powerful work arguing for the immediate abolition of slavery. In the southern United States I have talked with men and women whose grandparents were slaves, for not for another 1500 years did it seem right for civilised Christian nations to end what we now see to be a great evil. We look back appalled at Victorian slums and workhouses, or the hanging of a man for stealing a sheep. When our grand-children look back will they wonder why our prison system took so long to be reformed? The great majority of men and women coming into our prisons (which in ten years have seen a 50 per cent increase to 63,000 prisoners) are from the most deprived 30 per cent of society, where unemployment is at its highest and the cancer of poverty at its most crippling and shaming. Gandhi was right in declaring that the worst violence is poverty. It produces a dangerous mix of hopelessness and shame, and shame (especially in men) at being one of life's losers is the most potent cause of acts of violence that fill our prisons. A large proportion of prisoners have been permanently excluded from school and are illiterate and innumerate. Sixty per cent are using class A drugs at the point of entry. Many have been abused as children and have a shockingly low sense of self-worth; a fair proportion are mentally disturbed. If corrective justice is to be more than paying the price and making amends by 'doing time', then justice demands that a priority is the attempt to change people through education and a humane regime. Yet Sir David Ramsbotham, until recently the Government's Chief Inspector of Prisons, admits to being 'appalled' at what five years of prison visiting with a team of doctors, psychiatrists and educators have revealed in terms of overcrowding, squalor, lack of funding, lack of edu-cation, lack of hope. Unimaginative treatment of a prisoner, by taking away his or her sense of worth, may return them to the world with a sense of diminished responsibility. Many go out with resentment, as illiterate and innumerate as when they came in, and quickly reoffend. Ramsbotham kept on his desk a phrase of Winston Churchill from 1910, to the effect that the mood and tenor of a nation can be judged by the way it treats its criminals, and that there is a treasure in the heart of every person if only you can find it.[25] Those who have been damaged by the destructive effects of poverty should be able to find in their experience of prison what C. S. Lewis called 'a severe mercy', a place where the past may begin to be redeemed, and justice done in its fullest sense.

'I was a *stranger* and you took me in.' Among those held in detention in prison are many asylum-seekers. Last year some 70,000 people sought asylum in Britain. No government has yet found a way to balance control and compassion, a just and responsible sifting of the facts, in a situation where the huge demand for refuge has created criminal gangs who thrive off this form of human misery. The tabloid press write off a majority of them as 'bogus', and plays on fears that our nation is being swamped. In fact, the size of the ethnic minority in Britain is 7 per cent, many of whom are giving invaluable service to the community. Those we so easily term 'bogus' are economic migrants who may have no claim to asylum, but they may come from lands where the hardships they have to face, the abject poverty arising from civil war, are as severe as the political persecution from which others are fleeing. For among them are very many facing a genuine fear of torture, imprisonment or death under the many repressive regimes which litter our world.

In face of increasing numbers, every European government has drawn up harsher and harsher measures to keep asylum-seekers at bay. Rich countries now require a visa from those travelling from places likely to generate asylum-seekers. Unable to obtain them, the asylum-seeker has lost all legal means of access to our shores. The only option is to be smuggled to sanctuary or to forge your papers. For 15 years the numbers have defeated every attempt to keep pace with those lodging appeals and awaiting decisions, and many are imprisoned. Others, among whom are those traumatised and without English, are sent to different parts of the country, far away from doctors and counsellors at London's Medical Foundation for the Care of Victims of

Torture. All suffer further indignities in being forced to use the voucher scheme. If the rich nations of Europe are to meet the needs of people in genuine distress, it will be complex, difficult and costly. But one of the signs of a society still founded on, and impregnated with, Christian values, is an indiscriminate concern for justice, whether corrective or, in this case, distributive. In such a democracy, laws must be open to examination and, sometimes, challenged. And where we have got it wrong, in the past or the present, we should express our remorse in our readiness to think things through afresh.

All great Western literature before the mid-nineteenth century is permeated by Christian thought: it fed into the work of creative writers, with its themes of good and evil, justice and mercy, suffering and forgiveness. For Shakespeare, especially as he ages, the nature of justice, of mercy and forgiveness, become persistent themes. The tragedies all deal, in one way or another, with the nature of justice. The critic John Vyvyan (a fine scholar whose books are long out of print) sees Hamlet, learning the truth of his father's death, committing himself to revenge. But then he begins to reflect. He finds within himself a quality which rejects such a killing, a noble nature committed to an ignoble act.

> Hamlet cannot sweep to his revenge until his nobility has been overthrown. When the play opens, he has this nobility: when it ends, he has his revenge. All that lies between is his progressive overthrow, the gradual disowning of his higher self.

Shakespeare (like the gospels) is challenging us to reconsider what justice really is. He is demonstrating that if you yield to the law of vengeance, if you strictly apply the old code of 'an eye for an eye, a life for a life', you cast out love.

> Faced with the choice, nobility or revenge, [Shakespeare] unequivocally decided for nobility. But this implies a new ethical code, to the elaboration of which his later plays are

183

devoted. [In place of] retributive justice, what can we put in its place? His answer is, creative mercy.[26]

Hamlet neglects the law of Christ to follow the law of Moses, and all the great tragic heroes illustrate a single theme: each is tempted to be untrue to his own higher self, rejects the way of love and the pricking of conscience, and opens himself to evil. When love is cast out, as with Macbeth's ambition, Othello's jealousy and Lear's blind anger, justice becomes tyranny, and we watch the soul become a battleground where an inner war is bloodily played out. In the face of human wickedness, justice has two options: to find a punishment that will fit the crime, or to find some cure, some way of healing the evil, and it is this power of 'creative mercy' that Shakespeare so effectively works through in his last plays. It is a concept of justice based on the disclosure of God's justice and forgiveness in Christ.

So *The Winter's Tale* (1610) shows how Leontes' obsessive jealousy may in the end be forgiven and restored, in the face of injustice, by the power of his wife's enduring love. Six years earlier, in *Measure for Measure* (1604), Angelo (deputising for the absent Duke) rejects Isabella's plea for her brother's life, and she demands to know:

> How would you be
> If He, which is the top of judgment, should
> But judge you as you are? O think on that;
> And mercy then will breathe within your lips,
> Like man new made . . .
> Not the king's crown, nor the deputed sword,
> The marshal's truncheon, nor the judge's robe,
> Becomes them with one half so good a grace
> As mercy does.[27]

In one of Peter Brook's productions of the play he asked the actress to pause at this point until she felt the audience could take it no longer. Each night at that point there was anything up to a two-minute silence, 'a silence', writes

Brook, 'in which the abstract notion of mercy became concrete for that moment to those present'. The play ends with the forgiveness of Angelo by both the Duke and Isabella.

Finally, in *The Tempest* (1611), Prospero has the power to be revenged on those who have wronged him. He could have demanded justice. But it is one of Shakespeare's fundamental propositions

> that tragedy begets tragedy, for ever and ever, until someone has the strength, the courage and the understanding to say, Enough! . . . Enough of death for death, wife for wife, cut for thrust. Enough of this ever-widening sea of blood! . . . Let there be self-knowledge, love, creative mercy, regeneration, and man new made![28]

So all must be forgiven and set free. Even those two incarnate aspects of Prospero's own soul, the dark Caliban ('This thing of darkness I acknowledge mine'), his brutish, unregenerate nature, his shadow self; and the more joyful, freer spirit that is Ariel, are liberated in the end. And it is Ariel who, movingly, finally persuades Prospero to show mercy:

> ARIEL: They cannot budge till your release . . .
>
>         . . . Your charm so strongly works them,
>     That if you now beheld them, your affections
>     Would become tender.
> PROSPERO: Dost thou think so, spirit?
> ARIEL: Mine would, sir, were I human.[29]

Prospero, in the first act, had taught Ariel the word 'human', but at the end he must be reminded of what 'human' means. It means joining in the dance of forgiveness. So now, in perhaps the final words Shakespeare ever wrote for the stage, Prospero comes forward and addresses us:

> And my ending is despair,
> Unless I be relieved by prayer,
> Which pierces so that it assaults
> Mercy itself and frees all faults.

As you from crimes would pardoned be,
Let your indulgence set me free.[30]

# OCTOBER

## *The Dance of Love*

---

This wondrous miracle did Love devise,
For dancing is Love's proper exercise.

*Sir John Davies*[1]

So let us love, deare love, lyke as we ought,
Love is the lesson which the Lord us taught.

*Edmund Spenser*[2]

Beware you are not swallowed up in books! An
ounce of love is worth a pound of knowledge.

*John Wesley*[3]

love is something learned
like dancing.

*John Burnside*[4]

---

The woods are turning. In the welcome sun of a St Luke's
summer, there is spread out a patchwork of bronze, ochre
and darkest greens. The chocolate of the shedding beech,
the gold of larches, the scarlet of maples and the varied
lemon yellows of the ash, are set off by the many oaks and
birches which are still green. After the early frosts, the leaves
of the tall poplars rapidly fade; they drop from the higher

187

branches first, like balding men. Francis Kilvert, in his October diary for 1874, is searching for the right word to describe 'the shimmering, twinkling movement of the poplar leaves in the sun and wind. This afternoon I saw the word written on the poplar leaves. It was "dazzle". The dazzle of the poplars.' Sweet chestnuts (a tree introduced by the Romans) are ready for roasting, walnuts for pickling, and sloes waiting to be steeped in gin. Sycamore seeds come spinning down, and jays scream in the woods as, with hoarding squirrels, they hunt for nuts and acorns. Crab apples, vulgarly known as Scrogs, are being made into jelly – Shakespeare's crabs that in winter 'hiss in the bowl'.[5] In the hedgerows is the scarlet of hips and haws, a reminder of the rose hip syrup we drank in the War.

The last of the martins leave, and flocks of immigrant starlings arrive. Hedgehogs and dormice are hibernating, and tortoises. (Bitter experience taught me never to keep a tortoise and a retriever at the same time: the former's desire to hibernate is constantly frustrated by the latter's need to retrieve.) On the Backs at Cambridge the slow burning of the leaves will be producing thin coils of blue smoke, that most evocative of autumn sights and smells. In Olney, at the end of October 1790, that gentle depressive William Cowper (the self-styled 'stricken deer') writes:

> A yellow shower of leaves is falling continually from all the trees in the country . . . The consideration of my short continuance here, which was once grateful to me, now fills me with regret. I would live and live always.

In the Flemish Book of Hours two bay horses are dragging a wooden harrow, encouraged by a man with a thin whip; in the background a pair of white horses is pulling a plough; underneath a group of seven men dressed in white are playing marbles, with an eighth, perched on stilts, watching them; for the October occupation is **ploughing and sowing**. In one of his more uncomfortable sayings, Jesus warned: 'No one who has set his hand to the plough, and then looks back, is fit for the kingdom of God.'[6] And the secret of learning to dance is learning how to sow the seeds of love. For, if St John of the Cross got it right, 'when the evening of this life comes, we shall be judged on love'.

If those seeds are to be planted and nourished, there is only one starting-place: discovering what it means to be loved. For most of us, by parents; for the fortunate, by friends, husband, wife or partner; for all of us – if we did but know it, and more than we can conceive – by God. I have spent my life betting that there is a cause, an origin, of everything that exists, that (despite the darkness) there is a reason for beauty, compassion and goodness, and that to name the source from which they constantly spring, to name the true ground of love and to define it, is to name God. If we ask how we can experience this love, and therefore catch glimpses of God's nature, then the answer comes in two parts. One is an appeal to our hearts, the other to our heads. The first way is through other people, through knowing what it feels like to be valued and affirmed because I am uniquely me. The second way is through our reaction to the story of Jesus and the witness of his self-giving love, his claim that 'whoever has seen me has seen the Father'. To be persuaded that the meaning of all that Jesus was and did (sometimes explicit, always implicit) is that I am loved by God. It is to understand at last that to love fully is to be fully human, made 'in God's image' and therefore possessing this Godlike potential. Descartes defined 'human' in the words, 'Cogito, ergo sum' ('I think, therefore I am'); a better definition would be 'Amo ('I love'), ergo sum'.

'We love', writes St John, 'because he loved us first.' He is not saying 'we love *God* because he loved us first' (although that follows), but 'we become *capable* of love because we are loved'. When the American writer Raymond Carver was dying of cancer he wrote this short poem:

> And did you get what
> you wanted from this life, even so?
> I did.
> And what did you want?
> To call myself beloved, to feel myself
> beloved on the earth.[7]

It is only as you know yourself 'beloved on the earth' that in turn you become capable of loving. Carver spoke in terms of human loving: it is equally true of our experience of the divine. There are those who reject God on intellectual grounds, or who have been so battered by life that it seems a bad joke and who 'hand back their ticket'; there are many more who have somehow missed out in the love stakes, and who find it impossible to connect emotionally with such language. I have often preached (too easily) about the love of God on Sunday, and found myself on Monday seeking to console and encourage someone who has little sense of their own worth and, perhaps because of an unhappy childhood or a later painful rejection, find talk of the love of God hurtful and empty – even though, like a prize just out of reach, it may be a truth they long to possess. Talk of God as Father (or, sometimes worse, as Mother) or of the Trinity leaves them cold. Only the building of a relationship of trust, costly on both sides, in which there is the growth of friendship, proper listening, honesty and a continuing readiness to 'be there', may begin to persuade the un-persuaded that they are 'beloved on the earth' – and beyond it.

But if it is God who defines, indeed who *is*, the dance of love, then there is no escaping that most profound and mysterious form of all such dancing: the Trinity. Stevie Smith writes:

> Mrs Simpkins never had very much to do,
> So it occurred to her one day that the Trinity wasn't true
> Or at least but a garbled version of the truth

And that things had moved very far since the days of her
    youth.[8]

'Three persons in one God' certainly sounds a nonsense, but
only if we think of 'a person' in our terms. The difficulty is
that Christians need to speak of a truly personal God who
creates and sustains, who discloses himself by emptying
himself and giving himself in love, and whose life-giving
spirit unites and enlightens, yet our language won't stretch
that far. Paul Fiddes writes:

> When the early church fathers developed the doctrine of the
> Trinity they were not painting by numbers; they were finding
> concepts to express an *experience*. That is, they were trying to
> articulate the richness of the personality of God that they had
> found in the story of salvation and in their own experience . . .
> They must speak of the love of the Father, the grace of the
> Lord Jesus and the fellowship of the Holy Spirit, although they
> knew that the ultimate demand on their lives must come from
> one Lord.[9]

They conceived of God as a communion of 'persons', with
'Father', 'Son' and 'Holy Spirit' used as a kind of shorthand
to describe the movements *within a relationship*. We sometimes speak of the Trinity as the one who loves, the one
who is loved and the love between them, but even that is
inadequate, for it could equally describe a good marriage.
Though it may help us to understand that God cannot be
self-sufficient: he exists and is sustained by the mutual give
and take of love. And it is this reciprocity of self-giving
which gives birth to the universe, and which finally brings
forth creatures who may freely choose to share a little of
God's own awareness of what it means to love and be loved.
Rowan Williams, Archbishop of Wales, puts it like this:

> The whole story of creation, incarnation, and our incorpor-
> ation into Christ's body tells us that God desires us, as if we
> were God, as if we were that unconditional response to God's
> giving that God's self makes in the life of the Trinity. We are

> created so that we may be caught up in this, so that we may grow into the wholehearted love of God by learning that God loves us as God loves God.[10]

The God in whom I have come to believe, although infinitely Other and mysterious, is nevertheless one who acts only as agape acts. Such love longs for the independence, the free response, of that which is loved. So God chooses to limit his power, his omnipotence, because of the dictates of love. Love means letting the other be, and it is always persuasive, never coercive. To love sometimes means appearing defenceless and vulnerable, and it is then that it is at its most powerful. 'God knows', wrote Christoph Munzihirwa, Archbishop of Bukavu, Zaire, assassinated in 1996 for witnessing to his faith, and speaking of the incarnation, 'that there is no better way to express himself than through the weakness of a child. This is Love telling us that it comes unarmed.' The divine vulnerability is most expensively seen in the life, passion and death of Jesus. The first Christians came to believe that in this life and death God was, so to speak, abandoning himself to his creation, 'emptying himself' in Paul's phrase, 'bearing the human likeness, sharing the human lot',[11] putting himself in our hands. And (such is the compelling power of love) drawing us back into the dance. The technical Greek term for such divine 'self-emptying' is *kenosis*, and Pope John Paul, in a recent encyclical, places this concept at the centre of theology:

> The prime commitment of theology is seen to be the understanding of God's *kenosis*, a grand and mysterious truth for the human mind, which finds it inconceivable that suffering and death can express a love which gives itself and seeks nothing in return.[12]

It is indeed a radical truth about the nature of God and his relation to us, and one to which I shall return in reflecting on the dance of faith.

The Trinity needs to be seen, then, as movements in a constant dance, the God who is disclosed as Christlike always (as it were) going out of God's self in mutual love. The classic Greek notion of the static being of God is replaced by the church Fathers with an altogether more dynamic one, engendered by the interchange of love, one who is still engaged in the unfolding process of creation. By the Middle Ages some theologians used the image of the divine dance to describe the relationship of love within God, a kind of eternal round danced by the triune God out of which 'the rhythms of created beings who interpenetrate one another correspondingly arise like an echo'[13], though it did not take hold on the Christian imagination. Angels are envisaged in a never-ending circling dance round the throne of God; in Botticelli's *Nativity* they are performing one above the stable roof. They are showing that 'at the still centre of the turning world, there the dance is'; but the dance is a dance of love, with the dynamic image of a God who is both the dance and the dancer.

> O body swayed to music, O brightening glance,
> How can we know the dancer from the dance?[14]

But these are deep waters, and your sympathy may lie with Stevie Smith's Mrs Simpkins. So let me turn to something more manageable: love in human terms. Dietrich Bonhoeffer, in prison and awaiting almost certain death, wrote in a letter to a friend about our love for others and our love for God.

> God requires that we should love him eternally with our whole hearts, yet not so as to compromise or diminish our earthly affections, but as a kind of *cantus firmus* to which the other melodies of life provide the counterpoint. Where the ground bass is firm and clear, there is nothing to stop the counterpoint from being developed to the utmost of its limits ... Only a polyphony of this kind can give life a wholeness, and assure

us that nothing can go wrong so long as the *cantus firmus* is kept going . . . Put your faith in the *cantus firmus*.[15]

Although it is never entirely straightforward or clear-cut, love is often broadly thought of in terms either of *eros*, which is self-affirming, or *agape*, which is self-giving (and ultimately, self-sacrifice). With *eros*, which is motivated by desire, I look for someone to love who will satisfy and complete my own being. With *agape*, I give myself away, concerned to spend myself on the object of my love.

*Agape* is costly. As in the instinctive love of a mother for her child whatever he or she may do. There's a grim medieval poem which perfectly expresses this:

> A poor lad once and a lad so trim,
> Gave his heart to her who loved not him;
> Said she, 'Bring me tonight, you rogue,
> Your mother's heart to feed my dog.'

> To his mother's house went the young man,
> Killed her, cut out her heart, and ran.
> But as he was running, look you, he fell,
> And the heart rolled out on the ground as well.

> And the lad, as the heart was a-rolling, heard
> The heart was speaking and this was the word
> The heart was a-weeping, and crying so small:
> 'Are you hurt, my child, are you hurt at all?'[16]

In *Harry Potter and the Philosopher's Stone*, Quirrell, working for the evil Voldemort, is strangely impotent when he tries to kill Harry, who asks:

> 'Why couldn't Quirrell touch me?'
> 'Your mother died to save you. If there is one thing Voldemort cannot understand, it is love . . . Love as powerful as your mother's for you leaves its own mark. Not a visible sign . . . [but] to have been loved so deeply, even though the person who loved us is gone, will give us some protection for ever . . .

It was agony for Quirrell, full of hatred, greed and ambition . . .
to touch a person marked by something so good.'[17]

However trying we may find Paul's views on sex or the
role of women, his definition of *agape* is incomparable: that
which is patient and kind, does not envy others, is not quick
to take offence, keeps no score of wrongs, takes no pleasure
in the sins of other people, delights in the truth. The
opposite of love is not hate, but indifference, the failure to
care – or to care enough. It is a want of imagination, a lack
of empathy, an inability or a refusal to see in another human
being a creature as frail and as easily hurt as I can be. Simone
Weil wrote of how she loved the story of Perceval, who is
the only Arthurian knight to attain the Grail because he
was the only one to turn aside when it was within his grasp
and ask its suffering guardian, 'What are you going
through?' When someone is troubled, sick or dying, the
caring love of people who also know themselves to be vulnerable has a strangely stabilising and anchoring power.

Where *eros* and *agape* – the self-affirming and the self-
giving – meet is in that mutual commitment of one person
to another that historically has been in marriage, but
increasingly is seen in the commitment of partners. I say
'historically', yet by the early nineteenth century only about
half the population was formally married, and 'in the mid-
nineteenth century as many marriages ended through death
in the first fifteen years, as ended in divorce in the 1980s'.[18]
Our understanding of marriage is comparatively recent.
Social historians tell us that until well into the seventeenth
century love and companionship were secondary consider-
ations in the marriage relationship; but then so was the
place of women in ideas of marriage which did not rate
personal emotional satisfaction of much account. Today we
marry for love. In Louis de Bernière's novel, *Captain Corelli's
Mandolin*, Pelagia's father gives her this advice:

> Love is a temporary madness, it erupts like volcanoes and then
> it subsides. And when it subsides you have to make a decision.

> You have to work out whether your roots have become so
> entwined together that it is inconceivable that you should ever
> part. Because this is what love is. Love is not breathlessness, it
> is not excitement . . . No . . . that is just being in love, which
> any fool can do. Love itself is what is left over when being in
> love has burned away. It doesn't sound very exciting – but it
> is.[19]

It is exciting because it is for life, and because – if it succeeds –
it will prove life-changing. It is the most significant break of
the bond between parent and child. That first relationship
starts with total dependence and hopefully progresses to a
proper independence: the second begins with independence
and grows into a new and different kind of dependence; 'I'
plus 'I' equalling 'we', in a mystery that the Bible calls 'one
flesh'. This is at once the hardest and the most potentially
rewarding of all our creative adventures, for (if we get it
right) it both binds and liberates.

The binding is obvious, the liberating more subtle.
However happy or unhappy our childhood, most people
enter into marriage with certain wounds. Sometimes they
have to do with lack of worth or confidence, sometimes
with a deeper hurt that needs to be exorcised within this
new relationship of trust and affirmation. Unpacking the
promise 'to love and honour . . . *for better, for worse*', I hear
each saying: 'I, in all the mystery that is me, take the mystery
that is you as the one to whom I choose to give my un-
conditional love until the day I die; not just in good times
and bad, but with all the better and all the worse that goes
to make up the complex being that is me. You are flawed,
as I am, but I have chosen you because I love you.' Within
the intimate and secure relationship that marriage should
be there is then the chance, given patience, empathy and
the readiness to forgive and be forgiven, that each (in all the
tender intimacies of love-making, childbirth and family life)
will be cherished and affirmed beyond anything they have
ever known. Old wounds can be healed. It is self-giving love

(that most Godlike of our gifts) that lies at the heart of marriage, and the paradox of such love is simply this: the more we give ourselves away, the more we become our true selves. That is liberating.

Richard Hoggart, looking back on nearly 60 years of married love, compares this process of 'growing into one another, growing together like plants, intertwining without entirely interlocking, and certainly without submerging' to the violin and piano in Beethoven's Spring Sonata, not so much a coming together of two people as the emergence of a new unity. 'Intertwining without entirely interlocking', for in the last resort human beings are alone. We face birth and death alone. There is, deep within us, a private place, and not even the one who loves me most will ever know exactly what it feels like to be me. This aloneness is the other side of our uniqueness. When Robert Louis Stevenson was travelling in the Cévennes with his donkey Modestine, he wrote of how

> even while I was exulting in my solitude I became aware of a strange lack. I wished a companion to lie near me in the starlight, silent and not moving, but ever within touch. For there is a fellowship more quiet even than solitude, and which, rightly understood, is solitude made perfect.[20]

In the profound mystery of a lifetime of shared experience two people will be forever changed by, and become part of, the other. 'It is a deep love,' wrote Rilke, 'that of two solitudes who protect and greet and touch each other.' Yet those who marry, or who enter into an unwritten contract with a partner which is for them equally binding, know that in time one of them will have to face a desolating grief that will feel like being torn in two. And then the solitude opens like a wound. It is this grief that is the risk love takes, and it is this grief that is the last and most costly offering of love that one person may give to another. And let no one pretend that grief is somehow assuaged for those who have

faith in God and a belief in resurrection. Whatever our ultimate hope, the pain of parting is every bit as severe.

The scorching weight of grief we may feel when we lose
anyone we love – a parent, a child, or a friend – may be just
as painful. For many, especially the single, it is in those close
friendships, where we can be ourselves in the company of
those whom we trust, that we experience the support of an
affirming love. As with marriage, when death intervenes, it
is often the small things we miss most: the way he looked,
the things she thought funny, the memories we shared. In
her poem 'For Steve', Denise Levertov expresses this sudden
agonising absence:

> The morning after your midnight death
> I wake to Lieder –
> Schumann, Schubert, the Goethe settings.
> Why did I not make sure that you
> (and your partner also before his death,
> whose caberet songs would perhaps
> have pleased Franz Schubert) came to know
> this music?
> This is the way
> mourning always begins to take root
> and add itself to one's life. A new
> pearl-grey thread entering the weave:
> this longing to show, to share,
> which runs full tilt into absence.[21]

Richard Hoggart writes that

> to understand family relationships, to develop that sense of
> belonging, of companionship and compassion, is the spring-
> board from which we may move on to build wider and better
> relationships with others.[22]

Marriage as a springboard, an enabler: this is the second way
in which it can liberate us. Once you know that you are
loved, you are set free to enter more sympathetically into
the lives of those who, for whatever reason, have been

deprived of love; those who have been scarred by their marriage's irretrievable breakdown; those who are single through no choice of their own; and those who do not fit into the more conventional pattern of a monogamous man/woman relationship. Christians have never found it easy to bridge the divide between the ideal and the reality, the values of the kingdom where they conflict with those of the world, the tension between Christ's commands and Christ's compassion. When people are in need, whatever the cause may be, we too often show an illiberal and judgemental desire to hold the fort, to keep the rules at whatever cost, time and again making the best the enemy of the good; and as a result the God revealed as Christlike is popularly perceived to be not only remote but easily upset, judgemental and even somewhat prim.

Nowhere is this truer than in matters of human sexuality. We have loved definitions; we have felt safe knowing what are the proper bounds, even though they carry dangerous overtones of exclusion. But life for most people is not like that. Life is about exploring, hoping, struggling, yearning, longing for love and experiencing grief. It is often messy. It is about being knocked flat. It takes courage.We frequently get it wrong. At a time of rapid social change we need more than an appeal to moral codes that are so rigid that they fail to allow for human diversity, do not have a realistic understanding of sexual orientation, and apply generalised precepts to individual circumstances. We have to find ways of responding to the universal human need to find and give love that will keep faith with what we believe about the true worth of every human being; an approach that meets the unchanging test of what love of God and love of neighbour demands of us in terms of compassion, justice and forgiveness.

I believe that will mean (for example) understanding that the complications of the human psyche cannot be reduced to three sexual identification tags: hetero-, homo- and bi-. You cannot so simply (in James Fenton's words) 'colour-code the mysteries of the individual', ignoring the subtleties of our emotions and passions, measuring and defining love in terms of sexual orientation. There are many nuances in the world of human affections, and people often take a while to embrace their own inherent nature. Our childhood experiences act upon us, and sexual abuse can have a devastating effect on whether we come to celebrate or fear this most powerful of instincts. But for most of us, those nuances will resolve themselves into a clearly dominant erotic love for a member of the opposite sex; for a minority it will be an equally strong attraction to a member of their own. In most cases this is the result of a natural orientation, something given. That is no longer in question, though much destructive prejudice and ignorance still proves hurtful. Because people are easily hurt, and infinitely complex in their search for love, the truth about human relationships is always more complicated than we think. It is a truth born of experience that good marriages are the richest way for heterosexuals to experience a shared and ever-deepening love, and that it provides the most secure base for children to learn where the dance of love begins. It is true that casual or promiscuous genital sex, whether heterosexual or homosexual, is ultimately destructive, for it has everything to do with lust and little to do with love. It must also be true of those who are in a committed relationship of which *agape* is the defining mark, and which shows the marks of tenderness, faithfulness and trust, that this is something to be celebrated and affirmed. I have known and loved as friends a good number of gay people, and counselled others; some have lived a life of celibacy, some have lived with a partner. It would, I believe, have been a denial of our common redeemed humanity to have wished them to be other than they are.

Many ancient religious myths speak of the creation of the world as the dance of God. Hindus believe that the world was created by Shiva, the Lord of the Dance, who sends pulsating waves of sound through matter so that it dances.

Stone Age cave paintings show dancing shamans in animal dress. Human beings danced for joy, for love, for grief; they danced at sunrise, or to celebrate a birth or mark a death. There were (there still are) tribal dances, fertility dances, dances for rain or a good harvest. It is part of the human desire to be connected with – and control – the life forces. (Even morris dancing fits in somewhere.) And dance has always been a *community* activity. The sacred dance was a normal part of the Jewish worshipping life, and in the Old Testament the people dance round the sacred calf; after crossing the Red Sea Miriam takes a timbrel and dances and the women dance with her; David dances before the Ark of God; and celebrative dances occurred at times of festival.

There is an early Gnostic gospel called the Acts of John. In it, on the night of his arrest, Jesus calls his disciples to him and they form a circle, holding hands, and start to dance. Jesus then begins to sing a hymn:

> 'Glory be to the Father'. And we, going round in a circle, answered him:
> 'Amen.'
> 'Grace danceth. I would pipe; dance ye all.' 'Amen.'
> 'The whole of on high hath part in our dancing.' 'Amen.'
> 'Thou that danceth, perceive what I do, for there is this passion of the manhood, which I am about to suffer.' Thus having danced with us the Lord went forth.

Gustav Holst used part of this text for his *Hymn to Jesus*, and on the grave of his daughter Imogen are carved the words: 'The heavenly spheres all make music for us. All things join in the dance.' Certainly ritual dancing seems to have been part of the liturgical expression of the early church. The fourth-century bishop, Eusebius, writes of 'dancing in procession, at times set dances, and then circle-dances right and left', and there was particular emphasis on dancing at Epiphany, Easter and Pentecost. In the early Middle Ages the priests danced with the people on certain holy days as a sign of equality, though by the twelfth century priests (predictably) would only dance with other priests and deacons with deacons. The Dance of Death was widely practised in Europe, the figure of Death (a dancing corpse or skeleton) leading folk in a dance around the churchyard. William Tyndale, who first translated the Bible into English (and who first gave us the word 'compassion'), wrote in his Prologue to the New Testament:

> That we cal gospel is a greke word, and signyfyth good, mery, glad and joyfull tydings, that maketh mannes hert glad, and makyth hym synge, daunce, and leepe for joy.

At the Reformation, no doubt to the relief of the forerunners of those who today recoil at the thought of sharing the Peace, dancing ceased. The first edition of the Encyclopaedia in 1768 notes with distaste:

> Dancing is usually an effect and indication of joy. The Christians are not free from this superstition; for in Popish countries certain festivals, particularly those of the Sacrament and passion of our Lord, are celebrated with dancing.

Not that it has ever entirely died out. Dancing, as the world of ballet shows, is not only self-exhibition, but also self-exploration and self-expression, and liturgical dance is creeping back as a way of using the whole of one's body in worship. In that form of liturgical dance which is based on the Lord's Prayer, the Beatitudes or the Magnificat, once the repetitive steps are learned and you start to be carried by the music, you quickly lose any self-consciousness. It can be profoundly meditative and restorative (or so I'm told by one whose wise judgement I have long admired): it affirms both your own identity and your profound unity with everybody else. What Forster called 'talkative little Christianity' is so head-centred, so wordy, but dance affects the whole person. It can express more than can be said in words and touch the heart.

Recently, a dance company that works exclusively in prisons worked with Holloway prisoners over several weeks on a dance performance, and all the prisoners came to see it. David Ramsbotham was present. He tells me that the performance was watched in an absorbed and wondering silence by both prisoners and staff, that they were 'bowled over'. For what the prisoners saw was what their friends were achieving, a 'realisation that they were suddenly walking taller'.

Two years ago, one whole arm of Salisbury Cathedral Cloisters was filled by nearly 40,000 small terracotta figures, the sculptor Antony Gormley's *Field*. The idea came to him from images of thousands of people crossing the desert during the famine in Ethiopia. The figures, made to his instructions by communities in Merseyside, were each about a foot tall and roughly shaped, the only features on their circular heads two round holes for eyes. You stared at them, and 40,000 pairs of eyes stared back expectantly at you: the effect was both disturbing and strangely moving. Was it simply a crowd, or was it a community? It spoke to me of beseeching, of a kind of longing for what we might be. And what we might be is not a crowd but a community.

A community, as St Augustine wrote, is comprised of members united by a common love of something other than themselves. It is the place where people are known and valued individually, by their names. Kathleen Raine once said that unless you see a thing in the light of love, you do not see it at all. So with persons: love is the light in which I recognise your true origin and purpose, and you recognise mine. Life is not about egos, each protecting their 'me-ness'; it is about shared burden-bearing, persons learning to relate to other persons in the web of mutual exchange from the simplest level to the most profound. The final word to describe what it means to be human is not, in R. S. Thomas' bleak phrase, 'lonely'; it is 'community'. Jesus of Nazareth left no book behind him: he left a small, fragile community (the circle of the dance already ruptured by the action of Judas) and entrusted it with truths that within a few years of his death were to spread like wildfire as people were given a new vision of what human means. He spoke of the new life of the kingdom and he gave them in that shared meal on the night of his arrest a foretaste of it, of how life is meant to be. This is what we rehearse and enter into anew every time we celebrate the eucharist. I have written elsewhere[23] of what this means at the Christian level, as together we celebrate our new shared humanity in Christ. But it also connects to our shared *humanity* in the broadest sense, with how in our unjust world we *make the connection* between the breaking and sharing of bread (in the context of penitence, forgiveness and the symbolic exchanging of the Peace) and the universal human longing for a world which more effectively witnesses to the kingdom's values of justice and equity. Communion is about community; company ('cum'+ 'pane') means sharing bread. For Jesus the shared meal is integral to the life of the kingdom, or what some have called the City of God, where all things are made new and 'the leaves of the trees are for the healing of the nations'.[24] The novelist Charles Williams frequently writes of the City as the pattern of the new creation which embraces earth and heaven and was initiated on that first Easter Day. In *All Hallows Eve*, Lester Furnivall comes to see that in the City 'citizenship meant relationship, and knew it . . . What on earth is only in the happiest moments of friendship or love was now normal.'[25] In the salad days of my ministry I sometimes fell unthinkingly into the comfortable distinction between 'the church' and 'the world'. I quickly came to see that God is not so confined, that grace and compassion flourish broadly and without distinction, and that we should recognise and celebrate signs of the kingdom wherever they appear.

There have been many times when I have been caught up in a shared experience of something greater than myself, when I have felt, 'This is how life should be.' Only some of them have been in church, and many have involved dance. At a service in Westminster Abbey to celebrate an International HIV/AIDS Conference, where many were mortally sick, there was a moment after all the words had been spoken when a young black performer danced alone in the central space of the quire with such grace and tenderness that it touched something deep within us all. Within two years he was dead. On another night, after a group of two dozen Indian children from an orphanage in Calcutta had played Mozart in the nave, the boys returned, some with tabla drums to beat out the rhythm, others – the dancers – with scarlet, lemon, blue and green headbands and with long ribbons on their wrists. The beat grew faster and faster, the boys spinning and leaping and stamping in front of the statue of Isaac Newton and beside the grave of Charles Darwin, and the rapturous applause reflected the delight of an audience that, warmed by the beauty of Mozart, had been infected by the vitality of the dance with a deep sense of joy.

Last year, at the opening of the new Lowry art and theatre complex in Salford, two hundred local people acted out a verse cycle by a local poet. It celebrated the past and present of the post-industrial docklands landscape in which the Lowry stands. Percussionists, wrote Paul Vallely, beat out wild rhythms on the glass, steel and concrete fabric of the building, while dancers created ad hoc body sculptures on the moving escalators and

> barmen burst into operatic arias as they served up pints of Boddingtons, and thousands of children, youths and adults converged on the centre just as in a previous era they converged upon the local football ground in Lowry's famous matchstick-man celebration *Going to the Match*, which [is in] the gallery upstairs . . . It all hinted at something . . . that takes us to a level of human connectedness which is prior to the negotiations in which economics and politics embroil us.[26]

In the recent and unforgettable performance of *The Mysteries* at the National's Cottesloe Theatre, most of the packed audience were standing and moving among the players as they

acted out the old mystery plays of Creation, the birth, ministry, passion, death and resurrection of Jesus, and the Last
Judgement. At the end actors and audience were united as
they joined in a dynamic and joyful dance. It was the perfect
ending: a deep and liberating expression of that human
connectedness. I was carried back fifty years to the twice-
weekly dances in the village hall on Iona, when the island
community came together and for three hours found a noisy
unselfconscious unity in stately Gay Gordons and wild
eightsome reels.

There is a fine novel by Niall Williams, *As It Is in Heaven*,
which is about the healing power of music, landscape and
the difficulties and rewards of love. Philip falls passionately
in love with Gabriella, an Italian violinist. In almost the
final scene of the novel they set up a music school among
strangers in a remote village in County Clare, and extend
an open invitation to the villagers. Gradually, shyly, people
begin to arrive, many having come straight from a funeral.
Gabriella begins to plays to them.

> She played as if she were dancing . . . When [she] finished there
> was not a sound. There was only the astonished faces of those
> who had no idea they could be so moved by such music.

She is joined by a fiddler and people begin to dance. More
people arrive and the dance begins to possess them, until
they are

> dancing even beyond the hearing of the music and making
> steps and keeping time to the music that was already inside of
> them . . . They played and danced on and were like a sea, chan-
> ging moods like tides, now bright and quick, now slow with airs
> of sorrow. And while the moon was lost behind the coverings of
> thick cloud and the stars were put out in the western sky, the
> party continued . . . It was as if in those moments of music and
> dance each man and woman was seized with the knowledge
> of the boundless hardship and injustice of life and knew that
> this night . . . was one they would look back on from the edge

206

of life and realise that yes, there they had come as close as they ever had to true happiness.[27]

# *The Dance of Faith*

We dance round in a ring and suppose,
But the Secret sits in the middle and knows.

*Robert Frost*[1]

Denying, believing and doubting are to men what
running is to horses.

*Blaise Pascal*[2]

He that lives in hope danceth without musick.

*George Herbert*[3]

The nights are closing in, the landscape is muted and the
woods are silent. Maples continue to show flashes of orange
and scarlet and gold. The old Saxon name for November
was *Wind-monath*, wind-month, when the fishermen drew
their boats ashore and stopped fishing until spring arrived.
Many trees still hold some leaves, until the first storms
arrive. Then the leaves are piled up in brown and yellow
mountains, with the sweet chestnut leaves

> like great ragged scraps of fawn paper; the beech . . . like copper
> shavings, brittle and shiny and upcurled, as though ripped off
> with a colossal plane. Sycamore and poplar are like flat and

slippery yellow fish. Birch are like dead butterflies, oak like scorched paper.[4]

On the Norfolk salt marshes wintering Brent geese will be feeding. Wigeon fly in from Russia, pochard from Germany and Scotland, hooded crows from the Baltic. A few last martins and swallows are leaving, though gnats are still dancing in the sun; the male mosquitoes are dead, the blood-sucking females already hibernating, as are grass snakes and badgers. On cedars of Lebanon the barrel-shaped cones are flowering, while ivy is blooming on walls and dead branches, providing the main source of pollen and nectar as bees top up their winter stores. On 13 November 1872, in Dorset, Thomas Hardy writes:

> The first frost of autumn. Outdoor folk look reflective. The scarlet runners are dishevelled: geraniums wounded in the leaf, open-air cucumber leaves have collapsed like green umbrellas with all their stays broken.

And in mid-November 1798, in Hampshire, Jane Austen is enjoying the unusually fine weather,

> not very becoming perhaps early in the morning, but very pleasant out of doors at noon, and very wholesome – at least everybody fancies so, and imagination is everything.

The consistent November occupation in all Books of Hours is **gathering acorns for pigs**. Something to keep them going during a long, hard winter when resources are at their lowest. A bit like faith.

All the time I have been writing in my attic study I have sensed a number of shadowy figures lurking in opposite corners. In the blue corner is the 'wistful agnostic' who feels the dull ache of his inability to believe, her lack of faith, like the there- but-not-there of an amputated limb; and yet who cannot see how a post-Darwinian, twenty-first-century man or woman can retain faith in God with any kind of intellectual integrity. In the red corner, bloodied and defeated, are those who have been so damaged in childhood or so wounded in adult life as to make conventional words like 'love', 'forgiveness' and 'justice', meaningless and empty. And just outside, mocking from the stairs, is one in the angry shape of the scientist Richard Dawkins, who dismisses Christianity as 'a self-perpetuating mental virus'. Many others (not least the popular opinion-formers) crowd in behind him, joining in the currently fashionable sport of dismissing any form of religious belief with the closed mind of the most passionate fundamentalist.

The philosopher Anthony Grayling, writing recently to oppose church schools, likens a belief in Christianity to a belief in fairies. Howard Jacobson, a fine Jewish novelist, yet in his own words 'coming religiously from nowhere', nevertheless vigorously defends the teaching of religious education in schools, arguing:

> We are the poorer – no less intellectually than spiritually – if we do not acquire the wherewithal to believe ... or to disbelieve, [for] without inward understanding of the workings of belief, our disbelief isn't worth a candle. Hear Richard Dawkins inveighing against religion and you confront shallows in the human mind which you would never have imagined capable of supporting mental life. The pride [he] takes in himself as a man who has escaped superstition is nothing less than pride in having missed out on an education; for it trumpets ignorance of the emotional life of other men.

Jacobson defends religion as a friend of culture, as that which addresses the seriousness of life, and when he says 'religion' he means Christianity – 'without which we would not be who we are': the great New Testament themes and stories, as reconceived by Shakespeare, Milton, and Blake. As a Jew, he still remembers being locked away for half-an-hour a day with the other Jewish boys,

> listening to the Christians singing hymns ... feeling foreign,

aching to have what they have . . . their rock of ages, and then
again happy to have what I have, the unutterable name . . . We
may see ourselves bringing gifts, we Jews and Sikhs and
Muslims, increments of faith and understanding from which
this country can only profit. But we can no more suppose that
our systems of belief have an equal place in English culture
than we would allow Christianity to have an equal place in
ours . . . As for Grayling's atheism, I would . . . have that taught
as well. A fourth-form course. Intermediate Fairy Studies. And
Dawkins? Advanced Presumption.[5]

Such a boisterous defence from an unexpected quarter is a
reminder of that Christian faith which (at its best) has
radically redefined what we mean by God and what we mean
by human; which has sustained and motivated people on
their journey for two millennia; which has created schools
and universities to teach the young, hospitals and hospices
to care for the sick and the dying; which has inspired works
of art and music and literature that are universal and do not
age and which speak to that which is deepest within us. It
has enabled people in every generation to share the life of
a worshipping community in which the rites of passage –
birth and marriage and death – are properly marked and
celebrated, and where down the centuries, in the sacraments
of baptism and eucharist, people have found hope and
purpose, and come to know that they are loved. When all
this is casually dismissed as arising from a delusion which
intelligent men and women have now outgrown, it speaks
of an astonishing ignorance both of theology (the study of
the intellectual content and the validity of religious beliefs),
and of religion (the experience of individuals and
communities). The fact that in the past there have been
terrible things done in the name of God, and that in the
present some of the more extreme renderings of Christianity
leave most of us running for cover, is not the point. The
point is that post-Darwin, post-Holocaust, post-quantum
physics, post-structuralism, the dance of faith still retains its

integrity. Provided our image of God is not so constrained as to do both him and our own intelligence a grave disservice.

Many scientists recognise this. Professor Sir Brian Pippard, physicist and musician, spoke in his 1988 Cambridge Eddington Memorial Lecture of the impossibility of combining our *public* and *private* knowledge into a unitive and satisfactory description: what a scientist observes, say, of the dance of the atom and what a musician 'knows' of the dance of a Beethoven sonata. He recognises the scientist's temptation to dismiss religious experience as a delusion, and to be sceptical of

> antiquated cosmologies such as religions are apt to carry in their train; and to despise dogmas that imply a God whose grandeur does not match up to the grandeur of the universe he knows.

Yet he is critical of those who dismiss believers 'of transparent integrity' simply because such belief is

> inconvenient and unshared. We may lack the gift of belief ourselves, just as we may be tone-deaf; but it is not becoming in us to envy those whose lives are radiant with a truth which is no less true for being incommunicable. As scientists we have a craftsman's part to play in the City of God; we cannot receive the freedom of that city until we have learnt to respect the freedom of every citizen.[6]

It was Pascal who said that he was 'amazed at the audacity with which some people speak about God'; John Donne who saw Truth as standing on a huge hill,

> cragged, and steep . . . and he that will
> Reach her, about must, and about must go;[7]

and I have quoted earlier Isaac Newton's sense of being 'like a boy playing on the sea-shore', conscious of being surrounded by the great, undiscovered 'ocean of truth'. If our knowledge is like a small island set in an ocean of inexhaustible mystery, then the growth of the island does not lessen either the size or the mystery of the sea: it just increases the length of the shore a little. And perhaps we are most human, most what we are called to be, when we have one foot on that shore of what we know, and one foot in the mysterious, unknown ocean. This is where the poet and the painter stand, together with the best scientists and the wisest theologians: exploring, probing, digging deeper; and sometimes breaking through to a fresh realisation of truth. Art, science and theology meet and flower at the boundary of the known and the hidden. For all of us this is the dance, not of certainty, but of faith.

The recognition that there can be no other valid approach to the ineffable mystery, whether of the created world or of its Creator, has always been known by the theologian; it has been seen increasingly to apply equally to the scientist. As we saw, whereas Einstein's Theory of Relativity questioned both our position in, and our perception of, time and space, Heisenberg's Uncertainty Principle – and the Quantum theory to which it led – question our ability to know anything absolutely. They say that we can only know that aspect of reality that we are looking for, that our answers will always be answers to particular questions, and that if we ask different questions we shall get different answers. It is not truth, but our limited view of it, that proves limited and uncertain. Which in scientists like the distinguished physicist Richard Feynman leads to a certain humility. He argued passionately for science to embrace 'a philosophy of ignorance', for the scientist's freedom to doubt, and the value of an open mind if new discoveries are to be made. 'Doubt . . . in the sciences . . . is a thing of very great value.'[8] The scientist who makes a new discovery, following years of experimentation and testing at this boundary of the known and the unknown, has so often had to make a blind intuitive leap to produce a theory that may then be repeatedly tested and found to be consistent and trustworthy. Mind and heart have come together to produce that tingle of the spine which Vladimir Nabokov said was the most reliable guide, both in art and science, in the disclosure of truth.

Those of us who in faith explore that shoreline that stands between what our intellect tells us is firm ground and the elusive God our spirit longs for, may achieve a knowledge that is no less real for being unprovable other than in the evidence of changed lives. But we are complex creatures, and when we attempt to make sense of the world and explore our inner landscape there is a deep chasm that divides us. It is as wide as the Grand Canyon, and some are drawn to the North Rim and some to the South. This rift cuts through politics, social issues and religious traditions, for it reveals the needs and states of mind of very different personalities. To use a very broad brush: there are those – the North Rimmers – who want clear boundaries, who see life and belief and human behaviour in terms of black and white, and who need it clearly packaged and labelled; and there are others – the South Rimmers – with a more sceptical turn of mind, sensing mystery on every side, tolerant of religious and cultural diversity, knowing they seek an elusive God and that there is no easy way of escaping the dark. They stand with John Keats in his phrase 'negative capability' when describing the receptivity he believed to be necessary in a poet: that is the state 'when man is capable of being in uncertainties, Mysteries, doubts, without any irritable searching after fact or reason'.[9] (Keats regarded Shakespeare as the prime example of negative capability, able to identify so completely with his characters as to write about them with total empathy and understanding.) Those who opt for varying degrees of fundamentalism devise systems (and churches) which are exclusive rather than inclusive. They want certainty and control; a clear distinction between who is in and who is out, what is allowed and what is forbidden, what to believe and what not to believe. Such fundamentalism, in its political expression, is aggressive, dangerous and scary, ranging from the oppression of women to the Taliban's destruction of the ancient Buddhist statues. In its more extreme religious expression, it is scarcely less so. Richard Holloway writes:

> The fundamentalist is made anxious by the impermanence of things, the elusiveness and uncontrollability of the life of the spirit in human history. Like magicians, fundamentalists want to control the divine, have power over it, so that they can create an absolute system of knowledge and certainty, the very thing we long for in our anxiety and insecurity.[10]

By temperament a South Rimmer, I have often despaired at those who take a literalist view of the Bible, or who, by their clear distinction between the enlightened and the unenlightened, seem to exclude many who are searching or half-believing. It seems such a judgemental form of Christianity, over-simplistic, intolerant and blind to the fact that the Spirit works in all kinds of unlikely and surprising people and places, both inside and outside the church. They seem to forget that, first and foremost, the Christian Gospel is not about producing neat QED answers to life's problems, but about encountering mystery. Faith, like hope, is an attitude of the heart, a changed orientation of the spirit. It is to trust that love is at the heart of that Mystery for whom the English name is 'God'. And to do so in the face of the undeniable confusion, uncertainty and doubt which remain a natural part of all our lives. For me, and I know for many, the only kind of faith that it is possible to affirm is that of the father of the epileptic boy who comes to Jesus and begs that his child may be healed: 'Lord, I have faith; help me where faith falls short.'[11] Ten words which perfectly express the dilemma of that encounter with God which is at once a knowing and a not-knowing. In them we are stating a fact, not admitting a fault. Faith would not be faith if it did not fall short of certainty, if all ends were neatly tied up, all uncertainties resolved. There is something suspect about those who, in W. B. Yeats' words, are 'full of passionate intensity', the passion of total open-and-shut conviction. 'We are closer to

God when we are asking questions', writes Rabbi Abraham Joshua Heschel, 'than when we think we have the answers.'

In his poem 'The Pulley', George Herbert wrote that when God made us he contracted 'all the world's riches . . . into a span', but held back the ultimate gift of 'rest', leaving us unsatisfied and searching, with 'repining restlessnesse', so that

> If goodnesse leade him not, yet wearinesse
> May tosse him to my breast.[12]

It was Kierkegaard who argued that too much objective certainty deadens the very soul of faith. We cannot have infallible proof of the One for whom (being made in his likeness) we intuitively search, for such proof would devalue our response. All we have is the coin of faith, of which the flip side is doubt; and it must always carry with it, to affirm our precious gift of freedom, a touch of agnosticism, of not knowing all the answers. For this is what God asks of us: this is what makes our reaching out into the dark of such value to him. He invites our trust, even in the worst of times; yet such faith must always be conditional and incomplete. So Emily Dickinson can write:

> I stepped from Plank to Plank
> A slow and cautious way
> The Stars about my Head I felt
> About my Feet the Sea.
>
> I knew not but the next
> Would be my final inch –
> This gave me that precarious Gait
> Some call Experience.[13]

On the feast day of St Thomas, whose faith deserted him when told of the resurrection, Henri Nouwen notes in his diary that Thomas' other name was Didymus, meaning 'twin', and of how the church Fathers had written 'that all of us are "two people", a doubting one and a believing one'; we need the support and love of the worshipping community, he adds, 'to prevent our doubting person from becoming dominant and destroying our capacity for belief'.[14] Which is why the place for those who desire God but have not yet found him, or those who must still cross their fingers when reciting bits of the creed, is within the worshipping community and not outside it. Entry should not depend on signing on the dotted line. Entry depends on a desire to understand better. St Anselm famously said: 'Credo ut intelligam': 'I do not seek to understand so that I may believe, but believe *that I may* understand.' Doing always precedes understanding. We learn how to speak before understanding the rules of grammar and syntax. We encounter God before we seek to define him. 'God is known in proportion as he is loved,' ran the medieval tag; but we only learn how to love through being loved. In learning to dance, it is always that way round, and the first steps are the hardest.

Many have come to value that bleak but honest poet, R. S. Thomas, who stubbornly wrestled all his life with the paradox of the absence and presence of God: or rather, with his *apparent* absence and the moments when he realises the presence within that seeming absence; the sense of a room from which the one he seeks has just left. There are for him times

when a black frost is upon
One's whole being, and the heart
In its bone belfry hangs and is dumb;[15]

when

no God leans down
out of the air to take the hand
extended to him;[16]

he

> tests his faith
> On emptiness, nailing his questions
> One by one to an untenanted cross.[17]

Yet he keeps faith, aware that he is attempting to explore and convey a mystery which in the end is incommunicable in words; remaining kneeling in his silent church, or observing, with the keen eye of the birdwatcher, the natural world about him, coming to understand that

> it is matter is the scaffolding
> of spirit . . .
> it is the plain facts and natural happenings
> that conceal God and reveal him to us
> little by little under the mind's tooling.[18]

In one of his finest poems Thomas writes of gingerly sending out his prayer and waiting for its echo:

> leaning far out
> over an immense depth, letting
> your name go and waiting,
> somewhere between faith and doubt,
> for the echoes of its arrival.[19]

Many feel, in the world around them, God's marvellous echo rather than his calculable presence. 'Truly thou art a God who hidest thyself,'[20] complained Isaiah. But then, religion has always been more the story of longing rather than possessing. Thomas knows that words are powerless to reveal ultimate reality, that God is more likely to be sensed through an openness to Keats' 'uncertainties, Mysteries, doubts'. But more often than not, it is we who are absent, with our failure to give attention and our darting, wandering minds. So: 'you must remain kneeling'.[21] Literally or figuratively, for then, in the seeming absence, God's presence may be felt in that most intimate of relationships,

> the annihilation of difference,
> the consciousness of myself in you,
> of you in me.[22]

It is at the heart of our longing for the absent God that we discover his footprints, and sense that our desire to love him is born out of his love for us. So faith, which 'gives substance to our hopes and convinces us of realities we do not see',[23] discovers that God comes

As I had always known
he would come, unannounced,
remarkable merely for the absence of clamour.[24]

When the writer Philip Toynbee was dying of cancer he asked a priest who was visiting him how he came to be ordained.

He told me that he had tried several things first – engineering and psychiatric nursing among them – but this was the first pool he had stepped into in which he couldn't feel the bottom. A wonderful answer.[25]

But why are some aware of that bottomless pool and their need to explore it, while others ignore or shy away from the inner life of the spirit? It would seem to have to do with human intelligence, the fact that we are driven to ask ultimate questions and see meaning in our lives. IQ (Intelligence Quotient) is a familiar concept: it describes our rational intelligence. EQ and SQ have now joined the dance, attempts to widen the understanding of how our brain functions. EQ is our emotional, SQ our spiritual, quotient. There is in each of us a mixture of both IQ and EQ in differing degrees, a dance of head and heart. We think and we feel, but emotions – love, anger, fear – are so strong that they usually carry the day. Stories, novels, film, theatre, art, poetry and music, all appeal to our emotions. While those with a high IQ tend to be intelligent, ambitious, productive, emotionally cool and usually introspective, those with a high EQ tend to be outgoing and cheerful, socially at ease, good at handling relationships, sympathetic and caring.

But what of this newly fashionable concept of SQ? A high

SQ will not necessarily make me religious, but it will mean that I have a sense of something greater and other than myself that adds meaning and value to my life. SQ describes the intelligence with which we address such questions, seeing our lives in this wider context. It allows us to be creative, flexible and self-aware, inspired with a vision of how things might be changed for the better and recognising our power to change them. IQ, EQ and SQ should work in harmony, though they may function separately, individuals being high in one and low in another. They relate to the neural connections in the brain. Researchers in magneto-encephalographic technology (MEG), seeking a 'God-spot' in the brain, have focused on these neural connections which are situated in the brain's temporal lobes, and they have shown that when discussion turns to spiritual questions these areas light up. This does not witness to the existence of God: all it proves is that the brain has evolved in such a way as to ask questions of value and meaning. My brain is the bridge between my outer and inner worlds, and it brings us back to the mystery of how this thing called 'consciousness' has the power, not only to *analyse*, but also to *unite* the startling number of messages being fed into the brain's neural systems: shape, colour, sound, smell, touch. It seems that we all possess in some degree this higher order unitive intelligence that is SQ.[26] It is essentially holistic, so that those with low SQ find it hard to see beyond the immediate moment or place it within a wider framework of meaning, while those with high SQ make connections and recognise that the whole is always greater than the parts.

The great world faiths of Christianity, Judaism and Islam all affirm the validity of the human spirit. They share three great insights: the recognition of the infinite worth of each person; the belief that undergirding the creative process there is the divine will and an end-purpose; and a belief in a compassionate God who acts within history in certain specific ways. The central idea of theistic religion is 'that the Infinite pours itself out in love to the finite universe. This is the fundamental meaning of "revelation" '. David Ford has described asking a very experienced Roman Catholic priest what was the most common problem he met with in confession. He answered without hesitation: 'God'.[28] The misconception of God. The inability for whatever reason to see God as a God of love, forgiveness, tenderness and compassion. So often it is not faith that is the stumbling-block, especially when faith is understood as that reaching out towards what we most deeply desire, somewhere between doubt and conviction. The stumbling-block is our inability to believe and to trust that we are loved and valued for ourselves, 'to accept' (in Paul Tillich's phrase) 'that we are accepted'. Whoever we are and whatever we have done. Not because we deserve it, but because that is how God has once and for ever revealed himself to be. The God who reveals himself as Christlike is the only God on offer.

It remains true that all our language about God is provisional, Eliot's 'hints and guesses'. Yet the 'hints' have been sufficient for a faith founded on a seductive story that reached its climax in one man's birth, life, death and resurrection, to have captured the civilised world; and the 'guesses' that this man was indeed the unique (though not exhaustive) revelation of God have been persuasively tested in transformed lives. The author of the Fourth Gospel calls him 'the Word' (the Logos). In Greek thought the Logos is both the *self-expression* of God's own being and also the *creative power* by which the universe came into existence and is sustained. Jesus' first followers may have been monotheist Jews, but it did not take them long to assert that he was a unique human being disclosing – insofar as a person living in history could – the true nature of God's self-giving, suffering love. And John has no hesitation in affirming that this 'Word' was embodied, literally 'made flesh', in Jesus of Nazareth. In the words of one of my friends: it was, indeed, 'there from the beginning – but after all those dark millennia of gestation, we met a small human face, and recognised it as our own'.[29]

When I look back on my life, I cannot say that I have never doubted this extraordinary claim, or that there have not been times when I have resorted to stale and empty words, the sort of professional shorthand that trips too easily off the tongue of those of us who preach too many sermons. All I claim is that in my heart of hearts I have believed for most of my life that God *is*; that he is *as he is in Jesus*; and that no truth on earth is as important or as liberating. For if that is true then it changes everything: not only how I see God and how I see myself, but how I see the human race.

I love R. S. Thomas for his honesty. When he speaks of the elusive God and the loneliness of what it is to be human, he speaks out of a hunger and a need that has nothing to do with worldly success and everything to do with the restless, searching human spirit. Julian of Norwich, who lived through the Black Death, knew that faith in God brings no divine favours: 'He said not, "Thou shall not be tempested, thou shalt not be travailed, thou shalt not be afflicted"; but he said: "Thou shalt not be overcome".'[30] And towards the end of the *Four Quartets* Eliot quotes those other words of Dame Julian, which are at once a cry of hope and an act of faith: 'All shall be well, and all manner of thing shall be well'. The Christian echoes in that assertion are evident: the overarching love of God, the work of the Spirit in opening our eyes to truth, the life of the kingdom, the ultimate reconciliation of all things in Christ. But I hear in it all kinds of other human echoes. I hear in it the voice of Samuel Beckett's Malone in *Malone Dies*, somewhere between hopelessness and hope:

> Where I am, I don't know, I'll never know, in the silence you don't know, you must go on, I can't go on, I'll go on.[31]

I hear in it the final sentence of William Maxwell's fine novel *The Château*, where the old woman, lying awake at night and weary of life, reaches for the memoirs of a nineteenth-century missionary, 'who lived among the Chinese, and was close to God':

Mme Vienot puts what happened to him, his harsh but beauti-
fully dedicated life, between her and all silences, all creaking
noises, all failures, all searching for answers that cannot be
found.[32]

I hear it literally when the philosopher Ludwig Wittgenstein
speaks of his assurance that 'all is well' which comes to him
as he looks with wonder at the existence of his own hand.
I hear it in the words of the poet Jane Kenyon, both her
husband and herself having been diagnosed with cancer:

There are things in this life we must endure which are all but
unendurable, and yet I feel that there is a great goodness . . .
How, when there could have been nothing, does it happen
that there is love, kindness, beauty?[33]

I hear it in Auden's poem where he asserts that the poet's
task is to 'persuade us to rejoice', and that no matter what
our situation the call to praise and to rejoice are always
valid:

In the deserts of the heart
Let the healing fountain start,
In the prison of his days
Teach the free man how to praise.[34]

Faith (that intuitive confidence, if not in God, then in life)
is the belief that the forces on our side are greater than the
forces opposed to us. It may fall some way short of the belief
that 'God was in Christ reconciling the world to himself' or
the assured trust that 'underneath are the everlasting arms',
but wherever it appears it is to be celebrated. Bernard Levin
once described it as 'the current that warms and illuminates
and drives the world: the cause of yes against no'.[35] This is
not a cheap, unfounded optimism, but a deep and irrepress-
ible instinct that, for all its bruising pain and heartbreak,
these are not the final word about life. The final word is
love. As Levin says, if we emerge from a performance of *King
Lear* or *Hamlet* simply feeling that 'we have supp'd full with

horrors' and that the world is full of meaningless terror we have missed the point. In E. M. Forster's novel *Howard's End*, Helen is at a performance of Beethoven's Fifth Symphony in the old Queen's Hall. She hears the malignant goblins in the third movement which, with their assertion that the universe is meaningless, are scattered by the leap into the sunlit certainty of C major. But the goblins come back:

> Panic and emptiness! Panic and emptiness! Even the flaming ramparts of the world might fall. Beethoven chose to make it all right in the end . . . He brought back the gusts of splendour, the heroism, the youth, the magnificence of life and death, and, amid vast roarings of a superhuman joy, he led his Fifth Symphony to its conclusion. But the goblins were there. They could return. He had said so bravely, and that is why one can trust Beethoven when he says other things.[36]

Many years ago, when I worked at the BBC, I invited the playwright Dennis Potter to give a talk on Radio 4 in Lent. He spoke of the darkness of illness, and he asked, 'What, if anything, lies on the other side of the dark?' His answer had to do with giving attention to the present moment: even in pain, and lying awake in the small hours, to focus on what was happening to him and in him and around him, so that 'the actual sting of the moment became a point of such unexpected clarity that I could see it . . . as a widening chink of light through which I could look'.

> I understood then that God is not a palliative or a super-pill . . . but . . . someone present in the quick of one's own being . . . in the fibre and pulse of the world, and in the minute-by-minute drama of an ever-continuing, ever-poised, ever-accessible creation . . . I understood . . . that the world is being made right in front of us . . . and in living out our lives we give back piece by piece what has been given us to work and wrestle with. We share our own lives and find our own humanity in the long passage from innocence through the darkness of mortal distress . . . and apparent absurdity into the light that we know

is there if we have the patience and the courage to be still, to concentrate – to be alert.

'I am glad that I was here', said the Quaker, George Fox, at the end of his life.

'Now I am clear, I am full clear . . . All is well.'

All is well. Not by facile optimism, not in blinkered evasions, but in the richest and most active dimension of our humanity. It is the illumination we must and will ever seek on the other side of the dark.[37]

The circle of the dance of faith goes wider than we think.

# DECEMBER

## *Learning to Dance II*

---

there's a dance or two
in the old dame yet.

*Don Marquis*[1]

I have no desire to prove anything by dancing. I
just dance.

*Fred Astaire*

Death could drop from the dark
As easily as song.

*Isaac Rosenberg*[2]

the bright day is done,
And we are for the dark.

*Antony and Cleopatra*[3]

listen: there's a hell
of a good universe next door; let's go.

*e. e. cummings*[4]

---

For Thomas Hardy, the landscape turns in December from a
painting to an engraving. The last tints of autumn are gone
and most trees are revealed in their winter shapes, their
boughs 'bare ruin'd choirs, where late the sweet birds sang',[5]

their skeletoned forms standing out against the darkening sky of early evening. There is a strange grace about them, the knotty oak and the drooping ash. Some are hung with invasive clusters of mistletoe, which in the Middle Ages was thought capable of breaking the trances of epileptics, dispelling tumours, divining treasure and keeping witches at bay. The land has a sense of melancholy, only the holm oaks and the conifers, yew and cypress, fir and pine and cedar, supplying rare touches of colour and seeming darker than their summer green in the thin winter sunlight; and the holly, thick with scarlet berries if it has been a good spring. In the country only groundsel is in flower, and chick-weed and shepherd's purse, with an occasional late dandelion still holding its corner. Black-headed gulls fly deep inland in search of food, and starlings fill London squares at dusk. Snow seems to come more rarely in December than once it did: in 1922 it was so thick that Katherine Mansfield wrote that 'it clings to the branches like white new-born puppies'. On 4 December 1770, at Selborne, Gilbert White reported that 'most owls seem to hoot exactly in B flat'.

In the Books of Hours there were two occupations for December: **killing the pig** and **baking bread**. The Bedford Hours of 1423 show an alarmed pig kneeling by water, with a bearded man about to crack its skull with a large mallet; while a more animated scene on the sixteenth-century Flemish calendar shows women baking bread, and in the foreground a pig noisily having its throat cut, a woman catching the blood in a saucepan; in a lower panel eight plump villagers are having a tug-of-war on sledges. Death is unmistakably the flavour of the the year's end.

But first comes retirement.

> 'When all this is over', said the swineherd,
> 'I mean to retire, where
> Nobody will have heard about my special skills
> And conversation is mainly about the weather . . .

I want to lie awake at night
Listening to cream crawling to the top of the jug
And the water lying soft in the cistern.

I want to see an orchard where the trees grow in straight lines
And the yellow fox finds shelter between the navy-blue
    trunks,
Where it gets dark early in summer
And the apple-blossom is allowed to wither on the bough.'[6]

Memory is the strangest thing. Inside my head time is no longer linear, but co-existent, and I am all the ages I have ever been. Now that I am old (or is it elderly? Laurie Lee once asked: 'Why do they never say "old", always "elderly"? Elderly Tyme Dancing. Elderly King Cole was a merry elderly soul. The Elderly Bailey.'[7]), I still feel the same as I have always felt, and while the pattern was unpredictable before my story unfolded, I now see how it has all come together and (mostly) made sense. I wanted to be an actor, but chose to be a priest, and though there have been times when I wanted to escape, nothing else would have been half as satisfying. Increasingly my short-term memory lets me down. The elderly Henry James would tell the story of meeting a woman during his usual walk in Rye. He knew that he knew her, but he couldn't think who she was. He was wondering how to deal with the situation when she said, 'I've done up the joint into rissoles', and he realised with huge relief that she was his housekeeper. Long-term memory, however, allows you to harvest your life, to reconstruct it and find a meaning in it, an integrity. It is, as Proust said, a way of defeating time. For memories have little logical sequence about them: like dreams, they are fluid and surprising. As we reflect on the collage of our life, the most unexpected places and people pop up and jostle for attention without much logic or reason, and we can sort out what has been important and what has not mattered at all. The memory of those we have loved most remains as vivid as ever, while (hopefully) those who have tested us sorely are seen with wiser and more forgiving insight. And while St Paul may claim to have 'put away childish things', Seneca was nearer the mark when he wrote, 'It is not that age brings childhood back again. Age merely shows what children we remain.' And not entirely in a negative sense. John Updike, in reviewing what he calls Michael Sheldon's 'indignant biography' of Graham Greene, complains that

> the trouble with literary biographies . . . is that they mainly testify to the long worldly corruption of life, as documented deeds and days and disappointment pile up, and cannot convey the unearthly human innocence that attends, in the perpetual present tense of living, the self that seems the real one.[8]

I like 'the perpetual present tense of living', for it should never be 'I am who I was', but always 'I am who I am'.

Prospero, facing early retirement at the end of *The Tempest*, promised that 'every third thought shall be my grave'; which, comments John Updike, 'leave two thoughts to entertain above the ground: love one another, and seize the day'.[9] The last gets a little easier with age. With an increasingly limited time ahead, I think of those places I shall never see, and those things I shall never do, *and it doesn't matter*; and I think of missed opportunities, what has been called the 'sin of an unlived life', which does matter. There is a poem by Mary Oliver called *The Summer Day*, in which she spends her day being 'idle and blessed' and strolling through the fields, observing. It ends:

> Tell me, what else should I have done?
> Doesn't everything die at last, and too soon?
> Tell me, what is it you plan to do
> with your one wild and precious life?[10]

I often look at the faces of the old and wonder about their untold and often astonishing stories. Some reveal contentment and the beauty of their interior life. Others seem deeply scarred by suffering and discontent. Like the character in Vladimir Nabokov's *Speak, Memory*, of whom he writes:

> Misery was her native element; its fluctuations, its varying depths, alone gave her the impression of moving and living . . . [but] a sense of misery, and nothing else, is not enough to make a permanent soul. My enormous and morose Mademoiselle is all right on earth but impossible in eternity.[11]

Despite the dark and testing times, the sickness, the failures and the disappointments, I shall respond with a heartfelt 'Yes!' if that Jewish Rabbi is right and God's first question at the judgement will be 'Did you enjoy my creation?', for it has been a richly diverse and fulfilling life. And still is. But what I see more clearly now in the healing space of retirement is that, while bothering about details matters, how much time I have wasted in a kind of anxious perfectionism; how aware I have been of the beauty both of nature and the arts, but how much I have simply taken for granted; and, while I have always tried to put pastoral care at the top of the agenda, how much more loving I might have been. Thomas Traherne was right: 'Never was anything in this world loved too much, but many things have been loved in a false way: and all in too short a measure'.[12] So, I guess 'All in too short a measure' could have served as a subtitle to *Learning to Dance*.

When the writer Sylvia Townsend Warner was 65, she noted in her incomparable diaries:

> *14 October 1958*. In the evening the Amadeus played (Beethoven's) Opus 132; and I danced to the last movement, I rose up & danced, among the cats, & their saucers, and only when I was too far carried away to stop did I realise that I was behaving very oddly for my age – and that perhaps it was the last time I should dance for joy.[13]

Perhaps the genes that carried my bird-like grandmother past her century and my ever-competitive mother almost as far will work for me too, yet if you are wise, once you pass the Psalmist's three-score-years-and-ten your thoughts turn increasingly to what the Orthodox funeral service describes, in a good phrase, as our 'desired homeland'. For the hardest steps in this lifelong learning to dance are the final ones, when all that is predictable is the final outcome. A clear stream flows through the garden of a great house near my home: beneath the water lies a carved stone which bears the words: 'carries the moon carries the sun but keeps nothing'. Two things bind us together in our great human sameness and solidarity: birth and death. In each case the journey is into the unknown. In *King Lear* Edgar comforts his suicidal father with the words:

> Men must endure
> Their going hence, even as their coming hither:
> Ripeness is all.[14]

But many are unripe for death, which may come as a thief in the night. 'If only [we] could disintegrate like autumn leaves,' wrote Loren Eisley, 'dropping [our] substance like chlorophyll, would not our attitude toward death be different? Suppose we saw ourselves burning like maples in a golden autumn.'[15]

But it is not so simple. Henri Nouwen once said that those who have never looked their own death in the face can never really assist someone who is dying. There are some who drift into that slow and living death which is Alzheimer's, where the heavier cost is borne by those who love them. There are some who die suddenly, unprepared, in their sleep: they are often spoken of as the lucky ones. There are others who would prefer, given the choice, to die less suddenly, with more time to complete that unfinished business, and say goodbye. Certainly this can ease the burden of grief in those who are left behind. A handful of my close friends – Stewart, John, Terence, Giles – have died too young of cancer, and left an indelible memory of how the darkness may be faced with grace and courage. They lived out

Montaigne's hope that 'If I can, I will prevent my death from saying anything not first said by my life'. Each had lived in the light of Easter and the belief in resurrection.

No one dances alike. And the formal pattern of the dance changes all the time:

> The vagaries and checks, the graceful turns
> And not-so-graceful lurchings of the spirit,
> Which, had it never ventured such a caper,
> Had never known itself. To that bold dance,
> Which once was called the making of a soul
> And now is called the finding of a self,
> I pay the homage of an ardent mind.[16]

In this final phase of 'that bold dance, Which once was called the making of a soul' there may well be pain and suffering, though the two are not always the same. When you experience physical pain, that can be contained. One of the most important of medical breakthroughs has been in terms of palliative care, the control of pain that has been largely developed by the hospice movement which increasingly allows more and more people to die at home (with home nursing care), in hospital or in a hospice with little or no pain. But suffering touches the whole person, and spiritual pain needs equally to be addressed, for body, mind and spirit being such an indivisible whole, this deeper 'soul pain'– the pain of alienation with all its attendant anger or guilt, anxiety and disquiet – may increase our physical pain as well. When we come to die we need to be assured that we are loved, that we are much more than the sum of our rapidly disintegrating parts, that our life possesses meaning and value; and we may need to forgive or ask forgiveness for wounds given or received.

The lesson that haunts us all our lives, and that if we are wise we will learn sooner rather than later, is that love is indeed tested and 'proved in the letting-go'. Letting go of parents by children and children by parents; letting go of seeming securities, of the past, and of our countless possessions (even, sadly, books); and in the end, of our loved ones and even life itself. The Scottish poet, Norman MacCaig, has a small poem he calls 'Small Boy':

He picked up a pebble
and threw it into the sea.
And another, and another.
He couldn't stop.
He wasn't trying to fill the sea.
He wasn't trying to empty the beach.
He was just throwing away,
nothing else but.
Like a kitten playing
he was practising for the future
when there'll be so many things
he'll want to throw away
if only his fingers will unclench
and let them go.[17]

And the American poet, Mary Oliver, writes:

To live in this world

you must be able
to do three things:
to love what is mortal;
to hold it

against your bones knowing
your own life depends on it;
and, when the time comes to let it go,
to let it go.[18]

Ultimately, it is always a question of what we desire: what we really *want* and long for. Gerard Hughes writes that desire is the key to the spiritual journey, that

if only we have a strong enough desire for the things of God, to hunger and thirst after justice, to long for peace, to be able to love and be loved and to be wedded to truth, then we can let go of attachments which divert us from these things.[19]

For in the end we tend to get what we most deeply desire.

One of my underlying themes, sometimes implicit, sometimes explicit, has been that to be human is to know within you – and therefore within everyone else as well – the pattern of God, a God who is beyond all boundaries and all human conceiving; a God 'whose imperishable life is within us all'[20] and who desires that, before all else, we should desire him. I believe that this desire for God is often hidden, even to ourselves, for it appears in many disguises: sometimes it may take the form of a desire for knowledge or for truth; sometimes in the search for love. I scent it in an intuitive sense of my unmet potential, those glimpses of how human living and loving might be. It lies behind my wonder at the night sky, the unfolding sweep of evolution, the interplay of the forces of gravity, the perfection of the field daisy and the wild rose. I recognise it in my response to beauty in paint and words and music; in that deep satisfaction when in a symphony all comes together and is resolved in the harmony of the final movement; or when a novel's ending rings true to its promise; or when Odysseus finally returns home to Ithaca, his odyssey complete. I sense it (this unspoken desire for, and presence of, God) in the goodness incarnate in the mystery of ordinary/extraordinary people. It may be discerned at the heart of suffering and in its attendant compassion, wherever that is seen; and in every act of forgiveness and in each self-giving act of love. For things are at once simple and complex: the simple truth is that we are shaped (and judged) by our desires, and depending on what we desire most in this life – and beyond it – our spirits expand or they contract; they grow and blossom, or they shrivel up, like raisins in the sun. In his *Christian Discourses*, Kierkegaard writes:

> When the last time has arrived, and in the hour of death thou art lonesome and forsaken, thou wilt desire, as the very last

thing in the world of which thou art no longer a part, thou wilt desire what today thou dost desire.

Simple – but also complex, for we have so many longings and desires and attachments, and we find it so hard to discriminate between them and, finally, let them go.

If learning to live is hard enough, learning to die is much, much harder. In Alan Ayckbourn's play *House*, Trish says:

> The other evening I was ... watching the village children rehearsing their maypole dance. There they were, all clinging to their coloured ribbons as if their lives depended on it ... And I thought, that's how it is for all of us, really. When we're young we're each given a ribbon ... to cling on to, and once we have our ribbon we're taught the dance. And from then on, for the rest of our lives, we obediently move round and round our maypole, observing respective little set patterns ... keeping our distances, careful never to step on each other's toes ... clinging on to our ribbon, terrified of deviating in case we get hurt or lost or rejected. But the older we get, despite all our efforts, the more we get entangled with other people. Yet never for a minute do most of us ever dream of doing the obvious and just letting go.[21]

The trouble is that some of the ribbons are wondrous.

The final recorded words of Jesus are the Psalmist's words, set in the Jewish prayer book to be said before falling asleep: 'Father, into your hands I entrust my spirit.' They are the simplest, most childlike form of faith. Jesus had often spoken of such trust in God's overarching power and goodness as the only true way in which to live. And to die. When I come to die it will be the ultimate test of that trust in God that I have been trying to learn all my life. It will be the acid test of whether I am willing to let go of all that would bind me to earth, not just because I am old and tired and ready to depart, but because of my desire for God. Yet I hold back, for I cannot bear the thought of parting from those I love most in the world, nor of their grief; nor the thought of leaving the sights and sounds and scents that make this world so beautiful. One of the wistful delights of growing old is a new need to 'seize the day'. Each morning I say the prayer that begins: 'The night has passed and the day lies open before us,'[22] and most days I notice some simple wonder I thought I had outgrown. To believe that beyond death lies resurrection might be thought to make departing (and the grieving process) less painful. It doesn't. What it does is to change the whole context in which you see your life.

'We must all die; we are like water spilt on the ground, which cannot be gathered up again.'[23] 'The best thing about dying', said Sir John Astor, 'is that you don't have to pack.' Yet death is not about moving 'into the next room'. Within a few days the atoms that were 'me' will have been buried in the earth, where I shall be reduced to a skeleton in some three weeks and my bones return to dust (according to Hamlet's gravedigger) 'within some eight or nine year'; or they will have been consumed by fire. Any hope beyond death lies not with me but with God. For God is not a 'God of the dead, but of the living',[24] and 'no one else can satisfy the same need in God' as this uniquely created, uniquely loved creature that each one of us is in God's sight. I have lived and I shall die trusting that God will re-*member* me; that I shall be put together again. Of course this activity and personality that I call 'me' will no longer be expressed through the atoms of my familiar shape, for this body is worn out and has done its work, but what is still uniquely and recognisably me will be expressed elsewhere and in other conditions which I cannot even begin to imagine. When I say, 'I believe in the resurrection of the body', that is no crude literalism, a coming together again of all my scattered atoms, but rather a re-creation of everything that has made this particular embodied spirit me and not you. When in the twelfth century St Bernard of Clairvaux wrote of the four degrees of love, he says that the final degree of love, loving God with all our heart and soul and strength, will not be perfectly fulfilled this side of death, 'and yet our human substance will remain: *we shall still be ourselves*, but in another form, another glory and another power'.[25] I am not created for a relationship with God which is snuffed out with my last breath, nor to be lost in God like a drop of water in a river, but to be found in him in all my individuality. I have two grounds for such a hope: the first relates to my *incompleteness*, the second to *Easter*.

Recently I gave a series of retreat addresses under the title (stolen from a friend's book) of *The Longing for Home*. (It got transmuted by an unfriendly computer into *The Longing for Hove*, which placed me firmly in the Saga constituency.) While we can know nothing of what lies beyond death, there are all kinds of clues in our sense of incompleteness, a hunger for that which in this life just eludes our grasp, the need to glimpse in the confusion of our lives a purpose and a meaning. And they all point to home, the place where there is an end to all our searching; and where there is no need to explain, for everything is known. Here on earth there is beauty, but why is it so fleeting? There is joy, but why is it always achingly incomplete?

> Joy's trick is to supply
> Dry lips with what can cool and slake
> Leaving them dumbstruck also with an ache
> Nothing can satisfy.[26]

There is love in which two separate identities are united into the mysterious wholeness of 'one flesh', only one day to be painfully torn apart. The only truth that can integrate and make sense of our need for an ending, the harmonious resolution of the music, the satisfaction of our thirst for love, is that we are restless and dissatisfied until we rest in God. The truth that he is the source of my deepest experiences of love or forgiveness, of every intimation of beauty and moments of insight, of every stirring of compassion or anger at injustice, which stamp me as being made in his likeness. Not only is he their source, but their culmination; and to hope for 'heaven' (or the kingdom, or the City of God, choose which metaphor we will for what cannot be described) is to set our hunger in the context of that new quality of life which the writers of the New Testament call 'eternal' (and which they see beginning here and now). Faith, for them, means being grasped in the present by 'that which is to come'. In the words of Paul Tillich:

> The *coming* order is always coming, shaking *this* order, fighting with it, conquering it and conquered by it. [It] is always at hand. But one can never say: 'It is here! It is there!' One can never grasp it. *But one can be grasped by it.*[27]

In terms of evolution, the Christian faith is not long born. At certain critical points new forms of life have emerged, and new potentialities are realised, possibilities that could not have been guessed at before. Matter is informed by life in an ever-expanding variety of creatures, and eventually in a creature with self-consciousness and creativity, matter informed by spirit in the mystery of the person. Infinitely slowly, the true nature of the Creator-spirit is discerned, until in an extraordinary act of God's self-revelation a new stage of evolution begins. Our faith also evolves. It shifts and subtly changes as we change: how I saw life at twenty is not how I see it at seventy-plus. The answers to the questions are at once stranger and more lucid, those few on which I bet my life no less mysterious. At their centre lies Easter, which speaks of God inaugurating a new stage in creation. Even as the creation of human beings transcended that of animals, so – in what we call incarnation, cross and resurrection – God reveals in one unique human life what is possible for us, the true end and meaning of our lives. Without him we do not know what we are to be. The scientist/priest Arthur Peacocke puts it succinctly:

> Jesus manifested the kind of human life which . . . can become fully life with God, not only here and now, but eternally

beyond the threshold of death. Hence, for Christians, his imperative 'Follow me' constitutes a call for the transformation of humanity into a new kind of human being and becoming. What happened to Jesus, it was thought, could happen to all ... Jesus represents the consummation of the evolutionary creative process that God has been effecting in and through the world of matter.[28]

Men and women do not rise from the dead. But neither does a faith, sparked off by a small group of disillusioned men and women, catch fire and spread until it changes the world unless something quite extraordinary and totally unexpected happened in that remote part of the Roman Empire. We still know so little of the mystery of what informs a person, of what we mean by 'spirit', and we grossly underestimate the power of God to create and re-create. (Just as we seek to contain the Holy Spirit, this mysterious, hidden presence of God, powerful as wind, deceptive as fire; at work within and outside the church.) If we simply put our faith in reason and common sense, with Jesus as an exemplar of Christian life, we are nibbling at the edges of the Gospel. We ignore the fact that without the experience of Easter there would be no Gospel. No church, no sacraments, no story worth telling, no hope. Whatever the truth of the empty tomb, the upper room, the breakfast by the lakeside, and the walk to Emmaus, something wholly new took place, lives were profoundly changed, and (to those whose eyes have been opened) both life and death are redefined. It is as if, in the light of Easter, we stand with one foot in time and one foot in eternity, for it is in the risen Christ that we catch the scent of what God is and what we might be.

Two more images of the dance jostle for space. When Laurie Lee died on a summer evening in May, still rooted in the village where he was born, his wife and daughter recorded a transcendent moment: an extraordinary golden light, with a brilliant rainbow set against a black sky.

We heard his last breath ... and we went into the garden

and danced, and then picked masses of white tea roses, Dad's favourite – and sprinkled their petals on him. We had this extraordinary sensation rushing up through our feet and we just had to dance.[29]

Thomas Merton ends his spiritual classic, *Seeds of Contemplation*, with these words:

> The Lord plays and diverts Himself in the garden of His creation, and if we could let go of our own obsession with what we think is the meaning of it all, we might be able to . . . follow Him in His mysterious, cosmic dance. We do not have to go very far . . . to catch echoes of that dancing. When we are alone on a starlit night; when by chance we see the migrating birds in autumn descending on a grove of junipers to rest and eat; when we see children in a moment when they really are children . . . at such times the awakening, the turning inside out of all values, the 'newness', the emptiness and the purity of vision . . . provide a glimpse of the cosmic dance. For the world and time are the dance of the Lord in emptiness . . . [and] no despair of ours can alter the reality of things, or stain the joy of the cosmic dance which is always there. Indeed, we are in the midst of it, and it is in the midst of us, for it beats in our very blood, whether we want it to or not. Yet the fact remains that we are invited to forget ourselves on purpose, cast our awful solemnity to the winds and join in the general dance.[30]

That's it, really. Like Prospero,

> deeper than did ever plummet sound,
> I'll drown my book,

to be read by some, and then remaindered until, treading the paperback path to oblivion, its pages yellow and it falls to bits. Yet some of the truths it contains, nectar brought back to the hive while I have performed my version of the dance of the bees, will (I guess) go on feeding men and women who are hungry for God as long as we go on exchanging words on our common journey. But, though the book ends, the dance goes on: this endless round of remembering the past, learning to live for the day, and from time to time

> thinking a little about the future, that place
> where people are doing a dance we cannot imagine,
> a dance whose name we can only guess.[31]

On most days, I walk past George Herbert's memorial window in Salisbury Cathedral, and try to take to heart one of his briefest poems:

> Thou that hast giv'n so much to me,
> Give one thing more, a grateful heart.
> See how thy beggar works on thee
> > By art.
> Not thankful, when it pleaseth me;
> As if thy blessings had spare days:
> But such a heart, whose pulse may be
> > Thy praise.[32]

When Donald Nicholl was dying of cancer he quoted the words of a Russian poet, that gratitude (if not the highest) is the purest form of love, for when you are full of gratitude there is no room for anything else – recrimination or desire for revenge or self-pity. He began to record his gratitude for all those – individuals and communities – who had nurtured him throughout his life, and through his final diary entries two words echo like a heartbeat: *gratitude* and *grace*. I'll buy that for an epitaph. Or rather, I'll go on working at it, trusting that one day I may be confident enough to cast away my inhibitions and really learn to dance.

# NOTES

**Foreword**
1. Julian of Norwich, *Revelations of Divine Love* (Penguin Classics, 1966), ch. 11.
2. A. E. Housman, *Last Poems*, (Penguin, 1995).

**JANUARY: *The Dance of the Bees***
1. Alexander Pope, *An Essay in Criticism* I, pp. 362–3.
2. Quoted in the *Independent*, 21 September 1996.
3. Paul Potts, *Dante Called You Beatrice* (Eyre and Spottiswoode, 1961), p. 15.
4. Anthony Powell, *A Question of Upbringing* (Heinemann, 1951), p. 4.
5. Obituary in the *Independent,* 29 March 2000.
6. Michel de Montaigne, *Essays: Advice to the Reader* (Penguin, 1958).
7. Elizabeth Bishop, 'Questions of Travel', *Complete Poems* (Chatto & Windus, 1991), p. 93.
8. Edwin Muir, 'The Journey Back', *Collected Poems* (Faber, 1960), p. 168.
9. Leonard Woolf, *Beginning Again* (Hogarth Press, 1964).
10. Thomas Hardy, *The Woodlanders* (Macmillan, 1962), p.155.
11. C. Day Lewis, 'Walking Away', *The Complete Poems* (Sinclair-Stevenson, 1992), p. 546.
12. Barry Lopez, *About this Life* (The Harvill Press, 1998), pp. 143–4.
13. Virginia Woolf, *Journal* (1903), quoted in *Travels with Virginia Woolf*, ed. Jan Morris (Hogarth Press/Chatto & Windus, 1993).
14. E. M. Forster, *The Longest Journey* (Penguin, 1989).
15. William Golding, *A Moving Target* (Faber, 1982), p. 4.
16. Ronald Blythe, *Divine Landscapes* (Viking Penguin), 1986), p. 170.
17. Shakespeare, *Henry V*, Act 1, Scene 2.
18. Steve Jones, *Almost Like a Whale* (Anchor, 2000), pp. 171–2.
19. Rainer Maria Rilke, *Duino Elegies: The Seventh Elegy*, translated by J. B. Leishman and Stephen Spender (Hogarth Press, 1939), ll. 34–5, 39.
20. Letter to Witold von Hulewicz, 13.11.25, *Selected Letters of Rainer Maria Rilke* (Quartet Books, 1988), p. 392.

**FEBRUARY: *Learning to Dance***
1. Quoted in W. N. P. Barbellion, *The Journal of a Disappointed Man* (Alan Sutton, 1984), p. 167.
2. Alexander Pope, 'To Lord Bolingbroke', *Poems of Alexander Pope* (Penguin, 1950).
3. Italo Calvino, 'A Cinemagoer's Autobiography' in *The Road to San Giovanni* (Vintage, 1994), pp. 37–8, 51.

**MARCH:** *The Stillness at the Dance's Centre*

1. T. S. Eliot, *Four Quartets: Burnt Norton* (Faber, 1944), ll. 62–3.
2. Edward Thomas, 'Thaw' in *Collected Poems* (Faber, 1979).
3. Eliot, *Burnt Norton*, ll. 63, 66–7.
4. Quoted in Bill Moyers, *Healing and the Mind* (Doubleday, 1993), p. 129.
5. Thomas Hardy, *Under the Greenwood Tree* (Macmillan, 1912), ch.14.
6. Padraig J. Daly, *The Last Dreamers* (Dedalus, 1999), p. 77
7. Quoted in Helen Waddell, *Medieval Latin Lyrics* (Gollancz, 1976).
8. Saul Bellow in George Plimpton, *Writers at Work* (Viking, 1984), p. 190.
9. V. S. Pritchett, *Myth Makers: Chekhov, a doctor* (Random House, 1979).
10. Harry Williams, *Poverty, Chastity and Obedience* (Mitchell Beazley, 1975), p. 111.
11. Denise Levertov, 'Of Being', *The Stream & The Sapphire* (New Directions, 1997).
12. Isaiah 45:15 (AV).
13. R. S. Thomas, 'Pilgrimages', *Collected Poems 1945–1990* (J. M. Dent, 2000), p. 364.
14. Ludwig Wittgenstein, *Tractatus Logico-Philosophicus* (1922).
15. Thomas, 'Kneeling', *Collected Poems*, p. 199.
16. Eliot, *Four Quartets: East Coker*, III, ll. 23–8.
17. Rainer Maria Rilke, *Duino Elegies: Eighth Elegy* in *Selected Poetry*, ed. Stephen Mitchell (Vintage International, 1989), p. 193.
18. Ted Hughes, *Winter Pollen* (Faber, 1994), p. 29.
19. Victor Klemperer, *To the Bitter End: Diaries 1942–5* (Weidenfeld & Nicolson, 2000).
20. Quoted in Elizabeth Jennings, *Every Changing Shape* (Carcanet, 1996), p. 61.
21. In *This Sunrise of Wonder* (HarperCollins, 1995).
22. Gerard Manley Hopkins, 'As Kingfishers Catch Fire', *Collected Poems* (Oxford University Press, 1952).
23. Edwin Muir, *Collected Poems, 1921–1958* (Faber, 1960), p. 223.
24. Patrick White, *Flaws in the Glass* (Jonathan Cape, 1981).
25. Wallace Stevens, *Collected Poems* (Faber, 1955), p. 92.
26. John Kitching, quoted in *Otherworlds*, comp. Judith Nicholls (Faber, 1995).
27. Bernard MacLaverty, *Grace Notes* (Vintage, 1998), p. 270.
28. William Wordsworth, *The Prelude*, Bk V, ll. 604–5.
29. Sidney Smith, *Lady Holland: Memoir* (London, 1855).
30. Søren Kierkegaard, *The Lilies & The Birds*, tr. W. Lowrie (Oxford University Press, 1939).

**APRIL:** *The Dance of the Cosmos*

1. John Donne, *Poetical Works, An Anatomie of the World: The First Anniversary* (Oxford University Press, 1966), ll. 279–80.
2. Emily Dickinson, *The Poems of Emily Dickinson*, edited by Thomas H. Johnson (The Belknap Press of Harvard University Press), no. 632.

3. Peter de Vries, *The Glory of the Hummingbird* (Little Brown, 1974).

4. W. G. Sebald, *The Rings of Saturn* (The Harvill Press, 1998), p. 67.

5. John Milton, *Paradise Lost,* Book IV, ll. 208–10, 215–21.

6. Quoted in *The Faber Book of Science,* ed. John Carey (Faber, 1995), p. 25.

7. W. H. Auden, 'The Poet & The City' in *The Dyer's Hand* (Faber, 1963), p. 81.

8. Richard Dawkins, *Unweaving the Rainbow* (Allen Lane, The Penguin Press, 1998), p. x.

9. *God, Humanity and the Cosmos,* ed. Christopher Southgate (T. & T. Clark, 1999), p. 5.

10. Preface by John Gribbin in *Hubble's Universe* (Constable, 1996).

11. Dawkins, *Unweaving,* p. 116.

12. Ecclesiasticus 18:6–7.

13. L. T. More, *Isaac Newton* (1936), p. 664.

14. John Masefield, 'The Unending Sky: Sonnet V' in *Lollingdon Downs* (Heinemann, 1917).

15. Psalm 8:4–5.

16. Ecclesiasticus 18:8–10.

17. Alfred Noyes, *The Torch-Bearers* (Sheed and Ward, 1937).

18. Jacquetta Hawkes, *Man on Earth* (The Cresset Press, 1954), last page.

19. Arthur Peacocke, *Paths from Science towards God* (Oneworld, 2001), p. 72.

20. Stephen Hawking, *A Brief History of Time* (Bantam Press, 1990), p. 174.

21. John Gribbin and Martin Rees, *Cosmic Coincidences* (Bantam Books, 1989), p. 269.

22. Martin Rees, *Just Six Numbers: The Deep Forces that Shape the Universe* (Weidenfeld, 2000).

23. Paul Davies, *The Accidental Universe* (Cambridge University Press, 1982), pp. 82, 95.

24. Paul Davies, *The Mind of God* (Penguin, 1992), p. 16.

25. Martyn Skinner, from *Old Rectory* (Michael Russell Publishing, 1984).

26. Joseph B. Soloveitchik, *The Lonely Man of Faith* (New York, Doubleday, 1996).

27. Chet Raymo, *Skeptics and True Believers: The Exhilarating Connection between Science and Religion* (Vintage, 1999), p. 234.

28. R. S. Thomas, *The Forward Book of Poetry* (Forward Publishing (Agenda), 2000).

29. Raymo, *Skeptics,* p. 193.

30. Guiseppe Del Re, *The Cosmic Dance* (Templeton Foundation Press, 2000), p. 329.

31. ibid., p. 84.

32. Shakespeare, *The Merchant of Venice,* Act V, Scene 1.

33. John Dryden, 'A Song for St Cecilia's Day', i, *Oxford Book of English Verse* (Oxford, 1949).

34. Quoted in Kitty Ferguson, *The Fire in the Equations* (Bantam Press, 1994), p. 180.

35. Sir John Davies, *Orchestra, or a Poeme of Dancing* (1596).

36. Dante, *Divina Commedia. Paradiso* xxxiii, l. 45.
37. Shakespeare, *Troilus and Cressida*, Act I, Scene 3.
38. T. S. Eliot, *Four Quartets: Burnt Norton* (Faber, 1944), ll. 56–8.
39. Charles Williams, *The Greater Trumps* (Faber, 1932), pp. 94–5.

**MAY: *The Dance of Nature***

 1. Julian of Norwich, *Revelations of Divine Love* (Penguin Classics, 1966), ch. 11.
 2. Katherine Hepburn to Humphrey Bogart in *The African Queen*.
 3. A. S. Byatt, *The Biographer's Tale* (Chatto & Windus, 2000), p. 259.
 4. Elizabeth Bowen, *A World of Love* (Jonathan Cape, 1955).
 5. *The Parlement of the Three Ages*, tr. H. S. Bennett, quoted by G. M. Trevelyan, *Illustrated English Social History* (Pelican, 1966), p. 61.
 6. One of the eucharistic prayers from *Common Worship* (Church House Publishing, 2000).
 7. Paul Davies, *The Mind of God* (Penguin, 1992), p. 21.
 8. Job 38:22, 31.
 9. James Jeans, *The Mysterious Universe* (Cambridge University Press, 1931), p. 137.
10. Annie Dillard, *Living by Fiction* (New York, Harper & Row, 1982), p. 55.
11. Richard Feynham, *The Meaning of It All,* (Penguin, 1999), p. 12.
12. Jacob Bronowski, *The Ascent of Man* (BBC, 1973), p. 364.
13. Tom Stoppard, *Arcadia* (Faber, 1993), pp. 47–8, 73.
14. See further in Guiseppe Del Re, *The Cosmic Dance* (Templeton Foundation Press, 2000), pp. 108–9.
15. Bernard MacLaverty, *Grace Notes* (Vintage, 1998), pp. 196–7.
16. See 'April', n. 18.
17. Davies, *The Mind of God*, p. 175.
18. Steve Jones, *Almost Like a Whale* (Anchor, 2000), pp. 60–1.
19. Annie Dillard, *Pilgrim at Tinker's Creek* (Jonathan Cape, 1975), pp. 129, 132.
20. James Lovelock, *Homage to Gaia* (Oxford University Press, 2000), p. 2.
21. James Lovelock, *The Ages of Gaia* (Oxford University Press, 1988), p. 212.
22. Adam Ford, *Universe: God, Man and Science* (Hodder & Stoughton, 1986), p. 210.
23. Richard Mabey (ed.), *The Oxford Book of Nature Writing* (Oxford University Press, 1995), p. ix.
24. Rainer Maria Rilke, *Duino Elegies: Ninth Elegy, Selected Poetry*, ed. Stephen Mitchell (Vintage International, 1989), ll. 12–13.
25. Gerard Manley Hopkins, 'God's Grandeur', *Poems of Gerard Manley Hopkins* (Oxford University Press, 1952), ll. 6, 7, 10.
26. D. H. Lawrence, 'Lizard', *Selected Poems* (Penguin, 1960).
27. Quoted in J. Philip Newell, *The Book of Creation* (Canterbury Press, 1999), p. 38.
28. John Stewart Collis, *The Worm Forgives the Plough* (Charles Knight, 1973), pp. 270–1.

29. William Blake, 'A Memorable Fancy', *Complete Poems* (Penguin, 1977), l. 14.
30. Blake, 'Auguries of Innocence', ibid., l. 1.
31. George Eliot, *Middlemarch* (Penguin, 1994), p. 13.
32. St Augustine, *Confessions*, X, 6.
33. Martin Buber, *I and Thou*, tr. W. Kaufman (Macmillan, 1974), p. 127.
34. St Augustine, *Confessions*, VII, 7.
35. Coleridge, *Biographica Literaria 7* (Princeton University Press, 1983).
36. D. M. Black, 'Kew Gardens', *Collected Poems 1964–1987* (Polygon, 1991).

## JUNE: *The Dance of DNA*

1. St Augustine, *Confessions*, X, 8, 15.
2. James Wright, from 'The Undermining of the Defense Economy', *Complete Poems* (Bloodaxe, 1992).
3. Lewis Wolpert, *The Unnatural Nature of Science* (Faber, 1992), p. 456.
4. e. e. cummings, *Selected Poems 1923–1958* (Faber, 1958), p. 76.
5. William Cobbett, *Rural Rides* (1830).
6. Amy Clampitt, 'Westward', *Collected Poems* (Faber, 1998).
7. Arthur Peacocke, *Paths from Science towards God* (Oxford, Oneworld, 2000), p. 74.
8. Adam Ford, *Universe: God, Man and Science* (Hodder & Stoughton, 1986), p. 78.
9. A. S. Byatt, *The Biographer's Tale* (Chatto & Windus, 2000), pp. 156–7.
10. Shakespeare, *The Winter's Tale*, Act V, Scene 3.
11. Susan Greenfield, *The Private Life of the Brain* (Penguin, 2000), p. 168.
12. James Clerk-Maxwell, *Discourse on Molecules* 1873, quoted in *The Faber Book of Science*, ed. John Carey (Faber, 1995), p. 167.
13. Steve Jones, *Almost Like a Whale* (Anchor, 2000), pp. 88–9.
14. John Polkinghorne, *Scientists as Theologians* (SPCK, 1996), p. 47.
15. ibid., pp. 183, 214.
16. Arthur Peacocke, *Explorations in Science and Theology* (Templeton London Lectures, RSA, 1993), p. 12.
17. See Hans Küng, *Does God Exist?* (New York, Doubleday, 1980), p. 347.
18. John Kitching, quoted in *Otherworlds*, comp. Judith Nicholls (Faber, 1995), p. 3.
19. Sherwin B. Nuland, *How We Live* (Vintage, 1998), pp. 188–9.
20. Steven Rose, *Lifelines: Biology, Freedom, Determinism* (Penguin, 1997), p. 169.
21. John Burnside, from 'Geese', *The Asylum Dance* (Cape Poetry, 2000).
22. Chet Raymo, *Skeptics and true Believers: The Exhilarating Connection between Science and Religion* (Vintage, 1999), pp. 22–5.
23. John Donne, *Sermon*, Easter Day, 1627.
24. Jacob Bronowski, *The Ascent of Man* (BBC, 1973), p. 400.
25. Mary Midgley, *Science and Poetry* (Routledge, 2001), p. 2.
26. Quoted in *The Brain: Mystery of Matter and Mind* (US News Books, 1984), p. 23.

27. Midgley, *Science and Poetry*, p. 10.
28. See Bill Moyers (ed.), *Healing and the Mind* (New York, Doubleday, 1993), pp. 177–95.
29. Gerald Edelman and Giulio Tononi, *Conciousness: How Matter becomes Imagination* (Allen Lane, The Penguin Press, 2000).
30. Colin McGinn 'Can we solve the body/mind problem?' *Mind*, 98 (Oxford University Press, 1998).
31. Anne Stevenson, 'The Spirit is too Blunt an Instrument', *The Collected Poems 1955–1995* (Bloodaxe, 2000), p. 24.

## JULY: *The Dance of Words and Paint and Music*

1. Joseph Conrad, *The Nigger of the Narcissus*, Preface (1898).
2. William Faulkner, Nobel Prize acceptance speech, Stockholm, 10 December 1950.
3. Edith Wharton, *A Backward Glance*, (Everyman, 1993), ch. 10.
4. T. S. Eliot, *The Rock*, IX, *Collected Poems* (Faber, 1963).
5. Howard Root, 'Beginning All Over Again' in *Soundings*, ed. Alec Vidler (Cambridge University Press, 1962), pp. 17–18.
6. T. S. Eliot, *Four Quartets: Little Gidding* (Faber, 1944), V, ll 8–10.
7. Norman MacCaig, 'An Ordinary Day', *Collected Poems* (Chatto & Windus, 1985).
8. Ruth Padel, book review in the *Financial Times*, 17 March 2001.
9. Seamus Heaney, 'The Murmur of Malvern' in *The Government of the Tongue* (Faber, 1988), p. 23.
10. William Matthews, quoted in *The Sewanee Review* (The University of the South), Spring 1999.
11. E. M. Forster, *Howard's End* (Penguin Classics, 2000), pp. 101–2.
12. Ted Hughes, 'The Making of Poetry' in *Winter Pollen* (Faber, 1994), p. 24.
13. David Malouf, *The Great World* (Chatto & Windus, 1990), pp. 283–4.
14. A. E. Housman, 'The Name & Nature of Poetry' (1933) in *Selected Prose*, ed. John Carter (Cambridge University Press, 1961).
15. James MacMillan, interview in the *Independent*, 26 March 1999.
16. Thomas Traherne, *Centuries: The Second Century*, 90.
17. Simone Weil, *Waiting on God* (Routledge & Kegan Paul, 1952), p. 56.
18. Austin Farrer, 'Poetic Truth' in *Reflective Faith*, ed. Charles Conti (London 1972), p. 37.
19. Cecil Collins, Preface for *A Retrospective Exhibition Catalogue* (Tate Gallery, 1989).
20. R. S. Thomas, 'Pissarro: Kitchen Garden, Trees in Bloom', *Between Here and Now* (Macmillan, 1981).
21. Hughes, 'The Making of Poetry', p. 13.
22. Saul Bellow, *Ravelstein* (Viking, 2000).
23. Czeslaw Milosz, 'Esse in Uncollected Poems' in *The Collected Poems 1931–1987* (Penguin, 1988).
24. *Independent*, 2 September 2000.
25. George Steiner, *Real Presences* (Faber, 1989), p. 179.

26. C. S. Lewis, *The Weight of Glory* (SPCK, 1954), p. 8.

27. Oliver Soskice, quoted in Richard Harries, *Art and the Beauty of God* (Mowbray, 1993), p. 107.

28. Stanley Kunitz in Bill Moyers (ed.), *Healing and the Mind* (Doubleday, 1993), p. 249.

29. Amy Clampitt, 'Predecessors, Et Cetera' in *Essays* (University of Michigan Press 1991), p. 5.

30. Joseph Brodsky, *Of Grief and Reason* (Penguin, 1997), p. 323.

31. Jonathan Bate, *The Song of the Earth* (Picador, 2000), p. 64.

32. ibid., p. 282.

33. Seamus Heaney, talk on Radio 3, *Viewing the Century,* 23 January 2000.

34. W. H. Auden, 'In Memory of W. B. Yeats', *Collected Poems* (Faber, 1976), p. 198.

35. Brodsky, *Of Grief and Reason,* p. 61.

36. Hughes, 'The Making of Poetry', pp. 221–2.

37. Heaney, *The Government of the Tongue,* p. 107.

38. Shakespeare, *Twelfth Night,* Act I, Scene 1.

39. Bishop Keith Sutton in *Private Passions,* BBC Radio 3, 3 February 2001.

40. Janet Baker, 'Spirituality and Music', The Eric Abbott Memorial Lecture 1988.

41. Howard Goodall, *Big Bangs* (Vintage, 2001), p. 224.

42. Vikram Seth, *An Equal Music* (Phoenix, 1999), p. 101.

43. ibid., p. 110.

44. John Press 'After *Le Nozze di Figaro*', *A Girl with Beehive Hair* (Mandeville, 1986).

45. Bernard Levin, *Enthusiasms* (Jonathan Cape, 1983), p. 230.

46. Milosz, 'Pure Beauty', *The Collected Poems 1931–1987* (Penguin 1988), p. 363.

## AUGUST: *Dancing in the Dark*

1. George Herbert, *Outlandish Proverbs* (1640).

2. Samuel Beckett, Mr Tyler in *All That Fall, Complete Dramatic Works* (Faber, 1986).

3. Stanley Kunitz, 'An Old Cracked Tune', *Passing Through* (W. W. Norton, 1995), p. 21.

4. Albert Camus, *Lyrical and Critical Essays* (Random House, 1970), pp. 169–70.

5. Stevie Smith, 'I love', *Collected Poems* (Allen Lane, Penguin, 1975).

6. Shakespeare, *The Winter's Tale,* Act IV, Scene 3.

7. Elie Wiesel, *Night* (Bantam, 1960), p. 62.

8. Christopher Leach, *Letter to a Younger Son* (Arrow Books, 1981), p. 72.

9. George Eliot, *Middlemarch* (Penguin, 1994), Book 2, ch. 20.

10. Quoted in Richard Hoggart, *First and Last Things* (Aurum Press, 1999).

11. David Lodge, *Thinks* (Secker & Warburg, 2001), p. 108.

12. *The Diary of Virginia Woolf, Vol. III, 1925–30* (Penguin, 1982), p. 6.

13. Gerard Manley Hopkins, 'No worst, there is none', *The Poems of Gerard Manley Hopkins* (Oxford University Press, 1952), p. 106.

14. A. N. Wilson, *God's Funeral* (John Murray, 1999), p. 6.

15. Padraig J. Daly, 'Complaint', *The Last Dreamers* (Dedalus, 1999).

16. Daly, 'Ministers', *The Last Dreamers*.

17. Fyodor Dostoevsky, *The Brothers Karamazov* (Penguin Classics, 1993), Book 5, ch. 4.

18. Les Murray, 'The Beneficiaries', *Subhuman Redneck Poems* (Carcanet, 1996).

19. Arthur Peacocke, *Paths from Science towards God* (Oneworld, 2001), p. 86.

20. Julian of Norwich, *Revelations of Divine Love* (Penguin Classics, 1966), ch. 86.

21. Neil MacGregor, *Independent,* 21 April 2000.

22. Helen Waddell, *Peter Abelard* (Constable, 1933), pp 268–70.

23. Donald Hall, 'Without', *Without, Poems* (First Mariner Books, 1999), p. 17.

24. Reported by a prisoner, Fr Albert Reisterer, in *Christ in Dachau* (Newman Press, 1952).

25. Dietrich Bonhoeffer, *Letters and Papers from Prison* (SCM Press, 1953), p. 164.

26. Paul Fiddes, *The Creative Suffering of God* (Clarendon Press, 1988).

27. 2 Corinthians 12:9 and 1 Corinthians 1:25.

28. Austin Farrer, *Said or Sung* (Faith Press, 1960), pp. 34–5.

29. *Hymns Ancient & Modern*, New Standard 497.

30. ibid., 496.

31. Martin Buber, *I and Thou*, tr. R. Gregor Smith (T. & T. Clark, 1937), p. 52.

32. Richard Coles, from a broadcast talk reprinted in *Independent on Sunday*, 6 March 1994.

33. Romans 8:38–9.

34. Paul Fiddes, *Participating in God* (Darton, Longman & Todd, 2000), p. 286.

35. W. H. Auden, 'Herman Melville', *Collected Poems* (Faber, 1976), p. 200.

36. Wiesel, *Night*, p. 32.

37. ibid., pp. x–xi.

38. Julian of Norwich, *Revelations*, ch. 73.

## SEPTEMBER: *The Dance of Forgiveness*

1. Shakespeare, *King Lear*, Act III, Scene 8.

2. William Blake, from *Jerusalem*, Preface to ch. 3, *Selected Poems* (Penguin, 1988), p. 228.

3. R. S. Surtees, *Handley Cross* (R. S. Surtees Society), ch. 59.

4. Isaiah 5:2 (AV).

5. Matthew 7:16, 20.

6. Galatians 6:7.

7. Simone Weil, 'The Love of God and Affliction' in *Waiting on God* (Routledge & Kegan Paul, 1951), p. 69.

8. Quoted in Johann Christoph Arnold, *The Lost Art of Forgiving* (Plough Publishing, 1998).
9. Ecclesiasticus 28:2–3 (Jerusalem Bible).
10. John 1:16.
11. Austin Farrer, *Said or Sung* (The Faith Press, 1960), p. 59.
12. Laurens van der Post, *Night of the New Moon* (Hogarth Press, 1970), p. 154.
13. Eric Lomax, *The Railway Man* (Jonathan Cape, 1995), p. 276.
14. Mary McAleese, *Unreconciled Being – Love in Chaos* (Medio Media/ Arthur James 1997).
15. Seamus Heaney, from *The Cure at Troy* (Faber, 1990).
16. Desmond Tutu, *No Future without Forgiveness* (Rider, 1999), pp. 34–5, 219.
17. Isaiah 42:1–2, 4.
18. Amos 5:23–4.
19. Micah 6:8.
20. Luke 4:18–19.
21. Matthew 6:33.
22. For a startling analysis of the effect of hidden poverty in Britain see Nick Davies' *Dark Heart* (Vintage, 1998).
23. Lawrie Green, *The Impact of the Global* (Urban Theology Unit, 2001).
24. Matthew 25:45.
25. Interview with Sir David Ramsbotham, *Guardian*, 2 February 2001.
26. John Vyvyan, *The Shakespearean Ethic* (Chatto & Windus, 1959), pp. 28–9.
27. Shakespeare, *Measure for Measure*, Act II, Scene 2.
28. Vyvyan, *The Shakespearean Ethic*, p. 170.
29. Shakespeare, *The Tempest*, Act V, Scene 1.
30. ibid., 'Epilogue'.

## OCTOBER: *The Dance of Love*

1. Sir John Davies, *Orchestra, or a Poeme of Dancing* (1596).
2. Edmund Spenser, 'Epithalimion', Sonnet 68.
3. Quoted by Robert Southey, *Life of Wesley* (1820), ch. 16.
4. John Burnside, 'Roads', *The Asylum Dance* (Cape, 2000).
5. Shakespeare, *Love's Labours Lost*, Act V, Scene 2.
6. Luke 9:62.
7. Raymond Carver, 'All of Us', *The Collected Poems* (Harvill Press, 1996), p. 294.
8. Stevie Smith, 'Mrs Simpkins', *Selected Poems* (Penguin, 1975).
9. Paul Fiddes, *Participating in God* (Darton, Longman & Todd, 2000), p. 5.
10. Rowan Williams, 'The Body's Grace' in *Our Selves, Our Souls and Bodies*, ed. Charles Hefling (Boston/Cowley Publications, 1996).
11. Philippians 2:8.
12. Pope John Paul II, *Fides et Ratio*, Section 93.
13. Jürgen Moltmann, *God in Creation* (SCM Press, 1985), p. 307.

14. W. B. Yeats, 'Among School Children' in *The Poems* (Everyman, 1992), p. 263.
15. Dietrich Bonhoeffer, *Letters and Papers from Prison* (SCM Press, 1953), May 20 1944, p. 132.
16. Source untraced.
17. J. K. Rowling, *Harry Potter and the Philosopher's Stone* (Bloomsbury, 1997).
18. Janet Walker, *RSA Journal*, Vol. CXLIII (January 1995).
19. Louis de Bernières, *Captain Corelli's Mandolin* (Vintage, 1999), p. 345.
20. Robert Louis Stevenson, *Travels with a Donkey* (Collins; no year of publication given), p. 164.
21. Denise Levertov, 'For Steve', *Sands of the Well* (Bloodaxe, 1998).
22. Richard Hoggart, *First and Last Things* (Aurum Press, 1999).
23. In *Pray, Love, Remember* (Darton, Longman and Todd, 1998), ch. 9.
24. Revelation 22:2.
25. Charles Williams, *All Hallows' Eve* (Faber, 1945), p. 144.
26. Paul Vallely, *Independent*, 13 May 2000.
27. Niall Williams, *As It Is in Heaven* (Picador 1999), pp. 296–8.

**NOVEMBER: *The Dance of Faith***

1. Robert Frost, 'The Secret Sits', *The Poetry of Robert Frost* (Holt, Rinehart & Winston, 1967), p. 362.
2. Blaise Pascal, *Pensées*.
3. George Herbert, *Outlandish Proverbs* (1640), no. 1006.
4. H. E. Bates, *Through the Woods* (Victor Gollancz, 1936), p. 112.
5. Howard Jacobson, article in *Independent on Sunday*, 3 March 2001.
6. Brian Pippard, *The Invincible Ignorance of Science*, Eddington Memorial Lecture (January 1988), reprinted in 'Great Ideas Today', *Encyclopaedia Britannica* (1990), p. 337.
7. John Donne, *Satyre III*, ll 79–81.
8. Richard Feynman, *The Meaning of It All* (Penguin, 1998), p. 28.
9. John Keats, Letter to his brothers George and Thomas, 22 December 1817.
10. Richard Holloway, *Dancing on the Edge* (Fount, 1997), p. 49.
11. Mark 9:24 (NEB).
12. George Herbert, 'The Pulley', *A Choice of George Herbert's Verse*, ed. R. S. Thomas (Faber, 1967).
13. Emily Dickinson, *The Poems of Emily Dickinson*, edited by Thomas H. Johnson (The Belknap Press of Harvard University Press), no. 875.
14. Henri Nouwen, *The Genesee Diary* (New York, Doubleday & Co., 1981), p. 56.
15. R. S. Thomas, 'The Belfry', *Collected Poems 1945–1990* (J. M. Dent, 2000), p. 168.
16. Thomas, 'Emerging', *Collected Poems*, p. 355.
17. Thomas, 'In Church', *Collected Poems*, p. 180.
18. Thomas, 'Emerging', *Collected Poems*, p. 355.
19. Thomas, 'Waiting', *Collected Poems*, p. 347.

20. Isaiah 45:15 (AV).

21. Thomas, 'The Moon in Lleyn', *Collected Poems*, p. 282.

22. Thomas, 'Emerging', *Collected Poems*, p. 263.

24. Thomas, 'Suddenly', *Collected Poems*, p. 283.

25. Philip Toynbee, *End of a Journey*, 12 November 1980 (Bloomsbury, 1988).

26. I am indebted to Danah Zohar and Ian Marshall's *Spiritual Intelligence* (Bloomsbury, 2000).

27. John F. Haught, *God after Darwin* (Westview Press, 2000), p. 70.

28. David Ford, *The Shape of Living* (Fount, 1997), p. 28.

29. Words from a friend's letter.

30. Julian of Norwich, *Revelations of Divine Love* (Penguin Classics, 1966), ch. 68.

31. Samuel Beckett, *Malone Dies* (Calder & Boyar, 1970).

32. William Maxwell, *The Chateau* (Vintage Books, 1961).

33. Interviewed in Bill Moyers (ed.), *Healing and the Mind* (New York, Doubleday, 1993), p. 238.

34. W. H. Auden, 'In Memory of W. B. Yeats', *Collected Poems* (Faber, 1976), p. 197.

35. Article in *The Times*, 22 September 1978.

36. E. M. Forster, *Howard's End* (Penguin Classics, 2000), p. 47.

37. Dennis Potter, *The Other Side of the Dark*, unpublished talk on BBC Radio 4, 23 February 1977.

## DECEMBER: *Learning to Dance II*

1. Don Marquis, *Archy's Life of Mehitabel* (Faber, 1961), p. 188.

2. Isaac Rosenberg, 'Returning, We Hear the Larks', *Collected Works* (Chatto & Windus/Hogarth Press, 1984).

3. Shakespeare, *Antony and Cleopatra*, Act V, Scene 2.

4. e. e. cummings, *Selected Poems 1923–1958* (Faber, 1960), p. 56.

5. Shakespeare, 'Sonnet 73'.

6. Eilean Ní Chuillenáin, 'Swineherd', *The Second Voyage* (The Gallery Press, 1986).

7. Valerie Grove, *Laurie Lee* (Penguin, 2000), p. 518.

8. John Updike, *More Matter: Essays and Criticism* (Hamish Hamilton, 1999), p. 25.

9. ibid., p. 560.

10. Mary Oliver, 'The Summer Day', *New and Selected Poems* (Boston, Beacon Press, 1992), p. 94.

11. Vladimir Nabokov, *Speak, Memory: A Memoir* (Vintage, 1989), p. 117.

12. Thomas Traherne, *Centuries: The Second Century* (The Clarendon Press, 1960), p. 66.

13. *The Diaries of Sylvia Townsend Warner*, ed. Clare Harman (Chatto & Windus, 1994).

14. Shakespeare, *King Lear*, Act V, Scene 2.

15. *The Last Notebooks of Loren Eisley*, ed. Kenneth Heuer (Little Brown, 1987).
16. Ben Howard, 'The Holy Alls' in *The Sewanee Review* (Summer 2000).
17. Norman MacCaig, 'Small Boy', *Collected Poems* (Chatto & Windus, 1985).
18. Oliver, 'In Blackwater Woods', *New and Selected Poems*.
19. Gerard Hughes, *God, Where Are You?* (Darton, Longman & Todd, 1997), p. 166.
20. Wisdom of Solomon 12:1.
21. Alan Ayckbourn, *House*, Act II, Scene 1 (Faber, 2000).
22. From *Celebrating Common Prayer* (Mowbray, 1992).
23. 2 Samuel 14:14.
24. Mark 12:27.
25. St Bernard, *On the Love of God* (Mowbray, 1950), p. 67.
26. Richard Wilbur, 'Hamlen Brook', *New and Collected Poems* (Faber, 1989).
27. Paul Tillich, *Shaking of the Foundations* (Charles Scribner, 1996), p. 27. My italics.
28. Arthur Peacocke, *Paths from Science towards God* (Oneworld, 2001), pp. 147–8.
29. Grove, *Laurie Lee*, p. 510.
30. Thomas Merton, *Seeds of Contemplation* (Anthony Clarke, 1961), p. 230.
31. Billy Collins, 'Nostalgia', *Taking Off Emily Dickinson's Clothes* (Picador, 2000).
32. George Herbert, 'Gratefulness', *A Choice of George Herbert's Verse*, ed. R. S. Thomas (Faber, 1967).

# ACKNOWLEDGEMENTS

The author is grateful for permission to reprint extracts from the following:

'In Memory of W. B. Yeats' and 'Herman Melville' by W. H. Auden, from *Collected Poems* (Faber & Faber, 1976). Copyright © 1976 the executors of the Estate of W. H. Auden.

'Questions of Travel' by Elizabeth Bishop, from *Complete Poems* (Chatto & Windus, 1991). Reprinted by permission of Farrer, Straus & Giroux. All rights reserved.

'Kew Gardens' by D. M. Black, from *Collected Poems 1964–1987* (Polygon, 1991).

'Roads' and 'Geese' by John Burnside, from *The Asylum Dance* (Jonathan Cape, 2000). Reprinted by permission of The Random House Group Ltd.

'Lord of the Dance' by Sydney Carter. Reproduced by permission of Stainer & Bell Ltd, London, England.

'Westward' by Amy Clampitt, from *Collected Poems* (Faber & Faber, 1958).

'Nostalgia' by Billy Collins, from *Taking Off Emily Dickinson's Clothes* (Picador, 2000).

Eucharistic Prayer from *Common Worship* (Church House Publishing, 2000).

e. e. cummings, *Selected Poems 1923–1958* (Faber & Faber, 1958). Reprinted by permission of W. W. Norton & Company. All rights reserved.

'Thomas Merton' and 'Ministers' by Padraig Daly, from *The Last Dreamers* (Dedalus Press, Dublin, 1999).

Poem by Brenda Dawson, St Christopher's Hospice.

'no. 632' and 'no. 875' by Emily Dickinson. Reprinted by permission of the Publishers and Trustees of Amherst

College from *The Poems of Emily Dickinson*, edited by Thomas H. Johnson (The Belknap Press of Harvard University Press), © 1951, 1955, 1979 by the President and Fellows of Harvard College.

'East Coker', 'Burnt Norton' and 'Little Gidding' by T. S. Eliot, from *Four Quartets* (Faber & Faber, 1944).

*The Rock* IX by T. S. Eliot, from *Collected Poems* (Faber & Faber, 1963).

'The Secret Sits' by Robert Frost, from *The Poetry of Robert Frost*, edited by Edward Connery Lathem, the Estate of Robert Frost and Jonathan Cape as publisher. Used by permission of The Random House Group Ltd.

'Without' by Donald Hall, from *Without, Poems* (First Mariner Books, 1999). Reproduced by permission of Houghton Mifflin Company. All rights reserved.

*The Cure at Troy* by Seamus Heaney (Faber & Faber, 1990).

'An Old Cracked Tune' by Stanley Kunitz, from *Passing Through* (W. W. Norton, 1995).

'Of Being', by Denise Levertov, from *The Stream and the Sapphire* (New Directions, 1997).

'For Steve' by Denise Levertov, from *Sands of the Well* (Bloodaxe Books, 1998).

'Walking Away' by C. Day Lewis, from *The Complete Poems* (Sinclair-Stevenson, 1992). Copyright © 1992 in this edition The Estate of C. Day Lewis.

'An Ordinary Day' and 'Small Boy' by Norman MacCaig, from *Collected Poems* (Chatto & Windus, 1985). Reprinted by permission of The Random House Group Ltd.

'The Separate Notebooks, A Mirrored Gallery' by Czeslaw Milosz, from *The Collected Poems 1931–1987* (Viking, 1988). Copyright © Czeslaw Milosz Royalties, Inc., 1988. Reproduced by permission of Penguin Books Ltd.

'The Journey Back' and 'The Annunciation' by Edwin Muir, *Collected Poems, 1921–1958*, (Faber & Faber, 1960).

'The Beneficiaries' by Les Murray, from *Subhuman Redneck Poems* (Carcanet, 1996).

'Swineherd' by Eileen Ní Chuillenáin, from *The Second Voyage* (The Gallery Press, 1986). By kind permission of the author and The Gallery Press, Loughcrew, Oldcastle, County Meath, Ireland.

*The Torch-bearers* by Alfred Noyes (Sheed and Ward, 1937).

'The Summer Day' by Mary Oliver, from *House of Light* (Boston, Beacon Press, 1990). Copyright © 1990 Mary Oliver. Reprinted by permission of Beacon Press, Boston.

'In Blackwater Woods' by Mary Oliver, from *American Primitive*. Copyright © 1978, 1979, 1980, 1981, 1982, 1983 by Mary Oliver. First appeared in *Yankee Magazine*. By permission of Little, Brown and Company (Inc.).

'After *Le Nozze di Figaro*' by John Press, from *A Girl with Beehive Hair* (Mandeville, 1986).

'Seventh Elegy' and 'Eighth Elegy' by R. M. Rilke, from *Duino Elegies*, translated by J. B. Leishman and Stephen Spender, published by the Hogarth Press. Reprinted by permission of The Random House Group Ltd.

'Returning, we hear the larks' by Isaac Rosenberg, from *Collected Works* (Chatto & Windus/Hogarth Press, 1984).

*Old Rectory* by Martyn Skinner (Michael Russell Publishing, 1984).

'I love' by Stevie Smith, from *Collected Poems* (Allen Lane, Penguin, 1975). Copyright © the Estate of James McGibbon. Used by permission.

'Mrs Simpkins' by Stevie Smith, from *Selected Poems* (Penguin, 1975). Copyright © the Estate of James McGibbon. Used by permission.

'13 Ways of Looking at a Blackbird' by Wallace Stevens, from *Collected Poems* (Faber & Faber, 1955).

'The spirit is too blunt an instrument' by Anne Stevenson, from *Collected Poems* 1955–1995 (Bloodaxe Books, 2000).

'Thaw' by Edward Thomas, from *Collected Poems* (Faber & Faber, 1979).

'The Belfry', 'Pilgrimages', 'Kneeling', 'Emerging', 'In Church', 'Waiting', and 'Blackbird' by R. S. Thomas, from *Collected Poems 1945–1990* (J. M. Dent, 2000).

257

ACKNOWLEDGEMENTS

*Love's Endeavour, Love's Expense* by W. H. Vanstone (Darton, Longman and Todd, 1977). Used with permission.

'Hamlen Brook' by Richard Wilbur, *New and Collected Poems* (Faber & Faber, 1989).